Praise for *The Plug-In Drug*

"If you have children who watch television, you owe it to yourself—and them—to read this book."
— *The Christian Science Monitor*

"[Marie Winn] must be listened to. She has got hold of something so big it has escaped the rest of us."
— *The Washington Post*

"Parents and teachers—indeed, all who care about the survival of the human spirit—should read this thoroughly provocative book and take heed."
—Nancy Larrick, author of
A Parent's Guide to Children's Reading

"A thoughtful, lucid argument to the effect that television watching itself, rather than the contents of television programs, is what damages child development and family relations. The author draws on several disciplines . . . and blends their findings with her own research in a style that is unpretentious (no jargon) and effective."
— *The New Yorker*

"Extremely important . . . ought to be read by every parent."
— *Los Angeles Times*

PENGUIN BOOKS

THE PLUG-IN DRUG

MARIE WINN has written thirteen books, among them *Children Without Childhood, Unplugging the Plug-In Drug,* and *Red-Tails in Love: A Wildlife Drama in Central Park.* She has written for various publications including *The New York Times Magazine* and *Smithsonian,* and currently writes a column about birds and nature for *The Wall Street Journal.* Married to the documentary filmmaker Allan Miller, she lives in New York City within walking distance of two young grandchildren. She frequently visits two others in San Francisco and a great niece in England. All five children are growing up (and flourishing) without television.

MARIE WINN

THE
PLUG-IN
DRUG

Television, Computers
and
Family Life

**25th anniversary edition—completely
revised and updated**

PENGUIN BOOKS

PENGUIN BOOKS
Published by the Penguin Group
Penguin Putnam Inc., 375 Hudson Street
New York, New York 10014, U.S.A.
Penguin Books Ltd, 80 Strand,
London WC2R 0RL, England
Penguin Books Australia Ltd, 250 Camberwell Road, Camberwell,
Victoria 3124, Australia,
Penguin Books Canada Ltd, 10 Alcorn Avenue,
Toronto, Ontario, Canada M4V 3B2
Penguin Books India (P) Ltd, 11 Community Centre, Panchsheel Park,
New Delhi – 110 017, India
Penguin Books (N.Z.) Ltd, Cnr Rosedale ands Airborne Roads, Albany,
Rosebank, Johannesburg 2196, South Africa

Penguin Books Ltd, Registered Offices: Harmondsworth, Middlesex, England

First published in the United States of America by Viking Penguin Inc. 1977
First revised edition published in simultaneous hardcover and paperback
editions by Viking Penguin Inc. 1985
This second revised edition published in Penguin Books 2002

1 3 5 7 9 10 8 6 4 2

Grateful acknowledgment is made for permission to reprint the following copyrighted works:
Selections from "How to Tame the TV Monster" by T. Berry Brazelton, M.D., *Redbook,*
April 1972. Copyright © 1972 by Redbook Publishing Company.
By permission of Lescher & Lescher, Ltd.
"Dennis the Menace" cartoon by Hank Ketcham. Copyright © 1976 by Field Newspaper
Syndicate, Inc., T.M.® By permission of News America Syndicate
and Hank Ketcham Enterprises, Inc.
"Ousting the Stranger from the House" by Colman McCarthy, *Newsweek,* March 25, 1974.
Copyright © 1974 by Newsweek, Inc. All rights reserved. By permission of Newsweek.

Portions of this work appeared in Marie Winn's *Unplugging the Plug-In Drug* (Penguin, 1987).
Copyright © Marie Winn, 1987.

LIBRARY OF CONGRESS CATALOGING IN PUBLICATION DATA
Winn, Marie.
The plug-in drug : television, computers, and family life / Marie Winn—
25th anniversary ed., completely rev. and updated.
p.   cm.
Includes bibliographical references and index.
ISBN 0 14 20.0108 2
1. Television and children.   2. Television programs for children—United States.
3. Computers and children.   4. Computers and family.   5. Television and family.   I. Title.
HQ784.T4 W494 2002
302.23'45'083—dc21   2001058052

Printed in the United States of America/Set in Adobe Garamond

To Izzy, Abby, Eli, Clara,
and Sophy

Preface

The Good-Enough Family

All families are not created equal. Some seem to be spectacularly successful. Others are a total mess. Then somewhere between the heights and depths are most of the rest of us.

The Spectaculars are so comfortably in charge of their children's lives that they don't need to establish rules about television watching. Their family life is rich and satisfying. Television never seems to take precedence over human activities—conversations, games, leisurely meals, reading aloud—in this somewhat unreal family.

The troubled families at the other extreme are all too real: parents who don't get along or who've split up, who are abusive, addicted to alcohol or drugs, who don't understand the first thing about children and their needs, who are too immature, too disturbed, too self-absorbed to place any great value on family life, and whose children, consequently, are likely to have more than the usual share of difficulties. Though excessive television watching is a common symptom of family pathology, these families are not likely to find that watching less TV is going to make enough difference in their lives. They have too many other basic problems to deal with first.

The British psychiatrist D. W. Winnicott* once coined the phrase "good-enough mother" to describe a parent who may have considerable problems raising her children but still does a good enough job to avoid causing any serious psychological damage.

*Reference notes begin on page 305.

Similarly one might define a "good-enough family" as one neither so perfect as to be invulnerable to normal human weaknesses
nor so precariously balanced as to be swamped by troubles. Most
American families, I believe, fall into this category. The good-enough
family may have its shortcomings; nevertheless the parents care
deeply about their children's well-being and strive to make their family life as good as possible. They are the ones for whom television
control may make a crucial difference.

In the wide range of good-enough families some might be called
"better-than-good-enough," indeed, approaching the borders of
"spectacular" territory. Others are "barely-getting-by," rapidly head-
ing for deep trouble. For many of these families, how they control
television may decisively influence whether they go in one direction
or another. Yet television's powerful pull on children and parents
alike makes it far harder to control than most parents recognize.

The idea prevails, perhaps because of this book's negative title,
that my answer to parents' problems with television is to promote its
elimination altogether. But that has never been my purpose. I know
that my most persuasive arguments will never make television go
away, nor would I want it to. I am not an enemy of the medium nor
do I believe it is devoid of value.

My aim, instead, is to promote a new way of thinking about TV.
I believe that if parents understand the medium's power and look
squarely at the ways it affects their children and their family life, they
can begin taking the necessary steps to deal with it successfully. To
help parents and families with this difficult task is the purpose of
this book.

Note about the Twenty-fifth Anniversary Edition

In the early and mid-1970s I interviewed a great number of parents, children, teachers, social workers, television executives, school
principals, psychologists, and psychiatrists about television, then a

fairly new medium. The material from those interviews, conducted in Denver and New York City, formed the solid core of *The Plug-In Drug* when it was published in 1977.

During the next twenty-five years American society experienced great changes—changes in family configurations, in working patterns, in lifestyles and modes of expression. But as I began to talk to parents and experts in preparation for an updated edition of this book I found that nothing much had changed in regard to television.

People today have the same problems controlling the medium as my informants reported in the seventies. Teachers talk about the same problems getting kids to pay attention. Parents report the same effects on family life. Their descriptions of how they use television in the home are almost identical. Only the programs they mention in passing have changed. This is why I have retained almost all the parents', teachers', and experts' quotes about television that appeared in the earlier edition: they might have been uttered this morning.

While the extensive list of these informants appears in the acknowledgment section at the end of the book, almost all agreed, then and now, that anonymity allowed for greater honesty and freedom of expression on a subject as controversial as television use. Therefore in this edition as in earlier ones they are identified only generically— "A ten-year-old child" or "a mother of two preschool children" or "a third-grade teacher" or "a child psychiatrist." The quotes are offset and printed in italics. Other citations from scientific papers, books, articles, and surveys are offset and appear in regular type. Their sources are identified fully in the reference notes at the end of the book.

Of course all quotes about recent electronic technologies appear here for the first time: these machines hadn't found a place in the home twenty-five years ago. Most of the interviews about computers at home and in the classroom were conducted in 2001 with parents, teachers, and children in Schenectady, New York, and its environs, particularly the Scotia school district. I also spoke to a few other parents and teachers in New York City and San Francisco about their uses of video technologies. The names of all these informants appear in the acknowledgments.

About those new electronic technologies—notably the home computer, the VCR, and the video game terminal: in spite of advertisers' claims that these devices provide more "interactive" play experiences, parents recognize their essential similarities to television. The child is still watching things happening on a screen, whatever the source of the images. Parents can't help observing that their kids' involvement with these new amusements seems as unprofitable as television viewing, as likely to displace outdoor play, schoolwork, practice of musical instruments, hobbies, and leisure-time reading. Parents find it just as hard to control children's use of these other media as it is to control television. There's an addictive element about them all.

Consequently, when the word "television" appears in the pages that follow, it can almost always be expanded into the phrase "television and other electronic media." Because television remains by far the predominant screen medium, however, in the interest of simplicity and economy the word "television" is generally used alone.

Part V of this new edition deals directly with these other electronic media. Chapter 14 discusses computers in the classroom. Chapter 15 examines video games, VCRs, and various electronic playthings for the home. New sections on other recent developments in telecommunications are scattered throughout the book, the Teletubby phenomenon, the V-Chip, and Channel One among them. In addition, the chapters on television control, particularly those offering practical help to parents, have been expanded.

One last note: a great many new studies of television's effects on children have been completed since this book was first published, some of them offering concrete support for ideas that were only speculative when they originally appeared in *The Plug-In Drug*. I have included these findings to strengthen my argument, but with some hesitation. In truth, I don't really believe that scientific studies can ever provide solid proof about any of television's effects on children and families, and I don't believe that they are the only way to make a case for television control—the main subject of this book.

Common sense and parents' deep and trustworthy instincts must finally prevail in dealing with this complex issue. Parents *know* that something's amiss in their children's involvement with television. But a focus on program content often keeps them from recognizing what is really wrong. I hope this book will encourage parents to trust those instincts and strengthen their resolve to deal with television in a new way.

Contents

Part III. Television and the School Years

IV. How Parents Use Television

Part VII. No Television

CODA: The Television Generation   281

PART I

The Television Experience

Drawing by Ross; © 1974 The New Yorker Magazine, Inc.

1

It's Not What *You Watch*

Concern about the effects of television on children has centered almost exclusively upon the *content* of the programs children watch. Researchers devise complex and ingenious experiments to determine whether watching violent programs makes children more aggressive, or whether watching exemplary programs encourages "prosocial" behavior, as social scientists put it. Studies are conducted to discover whether television commercials make children greedy and materialistic or, as some have suggested, generous and spiritual. Investigators seek to discover whether television stereotypes affect children's ways of thinking, causing them to become prejudiced, or open-minded, or whatever.

The very nature of the television experience apart from the program content is rarely considered. Perhaps the ever-changing array of sights and sounds coming out of the machine—the wild variety of images meeting the eye and the barrage of human and inhuman sounds reaching the ear—fosters the illusion of a varied experience. It is easy to overlook a deceptively simple fact: one is always *watching television* when one is watching television rather than having any other experience.

Whether the program is *Sesame Street* or *Batman*, *Reading Rainbow*, or *The Flintstones*, there's a similarity of experience about all television watching. Certain specific physiological mechanisms of the eyes, ears, and brain respond to the stimuli emanating from the television screen regardless of the cognitive content of the programs. It is

3

a one-way transaction that requires the taking in of particular sensory material in a particular way, no matter what the material might be. There is, indeed, no other experience in a child's life that permits quite so much intake while demanding so little outflow.

The Concerns

Children under five, the age group most vulnerable to environmental influences, are also among television's heaviest users. According to the latest Nielsen Report, children in the 2–5 age group spend an average of 21.8 hours each week watching television, while children in the 6–11 group spend 18.3 hours watching. Other surveys indicate somewhat higher viewing times for the youngest viewers. Even the most conservative estimates indicate that preschool children in America are spending more than one quarter of their waking hours watching television.

For these youngest children the most troubling questions have little to do with program content: What are the effects upon the developing human organism of spending such a significant proportion of each day engaged in this particular activity? How does the television experience affect a child's language development, for instance? How does it influence the nascent imagination? Creativity? Is the child's perception of reality subtly altered by steady exposure to television unrealities?

For school-aged children concern necessarily centers on the impact of a heavy investment in television viewing on their school achievement, their physical and mental development, their social relations, and their development into active citizens of a democracy. For the investment is heavy indeed, and has been increasing over the decades. While 39 percent of nine-year-olds watched 3 to 5 hours of television daily in 1982, by 1999 that percentage was up to 47 percent. Meanwhile the questions remain: Do they read less or differently as a result of their TV viewing? Is their physical fitness diminished as a result of the hours spent sitting in front of a screen? Are their free-time activities less varied, less fulfilling?

What about effects on the family? How does the availability of television affect the ways parents raise their kids? Are new child-rearing strategies being adopted and old ones discarded because the television set is available for relief? How does watching television for several hours each day affect the child's abilities to form human relationships? What happens to family life as a result of family members' involvement with television?

These are questions of critical importance. The fact that they are rarely raised, that the meaning of the experience itself is rarely considered, signals the distorted view American parents take of television's impact on their children and families.

About the Content and Susceptible Kids

It would be foolish to say that the content of the programs children watch makes no difference at all. Obviously kids learn from what they see on the screen. Some of what they learn is useful and good, some washes over them without imparting much meaning, and some of it has a negative impact. All this, of course, is endlessly debated. But given the amount of time most children spend at the single experience of television watching, the question of whether the stuff they learn from programs is helpful or harmful pales in importance when compared to questions about the experience itself and the time devoted to it—whether *that* is helpful or harmful.

For example, children may acquire valuable information about wildlife from watching nature programs on television. But if the hours of watching fine nature documentaries affects children's relationship to *real-life nature,* if a walk in the woods begins to seem a bit boring when compared the to experience of lions pouncing on unsuspecting zebras in the Serengeti Plains, it begins to seem unprofitable to dwell on the educational value of those programs. And yet most discussions about television and children are entirely about the lions and zebras.

Similarly, it would be foolish to assert that all children are affected by television in the same way. Without a doubt some children are more susceptible to television than others. Research is needed to uncover just what the specific personality components might be that these children have in common, but while all children come to enjoy watching television, some children seem to *need* television far more than others and seem to be willing to watch endlessly.

A Scarsdale, New York, doctor and mother says:

> *I have three children, and each one has a very different relationship with the television set. I have to control the youngest one's viewing more strictly because she would watch all the time if she could. The older two are far more self-regulating and always have been.*

Family problems with television control are magnified by the presence of a TV-susceptible child. "We wouldn't have much trouble with TV if it weren't for Mary," or Danny or Tommy or Annie or countless others, goes the refrain. Most families with two or more children seem to have one such child, and often, it appears, it is the very child the parents perceive as having more problems in general—the shy or passive child, or the aggressive child, the child who has trouble getting along with other children. It is not hard to understand why a troubled or vulnerable child might form a deeper attachment to the safe, undemanding pleasures of television viewing. Meanwhile, in families with only one child, that child seems far more likely to develop the deep relationship with television that characterizes the TV-susceptible child, perhaps simply as a sibling replacement.

Even when other family members are lukewarm about television, one avid television fan in a family is sufficient to create a serious television problem. It is more difficult to engage in family activities and maintain a strong family feeling when one member would always rather be watching television.

In too many cases the TV-susceptible child brings the other family members, particularly the siblings, under his or her sphere of influence and they *all* end up watching more television than the parents might consider desirable. After all, the other kids in the family *do* enjoy watching television, though not with as much intensity as their susceptible sibling. It is not as hard for them to turn from other activities to television viewing as it seems to be for the television-loving child to leave the television set for the various alternatives presented by the parents or other children. The pull of television is too strong.

What Does *Not* Happen

There are undoubtedly perceptual factors unique to the television experience that affect the ways viewers respond to the medium; these may account for the somewhat hypnotic effect TV has on many people, and the difficulty they have tearing themselves away from the tube. But a great many of television's effects don't work directly. It's not so much a matter of what happens when one watches, but what does *not* happen during those hours spent before the screen. For children, this may prove to be television's major legacy.

Television's influence on a child's language development, for example, almost certainly does not depend on the richness of language the child hears during a program. The major effects will be indirect, resulting from the varied verbal experiences the child will *not* have had as a result of his or her time-consuming involvement with television—the hundreds or thousands of words *not* spoken and responded to by another human being, the questions *not* asked and answered, the conversations *not* had. Television's impact on child-rearing and on family life are almost entirely in this category.

Sociologist Urie Bronfenbrenner described this aspect of television's effect most dramatically:

> Like the sorceror of old, the television set casts its magic
> spell, freezing speech and action, turning the living into
> silent statues for as long as the enchantment lasts. The
> primary danger of the television screen lies not so much in
> the behavior it produces—although there is danger there—
> as in the behavior it prevents: the talks, the games, the family
> festivities and arguments through which much of the child's
> learning takes place and through which his character is
> formed. Turning on the television set can turn off the
> process that transforms children into people.

One of the clearest demonstrations of the displacement factor, as it has been called, is a unique study published under the title "The Impact of Television: A Natural Experiment in Three Communities." It documented the effects of television's arrival on a small Canadian town—"Notel"—that had been without television reception [due to geographic factors] for a decade into the television era.

University researchers, in advance of television's arrival, studied the television-free children and families, comparing them along a variety of lines with the populations of two demographically similar towns, one that had had only one TV channel available during the previous decade and another that had had many channels.

The findings were dramatic. Before television was introduced, the Notel children tested significantly higher than the kids in the other towns on tests of various skills. When re-tested a year after television's introduction, the Notel children's scores had gone down to the level of the kids in the other towns.

The researchers, however, did not attribute the declines to the act of television watching. Rather, they explained them by the fact that television watching displaced other more valuable experiences.

For example, before TV arrived in "Notel," the researchers found that its children tested significantly higher on a test of creativity than the kids in the other towns. Two years after the introduction of television, the "Notel" children's creativity scores had gone down to the level of the other towns. Can one conclude, therefore, that there is something about the act of watching television that makes kids less creative? Another explanation makes more sense: since the researchers found a significant correlation between high creativity scores and high participation in other leisure activities, and since these activities were significantly diminished when TV arrived in Notel, one can conclude that the change in scores was caused by the displacement of these other activities, rather than by the direct influence of viewing. Perhaps pursuing hobbies or crafts, going camping or joining clubs helps children develop new attention or concentration patterns, for example, or broadens their base of experience in a way that makes them more creative.

Similarly, the study found a negative effect on the Notel kids' reading competence two years after the arrival of television. How to explain it? "We suspect that a displacement process is involved. . . . The absence of reading practice is, in our view, more important than television per se." Obviously those hours a child spends watching television are hours she or he might have spent reading.

It's unfortunate indeed that in the years when television was a new medium, social scientists did not arrange for many such before-and-after experiments in a variety of communities. If the results had been similar to those in the Canadian study, it would have provided overwhelming proof of a causal relationship between TV viewing and declines in various academic areas, in creativity, in social participation of all sorts. The Canadian experiment is one of a tiny handful of such studies, and the only one on this continent. Unfortunately, it can never be replicated in Canada or the United States (or, indeed, in most of the Western world). The simple reason: communities without television to serve as the "before" in a before-and-after study no longer exist.

Why Do Parents Focus on Content?

Parents themselves, though often deeply troubled about television and its effects upon their children, center their concern primarily on the subject matter of the programs their children watch, rather than on the television experience itself. According to a recent comprehensive survey, seven in ten parents are more concerned with *what* their child watches than with how much.

In the recent past, many concerned parents joined Action for Children's Television (ACT), a parent-lobbyist organization that was influential between 1968 and 1992. Founded by a group of Boston mothers, ACT directed its efforts primarily toward the content of children's programs, especially toward eliminating violence and commercialism and encouraging the production of good entertainment programming for children.

During its heyday, ACT was greeted with enormous enthusiasm and gratitude by parents and educators. Who would have supposed that in its endeavors to improve programming for children ACT might have compounded rather than alleviated the television problems American families were confronting?

The fallacy of ACT's premise was epitomized in the words of one of its founders as she described the organization's goals: "We came to the realization that children watch a great deal of television that is not particularly designed for them, that parents have a perfect right to ask those responsible for programs aimed at the young to meet the *specific needs of children* [my italics] for at least a couple of hours during the day or evening.

But is it the specific needs of *children* that are at stake when parents demand better programming? Surely the fact that young children watch so much television reflects the needs of *parents* to find a convenient source of amusement for their children and a moment of quiet for themselves. When parents work to improve children's programming, it is their own need to assuage their anxieties about the possible effects of those hours of quiet, passive television watching on their children that underlies their actions. It makes parents feel less guilty if those hours seem "educational."

The needs of young children are quite different:

- Children need to develop a capacity for self-direction in order to liberate themselves from dependency. The television experience helps to perpetuate dependency.

- Children need to discover their own strengths and weaknesses in order to find fulfillment as adults in both work and play. Watching television does not lead to such discoveries; indeed, it only limits children's involvement in those real-life activities that might offer their abilities a genuine testing ground.

- Children need to acquire fundamental skills in communication—to learn to read, write, and express themselves flexibly and clearly—in order to function as social beings. The television experience does not further verbal development because it does not require any verbal participation on the child's part, merely passive intake.

- Children need to develop family skills in order to become successful parents themselves some day. These skills are a product of their everyday experiences as family members and their active participation in family life. There is every indication that television has a destructive effect upon family life, diminishing its richness and variety.

- Young children's need for fantasy is gratified far better by their own make-believe activities than by the adult-made fantasies they are offered on television.

- Young children's need for intellectual stimulation is met far better when they can learn by manipulating, touching, doing, rather than when they merely watch passively.

In spite of their good intentions, those who lobby for improved programming on TV may be doing more harm than good. The television experience is at best irrelevant and at worst detrimental to children's needs. Efforts to make television more attractive to parents and children by improving programming can only lead to the increased reliance of parents upon television as a baby-sitter, and the increased bondage of children to their television sets.

Oddly enough the television industry, though unwittingly, often demonstrates a greater understanding of the true needs of children than its most bitter critics. In defending his station's inferior children's programs, a network executive once stated, "If we were to [supply quality programs in the afternoon], a lot of people might say: 'How dare they lock the kids up for another two and a half hours? Let the kids go out and play and let them do their homework. And let them have a learning experience.' I don't think it's incumbent on *us* to provide them with a service that is specific in those terms."

It is unlikely that the networks avoid good programming for children because they want kids to watch less television. Nevertheless, the industry's cool indifference to the quality of children's television fare may indirectly prove to be more beneficial for children than the struggle of those who insist that fine children's programs be available at all times: conscientious parents are more likely to limit their children's television intake if only unsuitable programs are available.

Television Savants

Parents may overemphasize the importance of content because they assume that their children's television experience is the same as their own. But there's an essential difference between the two: adults have a vast backlog of real-life experiences that colors what they see; children do not. As adults watch television, their own present and past experiences, dreams, and fantasies come into play, transforming the material they see into something reflecting their own particular inner needs. Young children's life experiences are limited. They have barely emerged from the preverbal fog of infancy. It is disquieting to consider that hour after hour of television watching constitutes a *primary* activity for them. Their subsequent real-life activities will stir memories of television experiences, not, as for adult watchers, the other way around. To a certain extent children's early television experiences will serve to dehumanize, to mechanize, to make less real the realities and relationships they encounter in life. For them, real events will always carry subtle echoes of the television world. As a twenty-year-old who calculated that she had spent 20,000 hours of her life in front of a television set wrote:

> I didn't so much *watch* those shows when I was little; I let them wash over me. Now I study them like a psychiatrist on his own couch, looking hungrily for some clue inside the TV set to explain the person I have become.

Inevitably parents of young children turn their attention to the content of the programs their children watch because they have come to believe that television is an important source of learning. Parents like to point out this or that word or phrase or fact or skill their child has picked up from TV. But the television-based learning of the preschool child brings to mind the *idiot savant*, a profoundly retarded person who exhibits some remarkable abilities—one who can, for instance, mentally multiply five-digit numbers or perform other prodigious mathematical feats. Today's television-educated children can spout words and ideas they do not comprehend and facts they don't have the experience or knowledge to judge the accuracy of. Small children mimicking television commercials or repeating complex words or sentences they don't understand, these young *television savants* have no more ability to use their television-acquired material for their own human purposes than the defective pseudo-geniuses have of using their amazing mathematical manipulations for anything other than show.

A Strange and Wonderful Quiet

Because television is so wonderfully available as a child amuser and child defuser, capable of rendering a volatile three-year-old harmless at the flick of a switch, parents grow to depend upon it in the course of their daily lives. But as time goes on, television's role changes. From a simple source of entertainment provided by parents when they need a break from child care, television gradually becomes a powerful and disruptive presence in family life. Yet in spite of their increasing resentment at television's various intrusions, and despite their considerable guilt at not being able to control their children's viewing, parents do not take steps to extricate themselves from television's domination. They can no longer cope without it.

In 1948 Jack Gould, the first television critic of *The New York Times,* described the impact of the new medium on American families: "Children's hours on television admittedly are an insidious narcotic for the parent. With the tots fanned out on the floor in front of the receiver, a strange if wonderful quiet seems at hand. . . ."

At first glance it may appear that Gould's pen had slipped. Surely it was the strangely quiet children who were narcotized by the television set, not the parents. But indeed he had found the heart of the problem before the problem had fully materialized, long before anyone dreamed that one day children would spend more of their waking hours watching television than engaging in any other single activity. It is, in fact, the parents for whom television is an irresistible narcotic, not through their own viewing (although frequently this, too, is the case) but at a remove, through their children, fanned out in front of the receiver, strangely quiet. Surely there can be no more insidious a drug than one that you must administer to others in order to achieve an effect for yourself.

2

A Changed State of Consciousness

Television Zombies

"I think that watching television is a rather remarkable intellectual act in itself," said Dr. Edward Palmer, a former head of research at *Sesame Street*. "All the while kids are watching they're making hypotheses, anticipating, generalizing, remembering, and actively relating what they are seeing to their own lives."

Mothers' descriptions of their young children's behavior hardly bear out the notion that television viewing is a rich intellectual activity:

> *Charles settles in with all his equipment in front of the television set when he comes home from nursery school—his blanket and his thumb. Then he watches in a real trance. It's almost impossible to get his attention. He'll watch like that for hours, if I let him. But even though he doesn't seem quite awake, it's not as if he were asleep because it doesn't keep him from going to sleep at bedtime, whereas if he falls asleep at all during the day, even for half an hour, he has lots of trouble going to sleep at eight o'clock. I don't know what it is. He just seems mesmerized.*

> *My five-year-old goes into a trance when he watches TV. He just gets locked into what is happening on the screen. He's totally,*

absolutely absorbed when he watches and oblivious to anything else. If I speak to him while he's watching TV, he absolutely doesn't hear me. To get his attention I have to turn the set off. Then he snaps out of it.

Tom doesn't answer the phone when he watches TV, even though it rings loudly right next to him. He simply doesn't hear it.

Again and again parents describe, often with considerable anxiety, the trancelike nature of their children's television watching. The child's facial expression is transformed. The jaw is relaxed and hangs open slightly; the tongue rests on the front teeth (if there are any). The eyes have a glazed, vacuous look. Considering the infinite varieties of children's personalities and behavior patterns, there is a remarkable sameness of expression among television-watching children. They come out of the trance when the program ends or when they must go to the bathroom, and the obvious "snapping out" effect, as the face resumes a normal expression and the body returns to its normal state of semiperpetual motion, deepens the impression that the mental state of young children watching television is trancelike. There is certainly little indication that they are active and alert mentally.

The Shutdown Mechanism

Dr. T. Berry Brazelton, a pediatrician and writer about children, has speculated on the significance of the television trance. He describes an experiment involving newborn babies that may be relevant to the television trance:

We exposed a group of quietly resting babies to a disturbing visual stimulus—a bright operating room light—placed twenty-four inches from their heads. The light was on for three seconds, then off for one minute. The sequence was repeated twenty times. Throughout the test the babies were monitored for changes in their heartbeat, respiration and brain waves.

The first time the babies were exposed to the light stimulus they were visibly startled; however, the intensity of their reaction decreased rapidly after a few times. By the tenth time there were no changes in behavior, heartbeat or respiration. By the fifteenth stimulus, sleep patterns appeared on the electroencephalogram, although it was clear that their eyes were still taking in light. After twenty stimuli the babies awoke from the "induced" sleep to scream and thrash around.

Our experiment demonstrated that a newborn is not at the mercy of his environment. He has a marvelous mechanism, a shutdown device, for dealing with disturbing stimuli: he can tune them out and go into a sleeplike state. But if we can imagine the amount of energy a newborn baby expends in managing this kind of shutdown—energy he could put to better use—we can see how expensive this mechanism becomes.

Brazelton proceeds to link this shutdown mechanism to the television trance so common among young children:

Just like the operating room light, television creates an environment that assaults and overwhelms the child; he can respond to it only by bringing into play his shutdown mechanism, and thus becomes more passive. I have observed this in my own children and I have seen it in other people's children. As they sat in front of a television set that was blasting away, watching a film or horrors of varying kinds, the children were completely quiet . . . they were "hooked."

While the sensory assault of the television experience serves to activate an immediate passive response in many young viewers, the residual effects of such experiences during a child's early development may prove to be quite the opposite. Writing in the *American Journal of Psychiatry*, Dr. Matthew Dumont presented another possibility:

> I would like to suggest that the constant shifting of visual frames in television shows is related to the hyperkinetic syndrome. . . . Apart from the vapid and violent content of the programs, there are incessant changes of camera and focus, so that the viewer's reference point shifts every few seconds. This technique literally programs a short attention span. . . . I suggest that the hyperactive child is attempting to recapture the dynamic quality of the television screen by rapidly changing his perceptual orientation. . . .

Similarly another psychiatrist proposes that the frenetic, over-stimulating pace of *Sesame Street* and other programs geared to pre-school children may contribute to the frantic behavior observed with greater frequency among children today. These programs are "sensory overkill" for some preschoolers, who are not developmentally equipped to handle fast-paced electronic stimulation.

Concentration or Stupor?

Sesame Street's former educational director, Gerald S. Lesser, referred to children who seem to be in a trance while viewing television as "zombie viewers," and noted that the *Sesame Street* research department found nothing alarming about the phenomenon. In their opinion a zombie viewer might absorb just as much from watching *Sesame Street* as a child attending in a more natural, alert style. "Zombie viewing," wrote Lesser in his history of *Sesame Street*, "may either reflect intense concentration or stupor."

Until a scientific study of the television trance provides some conclusive answers, the question of whether it reflects concentration or stupor must be answered obliquely, by noting parents' general observations of their child's state of mind while watching television. Parents universally report that television watching induces a state of greater relaxation. Thus they frequently use television to soothe and sedate an overactive child.

A number of mothers report:

> *There are times when one doesn't want one's child to be so active. Half an hour before bedtime I don't want the kids getting worked up playing. I'd much rather they watch television quietly. It doesn't much matter* what *they watch.*

> *The school psychologist told me not to worry about Bill's TV watching. She said that he probably* needs *two hours of a* blah *activity when he gets home, to relax.*

> *When Davy gets home from school, the TV helps him relax. He's able to turn himself off a little bit with it, in a way.*

> *When the kids get home from school they need to decompress, and so I let them watch television then, even though the programs are lousy.*

This is not to say that children don't need "down time"—of course they do. But any activity that induces unwinding, decompression, or any other highly relaxed condition is not likely to involve intense mental concentration. It is more reasonable to suppose that this "*blah* activity" induces a more passive mental state than is normal in a child.

Passivity

Parents' observation of the passive nature of their children's television viewing often underlies their deepest anxieties about television's effects. The word "passivity" comes up again and again in talks with parents about their children's television experiences.

Is this anxiety a product of our society's orientation toward doing and achieving? Does the fact that parents prefer their child to read, for instance, rather than to view television merely reflect our society's preference for verbal rather than visual experience?

In bringing up a child from birth, each parent witnesses a remarkable progression from total passivity and receptivity to activity and successful manipulation. A mass of undeveloped nerves and powerful instincts, the newborn starts life with a steady, unfocused taking in. Certain biological mechanisms protect infants from too much intake: a predominance of sleep over waking protects them from sensory overload; "spitting up" or vomiting saves them from an excess of food. Unable to "act" in any purposeful way, their entire existence is bound up in receiving.

During their first three years children travel an enormous distance from this newborn stage. They achieve advanced muscle control and eye-hand coordination. They master crawling, walking, running, jumping. They learn to communicate by means of cries, smiles, whimpers, and then language. By three they are full of purpose, struggling to gratify their wants and desires without delay, eager to learn, to explore, to understand. In many ways they are almost the opposite of the purposeless, powerless creatures they were at birth.

The television experience is an unmistakable return to the passive mode of functioning for the small child. It is quite unlike any form of play. Since parental anxiety is often a finely tuned indicator that something is amiss in the child's life, parents' widespread anxiety about the passivity of their children's television experience may carry survival value for the child.

The Reentry Syndrome

Time after time parents note that their children's behavior seems to deteriorate *just after* they finish watching television. Because such behavior is frequently short-lived, parents hardly make note of it, but when asked specifically about their child's post-viewing behavior, many parents do confirm that some temporary crankiness or misbehavior often occurs at those times. Among their comments:

We notice that they always come away from an hour or two of television watching in a terrible state: cranky, captious, tired, ready to explode. They come away from the set and try to assuage some sort of inner dissatisfaction in some way—by drinking a lot, eating, jumping up and down aimlessly.

TV doesn't improve their disposition. They're grouchy and irritable right after they watch.

After watching, they're cross and hopped up.

The moment the set is turned off, there's a rapid rise in their inability to control themselves. They whine, they fuss, they absolutely regress. I'll send them to their room to settle down. And it takes them a while before they're back to normal.

When Anthony has spent a morning watching TV, he's not to be lived with. He's nervous, rude, inattentive, bored, doesn't know what to do with himself, and is quite disagreeable. Gradually he comes back to normal.

Immediately after watching television the kids' behavior plummets downward from the normal. There'll be wild running around and that sort of thing.

The main thing about television is the fact that there's a lot of energy there coming out at you, and you sit there passively, and it's going into you. When you turn that set off, it has to come out again. What I notice in my children is that it comes out in a very mindless way—mindless, spasmodic energy, a brief little temper tantrum, blowing up, pushing and shoving, being dissatisfied.

Post-television crankiness is an important signal to parents. Young children's behavior, after all, is a parent's most valuable source of information about their mental state and emotional and physical well-being, since small children rarely talk about their feelings. They hardly know what a feeling is.

When behavior takes a mysterious turn, when a child is disagreeable for no discernible reason or reacts in an unexpected way to both pleasant and unpleasant experiences—when, in short, a child's behavior does not follow the usual and simple rules of cause and effect as the parent understands them—then there's cause for anxiety. Invariably the child's inappropriate behavior pattern proves to have survival value when it is finally understood. A child, for instance, who comes home from nursery school each day in a wretched frame of mind, fussing and demanding attention, may provoke his or her parents to investigate what's happening at school; often serious problems are uncovered in this way, even though the child may never complain about school or the teacher, and may even claim that everything is fine at school.

Even more important to the child's well-being is the watchful parent's instinctive recognition that unexplained crankiness may be a symptom of oncoming sickness. Long before the child articulates any symptom, the knowledgeable mother or father, inspired by a peculiar behavior pattern, whips out the thermometer, often to discover that the child is feverish and sick. In such a case the child's crankiness is the organism's symptom that something is wrong; like all symptoms, its function is to help restore the body to its desired state of homeostasis. The parent proceeds to take steps to help restore the equilibrium that has, for some reason, been destroyed.

Another condition in a child's life regularly leads to behavior that appears to serve no rational purpose, yet proves to have survival value. That condition is sleep. A night of peaceful, pleasant sleep may be followed by a dismal irritability upon waking up, both in children and in adults. The mood does not seem to be a result of the pleasant or unpleasant aspects of the activity that preceded it. Rather, post-sleep crankiness represents a sort of reentry syndrome, as the mind moves from one state of consciousness into another. The organism seems to require a certain period of adjustment when making the transition from sleep to wakefulness, a period that is longer for some persons than others. Post-sleep crankiness offers a brief period of protection against the dangers inherent in normal human interactions. Leave me alone, the recent sleeper begs by means of such irritability, I'm not ready to deal with you as my usual self. I'm a different person at this moment and might function in the wrong way. Wait until I'm entirely awake. Then I'll behave reliably.

Bad behavior, to be sure, is sometimes purposefully used by children to get their way. In the case of post-television crankiness, however, the child's behavior is likely to lead to an undesired result: the parent might eliminate the desirable experience (television watching) in order to eliminate the subsequent undesirable behavior. It's logical to assume therefore that the post-television bad behavior is not like a child's whining and fussing to get a toy or a candy bar. It's provoked for some inner purpose that the child is unaware of.

Is post-television misbehavior a signal to parents that the child is fatigued and needs to rest? Why, then, do parents seem to consider television viewing a restful, relaxing activity and often encourage their overtired children to settle down before the television set? If anything, the child is probably in need of physical and mental activity.

It is far more likely that post-television crankiness serves a purpose similar to the unexplained behavior that appears at the onset of illness or at the end of sleep. It may either be a sign that something about the experience of television watching is harmful to the child and may have adverse developmental consequences, as in pre-sickness crankiness, or it may signal a transition from one state of consciousness to another (post-sleep irritability).

If post-television crankiness represents a reentry syndrome from one state of consciousness to another, this raises a particularly disquieting question: What, then, *is* the child's state of consciousness while watching television? It is clearly not sleep. Is it something other than waking? We are all familiar with drug-induced states of consciousness. Is the television-viewing child on some kind of trip, then, from which a transitional period of bad behavior is required before reentering the real world?

Television viewing the sickness, or television viewing the trip, or, worst of all, television viewing the sick trip—none of these possibilities bodes well. Surely if television viewing can be a trip, then, like the drug experience, it can become an addiction as well.

3

The Power of the Medium

Why Is It So Hard to Stop Watching?

A number of perceptual factors unique to the television experience may play a role in making it more fascinating and addictive than other vicarious experiences, factors to do with the nature of the electronic images on the screen and the ways the eye takes them in.

In real life we perceive but a tiny part of the visual panorama around us with the fovea, the sharp-focusing part of the eye, taking in the rest of the world with our fuzzy peripheral vision. But when we watch television we take in the entire frame of an image with our sharp foveal vision. Let's say that the image on the television screen depicts a whole room or a mountain landscape; if we were there in real life, we would be able to perceive only a very small part of the room or the landscape clearly with any single glance. On television, however, we can see the entire picture sharply. Our peripheral vision is not involved in viewing that scene; indeed, as the eye focuses upon the television screen and takes it all in sharply, the mind blots out the peripheral world entirely. Since in real life the periphery distracts and diffuses our attention, this absence of periphery may serve to abnormally heighten our attention to the television image.

Another unique feature of the television image is the remarkable activity of all contours on the television screen. While the normal contours of real-life objects and people are stationary, the electronic mechanism that creates images on a screen produces contours that move continuously, although the viewer is hardly aware of this movement. Since the eye is drawn to fixate more strongly on moving than on stationary objects, one result of the activity of television contours is to make them more attention-binding.

Yet another consequence of this contour activity is to make the eye defocus slightly when fixing its attention on the television screen. The reason is this: in viewing television the steadily changing visual activity of the contour causes the eye to have difficulties in fixating properly. In real life, when the eye does not fixate properly a signal is sent to the visual center of the brain, which then takes corrective steps. Since improper fixation is normally the result of an eye tremor or some physical dysfunction of the viewer rather than of the thing being viewed, the visual system tries to make corrections in the tremor or in some part of the viewer's visual system.

In viewing television, however, it's the visual activity at the contour of the image that causes the difficulties in fixation. Therefore it may be easier to give up striving for a perfect, focused fixation on a television picture, settling for a somewhat defocused fixation.

The sensory confusion that occurs as a result of the activity of television images is not unlike the state that occurs when the semicircular canals of the ears, which serve to maintain our balance and help the brain make the necessary adjustments to the body's movements, are confused by motion from external sources (as when one stands still and yet one's ear canals are moved this way and that by the motion of a car or ship or airplane). The unpleasant symptoms of seasickness or carsickness reflect this internal confusion.

The slight defocusing of the eyes while viewing television, while not as unpleasant as seasickness (it is barely perceptible, in fact), may nevertheless have subtle consequences that serve to make the television experience subtly dysfunctional for the organism. Research shows that defocusing of the eyes normally accompanies various fantasy and daydreaming states. Thus the material perceived on television may take on an air of unreality, a dreamlike quality. Indeed, similar visual-motor conflicts are frequently described as features of many drug experiences by users. This may be an explanation, at least in part, for the trancelike nature of so many viewers' television experiences, and may help to explain why the television image has so strong and hypnotic a fascination. It has even been suggested, though without any conclusive evidence to support it, that "early experiences with electronic displays are predisposing to later enjoyment of psychoactive drugs which produce similar perceptual effects."

All these perceptual anomalies may conspire to fascinate viewers and glue them to the television set. Meanwhile, High Definition television (HDTV), beginning to have a wide distribution in America, seems to have an even stronger fascination effect than normal TV. As a commentator on this technology wrote after first seeing an HDTV broadcast, "If there is anything to fear about HDTV it is the hypnotic power of its beauty. Normal television exerts this power even with its crudely resolved images. Who will be able to resist the seductions of this even more enveloping, involving visual universe?"

Of course there are variations in the attention-getting and attention-sustaining powers of television images, many of which depend on such factors as the amount of movement present on the screen at any given moment, and the velocity of change from image to image. It is a bit chilling to consider that the producers of the most influential program for preschool children, *Sesame Street,* employed modern technology in the form of a "distractor" machine to test each segment of their program to ensure that it would capture and hold the child's attention to the highest degree possible. With the help of the "distractor," the makers of *Sesame Street* found that fast-paced cartoons and fast-moving stories were most effective in sustaining a child's attention. This attitude toward young children and their television experiences seems cynical when compared to that of an executive of the British Broadcasting Corporation who declined to broadcast *Sesame Street* when it first went on the air.

She explained: "We're not trying to tie children to the television screen. If they go away and play halfway through our programs, that's fine."

Why It Captures the Child

If television had existed a century ago, would parents of that era, with their strong family structure and firm, authoritative ways, have managed to control the medium better than parents succeed in doing today? Not necessarily. There is something unique about the hold television has upon children, regardless of the sociological or methodological context.

Some of television's fascination may lie in its concentration of perceptual pleasures in a single quantum of experience: bright and ever-changing images, varied sounds and music, soothing repetition alternating with stunning change, all augmented by the cognitive fascinations of recognizable human figures and language. Whereas none of the single components of the television experience are nearly as satisfying as the basic, primitive pleasure of eating, for instance, or being cuddled, when taken all together in one package, these sensory stimulations may be powerfully gratifying.

Parents and others with intimate dealings with small children have a practical understanding of the importance of environmental stimulation. They know that infants can be distracted from physical pain or difficult emotional situations such as separation from their mother by having a shiny bracelet dangled before them or a lively song sung to them. Sometimes the sight of a particular color acts to soothe a fussing baby. Taking a crying baby to a window looking out on a busy street often has a quickly calming effect. The importance of outside stimuli is illustrated by experiments demonstrating that infants will inhibit their most crucial activity, sucking at the breast or bottle, when presented with something new to look at or listen to.

It might be postulated that children have a need for taking in sensory material, just as they have a need for taking in food and receiving affection. Fulfilling this need for sensory input, then, may be almost as pleasurable for the child as eating and cuddling. An indication of the special position television viewing holds in the young child's pleasure hierarchy is the frequency with which it is linked by psychiatrists, psychologists, and parents themselves with basic emotional gratification.

A child therapist reports:

> When I tell a parent to cut out television from a child's life because it is clearly having a detrimental effect, I often meet the same reaction that I do when I tell parents to take their five-year-old out of diapers and insist on his using the toilet, or to take the bottle away from a four-year-old. The mother says, "That's ridiculous. He's scared of the toilet. He'll never do it." Or, "That's impossible. He loves his bottle too much." Well, I've had the same reaction from parents when I bring up television. They're terrified. It just seems too terrible a deprivation to turn off the television set entirely. When they feel ready to take the chance and try my advice, they are always astonished at how easy it was. The only difference is that they don't slip back with the diapers and the bottle. But they do slip back with the television set.

Many parents make observations similar to this one:

> When Eric watches TV he uses his quilt—that's the only time he sucks his thumb. Not always, but usually. The only other time he uses his quilt is in bed.

A psychoanalyst notes:

> Parents don't like their kids watching television because it's so entrancing and captivating that it falls into the category of those

*forbidden, mildly damaging, and enjoyable experiences like
masturbation. They don't like to see their kid tune out, sitting
in the corner and playing with himself. And just so, they don't
like to see him sitting in the corner looking at the google-box for
hours on end. It's too pleasurable.*

Just as parents' understanding of the child's deep relationship to
food leads them to use food as a threat, a punishment, an incentive,
and a replacement for love, so, too, their understanding of the importance of television viewing in their child's life leads them to use
television as an important punishment and reward.

Almost 50 percent of the children recently interviewed in a large
survey reported that their parents used television deprivation as a
form of punishment. In all likelihood it has become the most widely
used punishment in America today.

"I catch myself using TV for discipline, telling Jimmy that he
can't watch if he doesn't behave, and my husband wisely tells me:
don't do that. But it's tempting. It's like no dessert," admits a mother
of a preschooler.

Television is also commonly used in toilet training today. Parents
place the potty in front of the television set to inspire the child to
"perform." Some parents also hold out promises of special television
programs as a reward for compliance with toilet-training requirements. Similarly, no-television is used as punishment for toilet-training lapses.

Parents intuitively understand the depth of their children's
involvement with television, an understanding partly informed by
observations of the intensity of their kids' viewing behavior and
partly by the extent of their grief when television is denied. This is
what ultimately keeps parents from turning off their sets, what allows
them to observe helplessly as their family life becomes increasingly
dominated by television.

Cookies or Heroin?

The word "addiction" is often used loosely and wryly in conversation. People will refer to themselves as "mystery-book addicts" or "cookie addicts." E. B. White wrote of his annual surge of interest in gardening: "We are hooked and are making an attempt to kick the habit." Yet nobody really believes that reading mysteries or ordering seeds by catalogue is serious enough to be compared with addictions to heroin or alcohol. In these cases the word "addiction" is used jokingly to denote a tendency to overindulge in some pleasurable activity.

People often refer to being "hooked on TV." Does this, too, fall into the lighthearted category of cookie eating and other pleasures that people pursue with unusual intensity? Or is there a kind of television viewing that falls into the more serious category of destructive addiction?

Not unlike drugs or alcohol, the television experience allows the participant to blot out the real world and enter into a pleasurable and passive mental state. To be sure, other experiences, notably reading, also provide a temporary respite from reality. But it's much easier to stop reading and return to reality than to stop watching television. The entry into another world offered by reading includes an easily accessible return ticket. The entry via television does not. In this way television viewing, for those vulnerable to addiction, is more like drinking or taking drugs—once you start it's hard to stop.

Just as alcoholics are only vaguely aware of their addiction, feeling that they control their drinking more than they really do ("I can cut it out any time I want—I just like to have three or four drinks before dinner"), many people overestimate their control over television watching. Even as they put off other activities to spend hour after hour watching television, they feel they could easily resume living in a different, less passive style. But somehow or other while the television set is present in their homes, it just stays on. With television's easy gratifications available, those other activities seem to take too much effort.

A heavy viewer (a college English instructor) observes:

> I find television almost irresistible. When the set is on, I cannot ignore it. I can't turn it off. I feel sapped, will-less, enervated. As I reach out to turn off the set, the strength goes out of my arms. So I sit there for hours and hours.

Self-confessed television addicts often feel they "ought" to do other things—but the fact that they don't read and don't plant their garden or sew or crochet or play games or have conversations means that those activities are no longer as desirable as television viewing. In a way, the lives of heavy viewers are as unbalanced by their television "habit" as drug addicts' or alcoholics' lives. They are living in a holding pattern, as it were, passing up the activities that lead to growth or development or a sense of accomplishment. This is one reason people talk about their television viewing so ruefully, so apologetically. They are aware that it is an unproductive experience, that by any human measure almost any other endeavor is more worthwhile.

It is the adverse effect of television viewing on the lives of so many people that makes it feel like a serious addiction. The television habit distorts the sense of time. It renders other experiences vague and curiously unreal while taking on a greater reality for itself. It weakens relationships by reducing and sometimes eliminating normal opportunities for talking, for communicating.

And yet television does not satisfy, else why would the viewer continue to watch hour after hour, day after day? "The measure of health," wrote the psychiatrist Lawrence Kubie, "is flexibility . . . and especially the freedom to cease when sated." But heavy television viewers can never be sated with their television experiences. These do not provide the true nourishment that satiation requires, and thus they find that they cannot stop watching.

A former heavy watcher, a filmmaker, describes a debilitating television habit:

I remember when we first got the set I'd watch for hours and hours, whenever I could, and I remember that feeling of tiredness and anxiety that always followed those orgies, a sense of time terribly wasted. It was like eating cotton candy; television promised so much richness, I couldn't wait for it, and then it just evaporated into air. I remember feeling terribly drained after watching for a long time.

Similarly a nursery-school teacher remembers her own childhood television experience:

I remember bingeing on television when I was a child and having that vapid feeling after watching hours of TV. I'd look forward to watching whenever I could, but it just didn't give back a real feeling of pleasure. It was like no orgasm, no catharsis, very frustrating. Television just wasn't giving me the promised satisfaction, and yet I kept on watching. It filled some sort of need, or had to do with an inability to get something started.

The testimonies of ex–television addicts often have the evangelistic overtones of stories heard at Alcoholics Anonymous meetings. A handbag repair-shop owner says:

I'd get on the subway home from work with the newspaper and immediately turn to the TV page to plan out my evening's watching. I'd come home and then we'd watch TV for the rest of the evening. We'd eat our dinner in the living room while watching, and we'd only talk every once in a while, during the ads, if at all. I'd watch anything, good, bad, or indifferent.
    All the while we were watching I'd feel terribly angry at myself for wasting all that time watching junk. I could never go to sleep until at least the eleven o'clock news, and then sometimes

I'd still stay up for the late-night talk show. I had a feeling that I had to watch the news programs, even though most of the time nothing much was happening and I could easily find out what by reading the paper the next morning. Usually my wife would fall asleep on the couch while I was watching. I'd get angry at her for doing that. Actually, I was angry at myself.

I had a collection of three years of back issues of different magazines, but I never got around to reading them. I never got around to sorting or labeling my collection of slides I had made when traveling. I only had time for television. We'd take the telephone off the hook while watching so we wouldn't be interrupted! We like classical music, but we never listened to any, never!

Then one day the set broke. I said to my wife, "Let's not fix it. Let's just see what happens." Well, that was the smartest thing we ever did. We haven't had a TV in the house since then.

Now I look back and I can hardly believe we could have lived like that. I feel that my mind was completely mummified for all those years. I was glued to that machine and couldn't get loose, somehow. It really frightens me to think of it. Yes, I'm frightened of TV now. I don't think I could control it if we had a set in the house again. I think it would take over no matter what I did.

Heavy television viewers often make comparisons between their viewing habits and substance addictions. Several decades ago, a lawyer reported:

I watch TV the way an alcoholic drinks. If I come home and sit in front of the TV, I'll watch any program at all, even if there's nothing on that especially appeals to me. Then the next thing I know it's eleven o'clock and I'm watching the Johnny Carson show, and I'll realize I've spent the whole evening watching TV. What's more, I can't stand Johnny Carson! But I'll still sit there watching him. I'm addicted to TV, when it's there, and I'm not happy about the addiction. I'll sit there getting madder and madder at myself for watching, but still I'll sit there. I can't turn it off.

Nor is the television addict always blind to the dysfunctional aspects of his addiction. A homemaker says:

Sometimes a friend will come over while I'm watching TV. I'll say, "Wait a second. Just let me finish watching this," and then I'll feel bad about that, letting the machine take precedence over people. And I'll do that for the stupidest programs, just because I have to watch, somehow.

In spite of the potentially destructive nature of television addiction, it is rarely taken seriously in American society. Critics mockingly refer to television as a "cultural barbiturate" and joke about "mainlining the tube." A spectacle called *Media Burn* perfectly illustrates the feeling of good fun that often surrounds the issue of television addiction. The event, which took place in San Francisco when television was still a young medium, involved the piling up of forty-four old television sets in the parking lot of the Cow Palace, soaking them with kerosene, and applying a torch. According to the programs distributed before the event, everybody was supposed to experience "a cathartic explosion" and "be free at last from the addiction to television."

The issue of television addiction takes on a more serious air when the addicts are our own children. A mother reports:

My ten-year-old is as hooked on TV as an alcoholic is hooked on drink. He tries to strike desperate bargains: "If you let me watch just ten more minutes, I won't watch at all tomorrow," he says. It's pathetic. It scares me.

A number of years ago a mother described her six-year-old son's need to watch:

We were in Israel last summer where the TV stations sign off for the night at about ten. Well, my son would turn on the set and watch the Arabic stations that were still on, even though he couldn't understand a word, just because he had to watch something.

Other signs of serious addiction come out in parents' descriptions of their children's viewing behavior:

We used to have very bad reception before we got on Cable TV. I'd come into the room and see my eight-year-old watching this terrible, blurry picture and I'd say, "Heavens, how can you see? Let me try to fix it," and he'd get frantic and scream, "Don't touch it!" It really worried me, that he wanted to watch so badly that he was even willing to watch a completely blurred image.

Another mother tells of her eight-year-old son's behavior when deprived of television:

There was a time when both TV sets were out for about two weeks, and Jerry reached a point where I felt that if he didn't watch something, he was really going to start climbing the walls. He was fidgety and nervous. He'd crawl all over the furniture. He just didn't know what to do with himself, and it seemed to get worse every day. I said to my husband, "He's having withdrawal symptoms," and I really think that's what it was. Finally I asked one of my friends if he could go and watch the Saturday cartoons at their house.

In the early 1980s Robin Smith, a graduate student at the University of Massachusetts in Amherst, conducted a research study on television addiction as part of a doctoral dissertation. Setting out to discover whether television viewing can truly be classified as an addiction according to a particular, narrow definition she had constructed from the work of various social scientists, Smith sent out a questionnaire to 984 adults in Springfield, Massachusetts, in which they were asked to rate their own behavior in regard to television viewing. Using a number of statistical tests to analyze the responses, the author concluded that the results failed to confirm that television addiction exists. "Television addiction does not appear to be a robust phenomenon," Smith wrote in that poetic yet obscure way academics sometimes have of expressing things.

Striving to understand why television is so widely considered an addiction, in the conclusion of her research paper Smith noted:

> . . . the popularity of television as "plug-in drug" is
> enduring. One possible source of this image lies in the
> nature of viewing experience. The only study to date that
> examines the nature of the viewing experience in adults
> found that television watching, of all life activities measured
> in the course of one week, was the least challenging,
> involved the least amount of skill, and was most relaxing.

If television viewing is so bereft of value by most measures of well-being, and yet takes up the greatest part of people's leisure hours, it becomes moot whether it is defined as an addiction or simply a powerful habit. As psychologists Robert Kubey and Mihaly Csikszentmihalyi concluded in their book about the television experience: "A long-held habit becomes so ingrained that it borders on addiction. A person may no longer be watching television because of simple want, but because he or she virtually has to. Other alternatives may seem to become progressively more remote. What might have been a choice years earlier is now a necessity."

Robert Kubey explains further: "While television can provide relaxation and entertainment . . . it still rarely delivers any lasting fulfillment. Only through active engagement with the worlds we inhabit and the people in them can we attain for ourselves the rewards and meaning that lead to psychological well-being."

4

The Experts

Dr. Spock and the Tube

For many decades after television's introduction into American society, long after viewing had come to take up more of the average child's waking time than any other single activity, the most popular child-care manuals paid little attention to the medium and the problems it had brought into the family. The few paragraphs they devoted to television referred only to the content of programs children were likely to watch. Excessive violence and sex were the dangers parents were warned about, not that excessive viewing might adversely effect their children's mental and emotional development.

Well into the television era, the most influential child-care guide of the 1960s, '70s, and '80s, Dr. Benjamin Spock's *Baby and Child Care,* made no mention at all of the role of television in the lives of the medium's most susceptible audience—very young children. As for school-aged children, early editions of Spock's manual took a casual view of their involvement with the medium: "In general, if a child is taking care of his homework, staying outside with his friends in the afternoon, coming to supper, going to bed when it's time, and not being frightened, I would be inclined to let him spend as much time with television and radio as he chooses," he advised parents, adding, "If the rest of the family is driven mad by having to watch or listen to a child's programs and if they can afford the expense, it's worth while to get him a set for his room."

By 1976 this phrase was deleted from all future editions of the book. Perhaps, as children's viewing hours continued to increase year after year it had become clear that this was a singularly ill-considered bit of advice. In the four versions that followed, Dr. Spock proposed that parents "come to a reasonable but definite understanding about which hours are for outdoors, for homework, for meals, and for programs." Though he was finally raising the subject of television control, he failed to include any further advice about how to achieve it.

By the seventh edition of *Baby and Child Care*, published in 1998, Dr. Spock and his new co-author had begun to take a strongly negative view of television. "Of all the media, television has the most pervasive influence on children," a new section on television begins. Unequivocally stating that television viewing promotes passivity and "requires zero mental activity on the viewer's part," that "watching TV is incompatible with creativity," and going on to suggest that television viewing "impairs children's ability to learn to read and fosters a short attention span," Dr. Spock came up with a perfect solution to this serious problem: "In my opinion, not having a TV at all seems to be a logical solution."

But in spite of his new conviction that the television experience is essentially passive and that it adversely affects creativity and attention spans, Dr. Spock retreated. "Since I recognize that this solution is far too extreme for most of you, there are some sound rules for making the best of television and minimizing its destructive effects on children," he wrote. The new rules he proposed focused almost entirely on program content: Pick wonderful videotapes for very young children instead of turning on the TV. Use the V-Chip to limit access to cable. Flatly forbid children to watch violent programs.

By shifting his attention from the experience to the content, he weakened his arguments about television's negative effects. He was suggesting, in effect, that by following his rules about picking fine programs and avoiding violence, everything would be okay. Thus the real problems of television control remained unaddressed in this expanded edition.

The Medical Establishment

Before 1995, though television had long been the single most time-consuming leisure-time activity in the lives of American children, the influential American Academy of Pediatrics focused almost entirely on matters of program content, especially television violence and its connection with aggressive behavior. There was one important exception: statistics had begun to show that obesity was on the increase among American children. In 1984 the AAP pinpointed television viewing as one of the causes of childhood obesity. It didn't matter what kind of programs they watched—too much television watching made kids fat.

In 1995 the doctors' organization issued a new sort of recommendation: "Parents should be encouraged to limit their children's daily television viewing to no more than 1 to 2 hours per day." For the first time an influential organization had out-and-out declared that the content of TV programs was not the only consideration for parents—that watching three hours of *Sesame Street* and *Barney* and *Mr. Rogers' Neighborhood,* all "high-quality" programs, might still not be acceptable for children.

Furthermore, the AAP proposed that pediatricians add TV viewing to their list of important subjects to bring up routinely with parents. The doctors were told to emphasize the importance of limiting television time, and to exhort parents to develop TV substitutes such as reading, pursuing hobbies, and imaginative play.

In August, 1999, the AAP took a bold step forward. In a new policy statement, the Academy noted that "research on early brain development shows that babies and toddlers have a critical need for direct interactions with parents and other significant caregivers for healthy brain growth . . ." Consequently, the august doctors' organization issued a new and radical guideline: "Pediatricians should urge parents to avoid television viewing for children under the age of 2 years."

"No TV for Toddlers" made front-page headlines in newspapers around the country. It had taken half a century, but the medical profession finally recognized television as a potential pathogen. Doctors were finally obliged to deal with it.

Physical Effects

If there is a single area in which television's impact has nothing to do with the content of programs, it's children's and adults' physical health. Among the issues:

• **Obesity**

The connection between obesity and excessive television viewing has been widely publicized. It was this incontrovertible correlation that drew the medical profession out of its torpor about children's TV viewing habits, impelling it to take up television as a health issue.

The explanation of why television viewing might lead to obesity seems obvious: 1. If you're watching, you're not doing something more active and 2. While you're watching you're likely to be snacking. But there may be more to it than that.

A researcher at Memphis State University monitored the metabolic rates of children watching a regular children's TV program [*The Wonder Years*] and discovered that as they watched, their metabolic rates dropped to a level somewhere between resting and sleeping. Had they been simply sitting and doing nothing at all, their level would have been significantly higher. The effect was even greater for children already overweight. Since the metabolic rate measures the number of calories a person uses up over time, this finding demonstrates that it's not merely a matter of TV watching displacing some form of exercise that encourages obesity. By reducing the metabolic rate, the act of TV watching itself makes kids more likely to become fat.

• Diabetes

Connected with the rise in obesity is a nationwide rise in diabetes—a 76 percent rise in cases among people in their thirties between 1990 and 1998. In a report in a professional journal, experts attributed the rise of diabetes to the rising weight of Americans which in turn they attributed to Americans' "increasing tendency to park themselves in front of television and computer screens."

• Decline in Overall Physical Fitness

A decline in overall physical fitness among American children has often been attributed to excessive TV watching. Very few people need proof of this connection. While kids used to play out of doors whenever possible during nonschool hours, today much of that time is spent in front of the tube. Television cartoons on weekends are more popular with children than their former weekend activities of bike-riding, roller-skating, playing baseball, and participating in other sports. Of course part of the reason kids spend less time playing outdoors has to do with changes in society during the last half-century: in most localities, it is no longer safe to send the kids outside to play without supervision. But better community opportunities for supervised play must be the answer to this problem, not more television watching.

• Sleep Disorders

Television viewing has been suggested as a possible causal factor in children's sleep disturbances. A report in the medical journal *Pediatrics* stated: "Health-care practitioners should be aware of the potential negative impact of television viewing at bedtime . . . In particular, the presence of a television set in the child's bedroom may be a relatively unrecognized, but important contributor to sleep problems in schoolchildren."

• *Low-back pain*
Researchers in Switzerland found that the amount of time spent watching television significantly increased the risk of low-back pain among schoolchildren.

5

Television and Violence: A Different Approach

First a Disclaimer

Violence is *the* big subject when people talk about television's impact on children. That's because most people believe implicitly that watching violent programs on TV leads to violence in real life. Everybody says it's true—the government, the PTA, the American Medical Association, virtually every group connected with children and their welfare. Before presenting an argument that goes against this strongly held belief, I feel obliged to make a disclaimer: I'm not saying that watching violence on television is good for children, nor am I saying that it's acceptable for kids to watch violent programs. My argument is about whether violent programs on television are responsible for the host of social ills people connect them with, and in particular, whether watching such programs makes children behave violently.

I would never deny that there's something deeply repugnant about the idea of children, particularly very young ones, seeing nasty, brutish behavior on their screens. Such images are scary and upsetting for some children. Violent programs are bound to influence many kids' ideas of what life is like, and may cause them to take on some superficial yet unattractive verbal and physical mannerisms. These will certainly influence the way the adult world behaves toward them: tough-talking and tough-acting little kids are likely to be treated less protectively. From this point of view the content of programs does matter. Parents *should* protect their kids from violent TV programs, just as the American Academy of Pediatrics, the national PTA, and the other child advocacy organizations suggest.

But that's not the whole issue. The inexorable focus on violent programming obscures greater problems that the medium brings into the home. Making TV violence the whipping boy for the level of violence in American society diverts attention and funds from other research and programs that might lead to valuable changes, including those dealing with excessive television viewing.

For families, focusing attention exclusively on this single issue gives the idea that violent programming is the major problem parents face with television. It allows parents to consider program content alone in making decisions about their kids' TV viewing, and diverts attention from the larger questions of how much time their kids watch, and what they are missing as a result. Perhaps parents don't want to hear this, having become dependent on television as a babysitter, a problem solver, a way to avoid dealing with their kids directly and with authority. With violence firmly established on center stage, they can successfully put off facing the need for real change.

Looking for a Link

Spurred on by the huge amount of violence on television, and by the scary possibility that viewing a lot of it might somehow make people behave more violently, social scientists have been looking for a connection between the two from television's earliest days. By the mid-1990s, more than 1000 studies investigating the effects of viewing televised violence had been completed. Many of these, some going back to the sixties and seventies, are used today to support the conclusion that television violence is, indeed, responsible for many of our society's ills.

Organizations such as the American Academy of Pediatrics and the National PTA consider the experimental evidence linking television violence and real-life violence good enough proof and urgently advise parents to monitor their children's viewing. Most parents are already solidly convinced that the connection has been proved, though they don't necessarily do anything about it.

Yet no direct, causal link has ever been demonstrated between the violence that millions of kids watch regularly on television, and the horrifying sort of behavior reflected in crime statistics. Indeed, relating the experimental findings to real violence in society is one of the major problems facing media researchers. While numerous studies show that kids act more aggressively after watching an hour of TV murder and mayhem, they show an increase in the ordinary forms of childhood aggression—pushing, shoving, hitting, and being verbally abusive—not rape or murder or any of the serious crimes included in crime statistics. As a comprehensive review of research on television violence undertaken by the American Psychological Society in the mid-1980s noted in this regard: "A great number of experimental studies demonstrate that after watching a violent program children of all ages will show more aggressive behavior. What has never been demonstrated is whether this increase in aggressiveness actually changes the child's behavior in ordinary life."

This, of course, jibes with most parents' intuitive understanding of how television affects their kids. While they suspect that all the violent stuff their kids watch on television day after day will rub off on them in subtle ways, nevertheless most parents feel reasonably certain that it won't turn their kids into juvenile delinquents. After all, the majority of American children are exposed to these violent programs regularly, while only a small segment of the viewing population becomes involved in serious crime.

It is particularly hard for parents to buy the idea that television instigates dangerous aggression when its function in the home is so different. There television cuts down on loud and boisterous play, prevents outbursts between brothers and sisters, and eliminates a number of potentially destructive household experiments children might be indulging in—playing with matches, for instance—were they not occupied by *Crime Stories* or *Miami Vice*.

The late Selma Fraiberg gave a sensible reason for rejecting a direct connection between normal children's viewing of violent programs and an epidemic of violence:

> I do not mean . . . that the vulgar fiction of television is capable of turning our children into delinquents. The influence of such fiction on children's attitudes and conduct is really more subtle. We need to remember that it is the parents who are the progenitors of conscience and that a child who has strong ties to his parents will not overthrow their teachings more easily than he could abandon his parents themselves. I do not think that any of us here needs to fear this kind of corruption of our children.

A further flaw in the argument that violence on television might cause children to behave more violently has been stated by a television critic who points out that if this were true, there would be a concomitant effect produced by the inevitable moralistic and "good" aspects of those same violent programs:

> If indeed the cumulative watching is turning us all, gradually, into depraved beings, then the cumulative watching of good must be turning us all, gradually, into saints! You cannot have one without the other. That is, unless you are prepared to demonstrate that evil is something like cholesterol—something that slowly accumulates and clogs the system, while good is something like spinach, easily digested and quickly excreted.

Making the Wrong Connection

Many studies purporting to connect violent TV content with violent behavior merely demonstrate a connection between television viewing [regardless of content] and aggressive behavior. For example, in the previously cited review of research by the American Psychological Association, the authors state: "The accumulated research clearly demonstrates a correlation between viewing violence and aggressive behavior—that is, heavy viewers behave more aggressively than light viewers." But by talking about *heavy viewers* rather than *viewers of violent programs* the authors prove nothing about the effects of viewing violent programs, only that viewing a lot of television, regardless of content, causes aggressiveness. This sort of unwarranted conclusion occurs again and again in scholarly discussions of television and its effects.

A widely cited experiment by Dr. Victor Cline, conducted in the 1970s, continues to be accepted as a demonstration that viewing violent programs blunts children's sensitivities to violence. In the study, researchers compared the responses of two groups of boys to a violent television program. One group had seen little or no TV in the previous two years while the other had watched an average of 42 hours a week for the same period of time. The researchers found that the heavy viewers were significantly less aroused by what they saw and concluded that the TV gourmands had been desensitized by gobbling up so many violent programs.

And yet Cline's two groups differed only in *how much* they had watched, not *what* they watched. The boys who had watched 42 hours of television a week showed diminished emotional responses, while the ones whose reactions were undulled had watched almost no television at all. Common sense suggests that 42 hours a week of *any* television program might tip the balance from reality to unreality in children's lives sufficiently to lower their arousal level. Six hours daily of the blandest, most peaceable programming seems just as likely to affect children's ability to respond normally to human realities as an equal amount of the blatantly violent programs that Cline and others are concerned about.

In January 2001, a new study on television and aggression was published in the journal *Archives of Pediatrics and Adolescent Medicine.* Its results were generally perceived as new evidence that watching violent TV programs makes kids more aggressive. In fact, like the Victor Cline study twenty-five years earlier, it demonstrated a different, though no less significant, finding: that watching less TV of any sort makes a difference.

In the new study, researchers from Stanford University enlisted as experimental subjects 192 third- and fourth-grade students attending two carefully matched public elementary schools in San Jose, California. After researchers observed the kids at the playground and interviewed their parents and peers, all participants were given "aggression ratings."

Then one school introduced a program that found imaginative ways to motivate the children to cut down their television, videotape, and video-game use. Over a six-month period the kids reduced their TV and video-game time by one-third, a substantial reduction. The other school served as a control—the kids spent their usual amount of time watching television and playing video games.

The results: when measured again, the kids who watched less TV had become less aggressive, while the control group remained at about the same level as before.

The experiment shows a significant connection between heavy TV viewing and aggression, and might have been useful in encouraging parents to cut down on their kids' hours in front of the tube. But the press construed the results as content-related: that watching less violence on TV was what made the kids less aggressive. The authors of the study may have contributed to this distorted view by introducing their paper with the words: "Violence is pervasive in television, movies and video games . . ."

Of course the experiment doesn't disprove that a connection between violent content and subsequent behavior exists; one can assume that since there's so much violence on TV, by cutting down viewing by a third, the kids were cutting down on a lot of viewing of violence. That, in fact, is what the authors did assume, citing previous studies on the subject. Nevertheless it does not mean that the experiment's results must be interpreted in that way.

Here are two alternative hypotheses that might explain why watching a lot of television would lead to increased aggression and cutting down would reduce aggression:

1. Television viewing substantially reduces that crucial set of experiences known as play. Several animal experiments have demonstrated the role of play in mitigating aggression. Could this not be true for humans as well? (See Play Deprivation, page 86.)

2. During the six-month period when TV was reduced substantially, there were surely some effects on parent-child relations at home. Perhaps the parents were more accessible to the kids during the hiatus. Perhaps they had to socialize them more. Whatever those changes were, they could have led to a decrease in aggressiveness among the kids.

Why is everybody so eager to suppose that it is the violence on TV that causes violence, even researchers whose studies demonstrate a different connection? Perhaps because if it's the content at fault, then something can easily be done about it: parents can turn off those violent programs. They can boycott stations and advertisers, get their legislators to pass laws, install V-Chips in their TV sets.

If parents are compelled to recognize that the problem resides not in the sock-bam-pow content, but in the great amounts of time their kids spend watching, then the solution is not so easy. It requires reducing the amount of time children watch, as the children did in the San Jose experiment. Or possibly eliminating television entirely from their children's lives, especially when they're very young. Few parents want to face that daunting prospect.

PART II

Television and Early Childhood

6

Television for Tots

Baby Viewers

Several decades ago parents looked forward to that wonderful moment when their demanding toddler would be transformed into a quiet video-tot just as eagerly as their counterparts do today. But in those days people believed that very little kids simply weren't cognitively ready to pay attention to a screen until they reached the age of about two and a half. Parents' own experience and much research supported that view.

During that era the child-development experts were neither surprised nor sorry that infants and young preschoolers did not seem to take to television the way older toddlers did. It appeared to be a clear survival mechanism on the part of the human organism during its earliest and most vulnerable stage. The experts understood the importance of those traditional activities young children have always engaged in—the great variety of physical and mental behaviors that fall into the category of play. These were precisely the activities that allowed young children to actively explore the world using all their senses. If very young children were to sit for hours watching images on a screen, their opportunities to engage in these vital activities would be diminished.

Though the experts said babies wouldn't watch TV, many parents couldn't help noticing that their babies were, indeed, attracted to the colors and moving shapes on the screen. The trouble was they weren't attracted for very long, not long enough for the parents' purposes—to be able to do tasks, make telephone calls, or simply take a break from child care. Perhaps there weren't the right kinds of programs available to fascinate the infant set. It was time for the researchers to get to work.

Some of the earliest studies of babies and their television-viewing potential were done in Japan, a country with high TV viewership at every age level. In 1986 a Japanese survey confounded the presuppositions that babies will not pay attention to television. It declared that one-third of the four- to five-month-old babies studied watched TV for an hour or more per day. They found that after the age of five months, infants begin to watch the screen "intently." The researchers found that by the time they reached their first birthday, 63 percent of babies in Japan were television viewers.

Are Japanese babies different in some particular way from American babies? There are probably other explanations. At the time the Japanese studies were done, though there were no real programs aimed especially at infants in the United States, Japan did have such a program. Entitled *With Mother*, it was especially created for babies and young toddlers. According to surveys, Japanese mothers made concerted efforts to have their babies exposed to this program, believing it to be beneficial to them.

Another finding might help explain the high rate of infant TV viewing found in the Japanese survey: more than seven out of ten respondents living near Tokyo reported that there was a TV set in the baby's room. One third of those babies could watch TV from their cribs. This does not seem to be the case in the U.S. although there are no statistics about babies and the proximity of television sets to their cribs. All this may change, as the TV status of American babies changes.

Marshall Haith, a professor of developmental psychology, may have been the first to create a videotape especially for infants and market it though catalogues and toy stores. That was in 1990, and parents who bought it discovered that their infants paid attention to it.

Within a few years videos for babies began showing up in video stores and baby catalogues. The market flourished. Yet babies remained the single segment of the American population that didn't officially watch television since they weren't included in statistical analyses such as the Nielsen Report.

In 1998 the first program in America ever to be targeted for babies and toddlers under the age of two arrived: *Teletubbies*. Produced by the BBC, *Teletubbies* had been a huge success in England. In 1997 spin-off merchandise from the program were the hottest-selling toys in the United Kingdom, generating over $40,000,000 [£23,000,000] for the BBC.

Teletubbies didn't slip onto the American scene quietly. Full-page advertisements in newspapers and magazines trumpeted the program's educational value. Ads were plastered on city buses. The program's producers appeared on talk shows to spread the word to parents. The PBS Web site promised that the show would "nourish children's thinking skills, teach them to listen, help build their curiosity, expand their imagination and increase their confidence." The irony of this set of claims is striking, considering that thinking, listening, curiosity, imagination, and self-confidence are precisely those attributes that television-viewing is said to affect in a negative way.

Among those who reacted indignantly to *Teletubbies* and to the very idea of a television program especially directed to babies was Alvin F. Poussaint, a professor of psychiatry at the Harvard Medical School. Writing with co-author Susan E. Linn in the magazine *The American Prospect,* he did not mince words in denouncing PBS, that trusted purveyor of *Mr. Rogers* and *Sesame Street,* for promoting *Teletubbies* on its network. "There is no documented evidence that *Teletubbies* has any educational value at all," he wrote. Responding to the producers' claim that children like the program, he retorted, "The fact that children like something, or parents think they do, does not mean that it is educational, or even good for them. Children like candy, too.

"Until more is known about the effects of television viewing on one-year-olds, and until longitudinal research determines exactly what, if anything, one-year-olds learn from *Teletubbies,* PBS officials should join the American Academy of Pediatrics and child development specialists around the country in actively discouraging parents from exposing their babies to television," Dr. Poussaint declared. He concluded his article with an exhortation: "Anyone who cares about children and has access to parents needs to urge them, earnestly, to keep their youngest, most vulnerable children away from the tube."

Sesame Street Revisited

In the past, real live people served as the principle training ground for children's language development. That is to say, it was understood that the more parents spoke to their children, read to them, listened to them and echoed back their sounds, the more likely they were to learn to use language well.

Today, since words and phrases similar to those parents speak emanate from the television set, many parents believe that young children will profit as much from giving their attention to a television program as they might if they spent that time talking and listening to a real person in real life. Indeed, with the almost universal acceptance of *Sesame Street* as a positive education experience for preschool children, many parents have come to feel that watching "educational" television programs may be a more profitable mental occupation than any they themselves might provide.

And yet the educational results of *Sesame Street* have been disappointing. The expectation that a program—carefully designed by the most eminent and knowledgeable child specialists—would bridge the gap between middle-class children who have had ample verbal opportunities at home and those children deprived of such opportunities has not been realized. Poor children have *not* caught up with their more advantaged peers, or even made significant gains of any sort, though they watch *Sesame Street* faithfully year after year. Schools have *not* had to readjust their first-grade curricula to accommodate a new breed of well-prepared *Sesame Street* graduates with higher levels of language maturity (the prevailing belief in the first years of the program). Although children exhibit certain small gains in number and letter recognition as a result of *Sesame Street,* their language skills do not show any significant or permanent gains as they progress through school.

Why, in the light of such small returns, do parents and educators continue to believe that this particular television program has such great value for young children? It is likely that much of the widespread belief in *Sesame Street*'s educational efficacy began with highly publicized evaluations of the programs results made by the Education Testing Service in 1970 and 1971. These findings indicated that the young watchers of *Sesame Street* did indeed make great gains as a result of their viewing experiences.

Five years later, however, as part of a larger project studying methods of evaluating and reviewing research, the Russell Sage Foundation published the results of a rigorous reevaluation of the original ETS evaluation in a book—*Sesame Street Revisited.* As the authors, a team of social scientists, painstakingly retraced the steps of the ETS researchers, they discovered some important discrepancies that led them to question seriously the original, highly positive findings regarding the impact of *Sesame Street.*

The authors of *Sesame Street Revisited* found that the group of children who had watched the most hours of *Sesame Street* in the ETS study and who exhibited the greatest cognitive gains did not merely watch so many hours by accident. As a specially selected experimental group they had been encouraged to watch in a particular way, receiving extra attention in the form of personal visits, promotional materials, and so on.

It was indeed the encouragement accompanying the experiment rather than the actual effects of the program material that caused those gains so widely publicized as proof of *Sesame Street*'s effectiveness, the authors believed. Yet another finding supported this view: among the "unencouraged" children involved in the original ETS evaluation, those who were the heaviest viewers of *Sesame Street* demonstrated fewer gains in cognitive skills than light viewers.

The Russell Sage study also found evidence that the gap between advantaged and disadvantaged children the program had been designed to narrow might actually have widened as a result of widespread *Sesame Street* viewing.

Noting that their negative findings about *Sesame Street*'s value were often met with skepticism or outright disbelief by parents of preschool children, the authors offered a number of explanations for parents' refusal to be persuaded that *Sesame Street,* though a delightful entertainment for young children, does not provide them with a particularly valuable learning experience:

- Parents are so impressed by any learning children achieve at early age that they believe the few things kids pick up by watching the program represent a far greater learning gain.
- Parents don't realize that children might have learned some of the things they seem to have learned from the program simply by environmental exploration.
- Parents are misled by the narrow gains in letter and number recognition that come from watching *Sesame Street* into assuming that the children are making gains in more general cognitive areas.
- Parents are influenced by the testimony of their friends about *their* children's gains from watching *Sesame Street.*

The authors also pointed out the favorable press that *Sesame Street* had received since its inception. "If the attitudes and beliefs of parents have indeed been influenced by this publicity," they write, "it too may have contributed towards overestimating the program's effects." It is interesting to note that while the positive findings of the ETS study had received prominent attention in the popular press, the Russell Sage study, a product of an equally respectable scientific organization, was largely ignored by the popular press at the time of its publication.

After the Russell Sage "revisit" to *Sesame Street,* no other substantial studies of the program's effects appeared for two decades. In 1995 the results of another study were released. Continuing the up-and-down cycle, once again a team of researchers concluded that *Sesame Street* had a positive impact on its target viewers—disadvantaged preschoolers.

But the new project's believability was jeopardized by an awkward fact: Children's Television Workshop, the parent organization of *Sesame Street,* partially supported the study and was responsible for choosing the researchers to design and perform it. Since the team chosen had published favorable findings about *Sesame Street* before, they were less likely to come up with a negative report.

The Echoes of *Sesame Street*

Though *Sesame Street* has enjoyed almost universal acclaim since its arrival in 1969, a few incisive voices have raised and continue to raise questions about the program's influence on its young viewers. The late Dorothy Cohen, a professor at the Bank Street College of Education, was perhaps the first child specialist to speak out against the show's particular quick-cut, fast-action format. In a paper that attracted much attention among educators, she wrote: "While some children enter kindergarten and even nursery school recognizing letters as a result of the emphasis placed on such recognition by *Sesame Street,* there is also, if we are to believe experienced teachers, a decrease in imaginative play and an increase in aimless running around, noninvolvement in play materials, low frustration tolerance, poor persistence, and confusion about reality and fantasy."

Other child experts, notably Yale University psychologists Dorothy and Jerome Singer, also singled out the show's fast pace for criticism. In 1979 they argued that the show created "a psychological orientation in children that leads to a shortened attention span, a lack of reflectiveness and an expectation of rapid change in the broader environment." Today the Singers, now co-directors of the Yale University Family Television Research and Consultation center, write that although the quote represented their views in the late seventies, "since then *Sesame Street* has gradually heeded this and other criticisms and has modified pace, increased emphasis on sound and phonics [not only the names of letters], has increased emphasis on 'prosocial' skills, etc."

Educator and author Jane Healy has been one of *Sesame Street*'s most incisive critics since the program first came on the air. In her book *Endangered Minds,* it is not so much the program's pace, but the whole notion of teaching reading to preschoolers that Healy questions. "*Sesame Street* has popularized the erroneous belief that it is appropriate for most preschoolers to learn to read. . . . Misguided efforts to train preschoolers in skills more appropriate for kindergarten or first grade diverts valuable time and attention from their real learning needs," she writes. As Healy and every early childhood educator know, these needs require active, hands-on experiences, experiences that fall into the category of play, not television learning.

In her book Healy does not come up with much to praise about the program. She notes that although it has provided children with unifying cultural symbols such as Big Bird and Ernie, it has also helped sell a lot of related products. And while the program makes a serious effort to give positive messages about important subjects such as cultural diversity, handicaps, and the like, Healy observes that most of those messages go over the heads of its audience.

But why be so earnest about it—why single out this charming, well-produced program for criticism? What if *Sesame Street* has not fulfilled its original goal of reducing the gap between advantaged and disadvantaged children—a goal that may have been unrealistic in the first place? The program's fun, isn't it? Surely kids will pick up what they didn't learn on the program when they get to school.

The problem lies in *Sesame Street*'s unique reputation as an important educational experience for young children, and its consequent role in promoting television viewing even among parents who might feel an instinctive resistance to plugging such young children in. As hundreds of parents have noted in interviews about their children's television experiences, many of them appearing in these pages, *Sesame Street* marks their child's transition into television viewing.

For many thousands, perhaps millions of children, the echoes of *Sesame Street* continue to reverberate long after they move on to other programs. As Tannis MacBeth Williams has pointed out in *The Impact of Television,* for those millions of children who have learned letters and numbers by watching the program, that first part of the process was fun. But the next stage is not. "It requires slogging practice," she observes. And that practice, she reminds the reader, cannot come from television viewing. Meanwhile, for the less able learners—who require even more practice than those who pick up reading quickly—practicing may come to seem even less pleasant and television even more attractive.

How Much Do They Understand?

Much evidence suggests that the viewing of television by very young children does not lead to significant learning gains. Why should this be? A number of studies of children's actual comprehension of television material find that while children clearly enjoy watching particular programs intended for their age group, and may be quite attentive while they watch, their understanding of what is happening on the screen is very small indeed.

In one study, preschoolers' comprehension of an informational television program designed for their age group was measured by a standard evaluation procedure. A majority of the children understood less than half the tested information. Since the children who were asked some questions midway through the program segment showed no better comprehension than those who were asked all the questions at the end of the program, the possibility was eliminated that memory, not comprehension, was the deciding factor.

In another study, children aged four, seven, and ten years were shown a twenty-minute fairy tale of a kind commonly seen on television. After they saw the film the children's comprehension of the story was tested. Only 20 percent of the four-year-olds showed that they had understood the story line. The older children's comprehension was far superior. The authors conclude that "preschool children were unable to either remember what they had seen with any fidelity or to interpret accurately why the characters acted as they did."

In a third study, four-year-olds were shown a movie of a man performing a series of acts such as building a particular kind of block tower, putting a toy on top, and walking away. Twenty similar behaviors were shown in the film. The children were told before viewing that they would later be asked to do what the man did in the film. But the children did not learn the activities by watching them on film. They were able to reproduce only six of the twenty acts.

A second group of four-year-olds, however, who viewed the films in the company of an experimenter who verbally described each act as it was performed on the film, demonstrated far greater comprehension, or at least retention, of the filmed material. These children showed a 50 percent increase in ability to correctly reenact the filmed activities.

More recently researchers investigating the viewing habits of preschoolers noted that mothers were often far more critical of the programs than their preschoolers were. "In their evaluation of one program," they write, "mothers complained that there were too many characters to follow. This was not a problem for their young children *because the kids simply didn't try to follow all of them.*" [my emphasis].

The researchers concluded: "Post-viewing interviews with preschoolers strongly indicate that their enjoyment of a program is often independent from their comprehension of the content. In repeated instances, the child was watching with rapt attention but with limited understanding of the story line or theme.

While researchers find that comprehension and retention of what children see on television does increase with age, certain findings show that even children as old as eight do not remember much of what they see and hear on television, and that even in programs especially designed for children, such as *Sesame Street,* retention by preschool and kindergarten children is very low, suggesting that comprehension is low as well.

Parents, of course, have their own evidence of young children's lack of comprehension: they see their own kids engrossed in programs they cannot possibly understand.

A mother reports:

> *My four-year-old loves and adores television and would watch it twenty-four hours a day if we let him. The other afternoon he watched the economic mini-summits on television, and you have to be some sort of nut if you sit there and watch those, even* if you understand them!

A father of a five-year-old relates:

> *My son and I were lying on the bed together the other night, watching a program about labor unrest in Cornwall, and he*

was absolutely fascinated. I said to him, "Would you like me to explain this to you?" and he said, "No Daddy, I'm just watching."

If watching *Sesame Street* does not bring about the same sort of cognitive gains that real-life linguistic experiences provide, and if young children spend thousands of hours engrossed in watching programs whose content they don't understand, what, then, *is* going on when they watch television? What sort of mental activity are they engaging in while viewing? And what effect might their involvement with this particular form of mental activity, so different from all other waking activities, have on their mental development?

7

Television and the Brain

When children want to know why they can't watch all the television they want, parents often resort to answers that suggest, with mock humor, that too much television will have deleterious effects on the brain. "It will turn your brains to mush" and "It will rot the brain" are phrases frequently used by parents trying to express their barely formed and unarticulated anxieties about the television experience.

The possible effects of heavy involvement with television on a child's brain development clearly do not lie in the direction of brain-rot or "brain-mush"; several generations of children raised watching television have come to maturity showing no signs of a downward trend in overall intelligence. And yet there *are* aspects of brain development that may be significantly affected by regular exposure to the television experience, though they cannot be measured by means of a simple IQ test. An understanding of certain aspects of brain physiology may clarify the potential neurological impact of the television experience.

Brain Changes

Are a child's real-life experiences capable of producing changes within the brain? In a discussion of television's impact on children, it is a highly relevant question, for if environmental factors *can* affect brain development, then a time-consuming experience such as television-watching must be considered as a source of neurological change, either a positive or a negative one.

For a long time most scientists believed that brain capacity and development were genetically predetermined and unaffected by the events and experiences of life. An experiment published in 1972 first indicated that there were, indeed, many aspects of brain anatomy and chemistry that could be significantly altered by stimulation or lack of it. These experiments, investigating brain changes in animals raised in impoverished environments (bare cages with little outside stimulation) compared with changes in animals raised in enriched environments (cages filled with toys and equipment, and numerous opportunities to engage in stimulating activities), demonstrated an increase in weight of the cerebral cortex as well as increased brain enzyme activity among those animals raised in enriched environments. The rats from the enriched environments ran better mazes than the deprived rats, showing that the brain changes led to increased mental capacity.

What about those three- or four-year-olds who spend two or three or four hours a day watching television images? Might this be considered an "enriched environment"? After all, there are many images and sounds coming out of the television set, and the child takes them in.

Dr. Marian Cleeves Diamond, professor of neuroanatomy at the University of California and one of the authors of that landmark study, proposes an answer to that question. Presenting her findings about brain changes at a government conference on television and children, Dr. Diamond made no direct connections between her study and the effects of television viewing on young children. She did not suggest, for instance, that a comparison might be made between the deprived rats and children deprived of play experiences as a result of excessive television watching. Scientists don't make speculative judgments of that sort. But her final comment to the audience of educators and researchers came as close as a scientist ever comes to making a straightforward conclusion based on gut feelings rather than on hard and fast evidence.

"[T]he reason I was brought here today was to mention that the investigators have shown that if rats sit alone in cages watching those rats in enriched environments, the brains of the watching rats do not demonstrate measurable changes. It is important to interact with the objects, to explore, to investigate, both physically and mentally." Clearly she was talking about television.

Research conducted during the next two decades removed any doubt about the impact of early brain stimulation on a child's later cognitive development.

In 1987, using Positron Emission Tomography (PET scans), Dr. Harry Chugani, a professor of neurology at Wayne State University, and colleagues measured changes in the brain's metabolic activity in various areas over time. In this way they were able to demonstrate that environmental factors can alter neuron pathways during early childhood and long after.

According to other neuroscientists, among the most important of the environmental factors that might affect neurological development are the language and eye contact an infant is exposed to. Indeed, some researchers say that the number of words an infant hears each day is the single most important predictor of later intelligence, school success and social competence. But there's one catch. As a *New York Times* science writer concluded, "The words have to come from an attentive, engaged human being. As far as anyone has been able to determine, radio and television do not work."

Critical Early Experience

Since very young children are among America's heaviest television viewers, it is important to look at a body of experimental as well as naturalistic evidence suggesting that the experiences of the early years, when the organism is growing and developing most rapidly, have a greater effect on brain development than those occurring in later years.

One of many such experiments demonstrating the greater importance of early environmental stimulation was performed several decades ago with kittens as the experimental subjects: The eyes of newborn kittens were stitched together to prevent them from seeing. By this means they were kept in darkness for three months. When the animals' eyes were opened, the researchers discovered that they did not proceed to acquire vision as they normally would have done a few days after birth. In the absence of visual stimulation within the first months of life, the kittens' visual system proved to be permanently damaged—the brain center responsible for vision did not function properly, for some reason. However, when the eyes of older kittens who had already acquired normal vision, or of adult cats, were artificially closed for an equal period of time, no optical damage resulted. Other experiments with chimpanzees support the theory that in the early stages of an organism's development there are sensitive periods of growth during which the presence or absence of certain experiences is critical for normal brain development.

While it is difficult to draw direct conclusions about human experience from animal experiments, old studies of infants and young children reared in sterile hospital wards, orphanages, and other institutions, all as impoverished in terms of mental stimulation as the bare cages of the rats in the animal experiments, support the findings of such experiments. The institutionalized children grew up with irreversible mental deficits.

Further evidence of the impact of environmental stimulation on brain development is provided by Head Start and other large-scale early education programs for young children. These have indicated, although not yet rigorously, that persistent sensory enrichment can lead to gains in mental ability. But the intervention must not come too late: a great body of social evidence suggests that the deficits of an environmentally impoverished early childhood are hard to make up for by remedial programs and opportunities for mental stimulation in later childhood.

A Caveat

In recent years there has been a popular movement emphasizing the critical importance of infancy and the years up to the age of three in child development. Parents are exhorted to play Mozart tapes for their babies, and to fill their cribs with stimulating black and white mobiles and toys to "ensure optimal brain development." Parents might infer, from the proponents of this movement, that there is nothing much they can do after three. It might even seem that they needn't worry about how much television their four- or five- or nine-year-old watches—the crucial moment that determines whether their child will make the honor roll or require remedial reading has passed.

Yet the term *early childhood,* as it is generally used in education, includes children up to the age of eight or nine. In fact, while there may, indeed, be certain sensitive developmental periods during the first three years, there is no question that important development goes on for at least another decade, and perhaps even longer. As John Bruer has pointed out in his book *The Myth of the First Three Years,* most of the neurological evidence of the last twenty-five years indicates that critical brain cell maturation continues at least until the age of eleven.

In the PET scan studies cited above, Chugani and his associates found that the years between three and nine are the most significant from the viewpoint of neurological development. Indeed, they go on to conclude: "our findings support the commonly accepted view that brain maturation in humans proceeds at least into the second decade of life." Still other studies show brain cell growth continuing until adolescence, and perhaps throughout life.

Nonverbal Thinking

It's hard to conceive of what goes on in children's minds before they learn to speak or understand words. Our own perception of thinking is so bound up with the notion of some sort of inner language that the nature of nonverbal thought is almost unthinkable. And yet there is experimental evidence to prove its existence. Researchers have demonstrated that infants as young as three months of age can differentiate between pictures of a regular human face and a discrepant image, one, say, with three eyes. Something akin to thinking must be going on as infants compare the picture of the "wrong" face with their internalized experience of regular human faces. A "thought" of a regular, two-eyed human face must exist in the child's mind, an image unaccompanied by words (since the child is months away from language acquisition), and yet activated somehow by the discrepant image. This is how children learn. Until the advent of language they will continue to absorb experience by means of a nonverbal form of thought.

By the second birthday, language has become a dominant force in a normal child's life. The symbolic labeling of all objects and events dominates all mental efforts from this point on. It is reasonable to assume that once language develops, the brain starts to specialize and verbal thinking begins to play an increasingly important role in children's cognitive development. With the ability to speak and understand, children become more active participants in thought and concept development, and nonverbal thinking ceases to serve its original function as the major source of learning. Now begins a journey of mental development that uniquely defines each child as a human being—animals, after all, depend exclusively upon nonverbal forms of thinking.

But the organism's first form of mental functioning, that nonverbal mode of thinking in operation when an infant reacts with heightened attention to a three-eyed face, does not simply vanish when verbal thinking sets in. Undoubtedly the two forms of thinking continue to function side by side throughout life.

Verbal thought is used whenever words, symbols, logic, or focal organization is required. Nonverbal functioning may be seen when the mind shifts into a qualitatively different state, as in those moments when one seems to be washed over by sensations unaccompanied by the usual mental manipulations. Staring into a flickering fireplace is an example of a nonverbal form of mental operation: the mind perceives the changing movements of the flames—the visual stimuli are obviously received by the brain's sense receptors—and yet no verbal manipulations occur. A mode of mental functioning that requires nothing but intake and acceptance is in operation under such circumstances.

For adults, nonverbal mental activities carry connotations of relaxation from the difficulties of logical thinking and promise a much desired achievement of peace and serenity. But for young children in their formative, language-learning years, any extended regression into nonverbal mental functioning such as the television experience offers is a potential setback. As they take in television words and images hour after hour, day after day, with little of the mental effort that forming their own thoughts and feelings and molding them into words would require, as they relax year after year, a pattern emphasizing nonverbal cognition becomes established.

Young children have a built-in need for mental activity. They are learning machines, "absorbent minds," gluttons for experience. In a culture that depends upon a precise and effective use of spoken and written language, children's optimal development requires not merely adequate, but abundant, opportunities to manipulate, to learn, to synthesize experience. Only their parents, fatigued by their offsprings' incessant demands for learning in the broadest sense of the word (learning that may involve whining, screaming, throwing things, pestering), require the "relaxation" afforded by setting the kids before the television screen, thus causing them to become, once again, the passive captives of their own sensations.

Brain Hemispheres

Television's impact on the developing brain may be closely connected to the particular ways in which the brain is organized to handle verbal and nonverbal material.

The cerebral cortex, that part of the brain responsible for the forms of higher thinking that distinguish human beings from lower animals, is not a single unit. It is composed of two separate hemispheres connected by a tangled mass of fibers. But unlike symmetrical organs such as the kidneys or lungs, in which each part is a precise duplicate of the other, each brain hemisphere has a number of unique and specialized functions. The left hemisphere, it has long been known, operates most of the brain's verbal and logical activities. For this reason it is often called the "dominant" hemisphere. The specific functions of the right hemisphere are less clearly understood, but it is known to be involved with spatial, visual, and perhaps affective activities.

Thus it happens that when an adult suffers a stroke in the left cerebral hemisphere, he or she is highly likely to lose all language capacity, while a right-hemisphere lesion will lead to a loss in face-recognition capacity, for instance, or in shape recognition ability, or in certain musical abilities such as tone recognition. After right-hemisphere surgery, patients may find it difficult to solve visual or tactile mazes, while patients undergoing similar operations on the left hemisphere perform well on such tests but show diminished abilities on verbal tests.

Many of the evident dualities in human nature and the qualitative differences found in ways of mental functioning undoubtedly have their origins in the brain's peculiarly asymmetrical organization. There are two kinds of "intelligence," for instance, tested on standard

IQ tests—verbal-logical and spatial. Many people are disproportionately endowed with one or the other of these abilities. Such a discrepancy may well have a neurological basis. Many people have come to believe that there are many more "intelligences" than those two.

The clear division of human memory into two categories—verbal and visual—provides further support for the idea that there exist two discrete ways of thinking. Experimental evidence shows that the processes involved in remembering what we see are quite different from those by which we remember what we read or hear as words. In everyday life this disparity is reflected in the common experience of recognizing the face of a person one has met before (visual memory), but failing to remember the person's name or even the circumstances under which the original meeting took place (verbal memory).

But hemisphere specialization, accompanied by two separate forms of mental organization, characterizes the adult brain alone. A very different situation exists in regard to the brain of a young child.

Until a child begins to acquire language, usually at the beginning of its second year, each hemisphere of the cerebral cortex seems to be equally developed in verbal capacity. Researchers have learned, for instance, that lesions of the left hemisphere in children under the age of two are no more injurious to their future language development than lesions in the right hemisphere, whereas adults with similar injuries suffer permanent linguistic losses. Children with left-hemisphere damage occurring after the onset of language but before the age of four may suffer temporary linguistic difficulties, but in almost all cases language is quickly restored. Brain injuries incurred before the early teens also carry a good prognosis for recovery of language ability.

But when damage occurs after this critical period, the outlook is poor. Whatever disability has been suffered is generally permanent. Since neurological evidence shows that it is around the age of twelve that the brain attains its final state of maturity in terms of structure and biochemistry, it appears that certain functions such as brain specialization lock into place at that time.

The fact that the brain of a young child is different in important ways from an adult brain may help us to localize the areas of television's possible neurological impact on a child. If during those formative years when the brain is in transition from its original, unspecialized state to one in which each hemisphere takes on a specific function, children engage in a repeated and time-consuming nonverbal, primarily visual activity—if, in effect, they receive excessive stimulation for the right-hemisphere forms of mental functioning—might this not have a discernible effect on their neurological development?

There are some indications that television viewing functions as just such a nonverbal, visual experience in the lives of young children. One is the trancelike state that characterizes many children's viewing behavior. It suggests that normal, active cognition is temporarily replaced by a state of mind more akin to meditation or other right-hemisphere–mediated states. The use of television, moreover, as a pacifying agent, a relaxant for overstimulated children and a sedative for troublesome ones, points up the nonverbal nature of the television experience.

Further evidence of the nonverbal effect of children's television experiences is seen in television's failure to act as an adequate replacement for real-life linguistic opportunities. The director of a Harlem center for deprived preschool children reports that child after child arrives at his school virtually mute, unable to speak a single intelligible sentence, although medical examinations reveal no clinical deficiencies, either physical or mental. "It is usually diagnosed as a speech defect," he observes, "but most often I have found it to be simply the result of hearing bad English, listening to nothing but television, and being spoken to hardly at all."

A Commitment to Language

Television viewing, to be sure, will not prevent a normal child from learning to speak. Only in cases of gross deprivation where children are almost totally isolated from human sounds will they not proceed according to a fairly universal language-learning schedule and fail to acquire the rudiments of speech.

It's not the child's actual acquisition of language, but the *commitment* to language as a means of expression and to the verbal mode as the ultimate source of fulfillment that's at stake. Such a commitment may have a physiological basis in the balance of right- and left-hemisphere development.

For young children who have only recently made the transition from nonverbal to verbal thought, much depends on their opportunities to exercise their growing verbal skills. The greater the children's verbal opportunities, the greater the likelihood that their language will grow in complexity and that their verbal thinking abilities will sharpen. The fewer their opportunities, on the other hand, the greater the likelihood that certain linguistic areas will remain undeveloped or underdeveloped as critical time periods come and go.

If those thousands and thousands of hours young children spend viewing television *do* serve as a source of verbal stimulation and *do* help to develop the verbal centers of the brain, if all those fine adult words and phrases coming out of the television set *do* function as effectively as real-life talking and listening, then surely children who watch a great deal of TV would surpass in verbal skills those who watch little TV. This does not appear to be the case. Indeed, a carefully controlled study designed to explore the relationship between television viewing and the language spoken by preschool children discovered an inverse relationship between viewing time and performance on tests of language development: the children in the study who viewed more television at home demonstrated lower language levels.

8

Television and Play

Less Play

"Suppose there wasn't any TV—what do you think your child would do with the time now spent watching TV?"

This was one of the questions addressed to a large number of mothers of first-graders in a survey published in the 1972 Surgeon General's _Report on Television and Social Behavior._ Not unexpectedly, 90 percent of the mothers answered that their child would be _playing_ in some form or another if he or she were not watching television.

It hardly requires a team of social scientists to demonstrate that television viewing keeps children from playing, for play is the major occupation of childhood. Any new activity that takes up so many hours of children's time is bound to make considerable inroads into their play time.

Virtually all the activities preschool children normally engage in during their waking hours (except television viewing) fall into the category of play. When a three-year-old child builds a block castle with another child, this activity is easily defined as play. But when a child pulls all the books out of a bookcase, or tags along behind a grown-up pretending to sweep the floor, or picks up the phone and has a make-believe conversation, or scribbles all over the wall, or hides with a teddy bear under the bed—that child is still playing. Clearly the two- or three- or four-year-olds who spend two or three or four hours daily watching television are spending significantly less time playing than if they did not watch television at all.

Not only does television viewing lead to a reduction in play time; there is evidence to suggest that it has affected the very nature of children's play, particularly indoor play at home or in school.

The Meaning of Play

The "playful" nature of children's play often obscures its importance. Far from being a mere diversion or pleasant time-filler, play involves a critical variety of behaviors that serve important purposes in the child's social, emotional, and intellectual development. Indeed, the universal appearance of play throughout the animal kingdom, and the growing complexity of play as one ascends the phylogenetic ladder, confirms the idea that play must have some survival value for all species that engage in it. To discover what these values are, it's useful to distinguish the different forms of play that children universally engage in, from the earliest stages that occur even before the child is attracted by the television set, to those advanced forms that may be displaced by television viewing.

Babies' first instinctive gropings and tastings and smellings, which become increasingly purposeful during the first year of life, may be seen as the beginnings of play, helping them gain their first understandings of their own selves in relation to their environment. By acting out innate instincts to explore, children begin to differentiate themselves from their parents and the world at large, and begin to learn some things about their environment.

In addition to providing basic understandings, young children's manipulations allow them to practice the important physical skills they are in the process of developing. In reaching for a toy, for instance, the child is developing eye-hand coordination, a crucial survival ability.

Not merely do infants explore by touching, tasting, or smelling, but verbally as well, by babbling and making a variety of sounds. A babbling child is clearly practicing oral skills, making sounds in a purposeful way with an evident interest in the results as well as the process. These verbal experiments are important precursors to language acquisition.

Another form of play involves imitation. Even before the first birthday a child will imitate certain adult movements and gestures in a playful way. (The parents clap their hands and the child claps back.) These mimicking games provide the first opportunities for a true two-way communication even before speech is acquired. By this means children begin to progress from a state of total receptivity to a relationship in which they are able to contribute something themselves. Imitative play also includes another important stage of language learning, during which children move on from random babbling to a deliberate imitation of the sounds produced by the people around them.

A form of play fulfilling a different function is seen when babies indulge in the game of peek-a-boo. In this rudimentary version of imaginative play children begin to use play to serve their inner needs. They have but recently made the uncomfortable discovery that the adults in their world, those all-important providers of food, warmth, and security, are not actually a permanent part of themselves but unpredictable creatures who can and do on occasion leave them. The symbolic reenactment of this painful separation in peek-a-boo may be what makes the game so universally delightful to babies. Thus play helps to make difficult aspects of reality more acceptable to the young child.

In children's later, more complex forms of imaginative play they similarly find ways to work out difficulties and adjust the realities of life to their inner requirements. In make-believe play children can take on the roles of their parents and redress grievances that have caused them suffering; they can reenact painful scenes from everyday life and transform them into more satisfactory experiences. In play they can expose, and perhaps exorcise, fears that they cannot articulate in any other way.

More important, perhaps, is the opportunity imaginative play affords children to become active users rather than passive recipients of experience. Things seem to happen to young children, to be done to them, and they are well aware of their general impotence in the power hierarchy of the world. But in the course of their make-believe play they are allowed to reverse this balance. By means of make-believe, children structure a world for themselves in which they have the power to act and to affect people and events. By this temporary reversal of the power balance, young children are able to accept their position in the real world, a position, they are dimly aware, that is also temporary.

Perhaps the most important function served by play in children's lives does not reside in the specific forms of play, but in the social circumstances that surround it. At first, very young children do not really play "with" other children, although the presence of other children may delight and stimulate them. They play alone or engage in what is called "parallel play," that is, they pursue their own activity in the presence of others without incorporating them into their play. But around the age of three or four the child begins to take part in a more truly social form of play with other children, play involving give and take and a certain amount of mutual cooperation.

Without a doubt social play presents more difficulties than solitary or parallel play or play with an indulgent parent. Playing with others requires a child to suppress his or her own wishes and desires to a certain degree. This is not an ability most children are born with: self-control must be learned. They must also discover the difficulties that attend the varying levels of aggression normally existing among their playmates. More aggressive children must learn to find less pushy ways to achieve their ends, while milder-natured children must learn to protect themselves and to maintain their integrity in the face of more forceful companions.

As children grow and the course of their play, exploratory as well as imaginative, becomes increasingly social, their ability to control their own behavior and to influence the actions of others becomes increasingly important to their success as social creatures. While aspects of play continue to fulfill many of the same functions they once served—physical-skill-developing as well as psychological-tension-relieving functions—now the acquisition of social skills and impulse control becomes the critical factor in children's play. Losing gracefully, learning to give in, getting along peacefully with others, all these are skills that children develop as they learn to play successfully with other children. The survival value of such skills in human adult life is obvious, although wars and the violence within societies and families attest to mankind's imperfect attainment of them.

Ultimately, childhood play colors the rest of life, long after a child grows up. As anthropologist Edward Norbeck wrote: "The primary purpose of play has a deeper importance for every individual. Playing children are motivated primarily to enjoy living. This is the major rehearsal value of play and games, for without the ability to enjoy life, the long years of adulthood can be dull and wearisome.

An Experiment of Nature

The ideal way to discover the effects of television viewing upon young children's play would be to compare the behavior of a large, carefully selected sample of television-watching children at play with that of a matched group of non-watchers. Such an experiment cannot be performed today for a simple reason: virtually all young children watch considerable amounts of television.

Nevertheless, such an experiment comparing the play of television and non-television children was once performed. The results, however, went unnoticed, perhaps because it was not deliberately designed but rather what might be called an "experiment of nature." It took place in America's nursery schools, kindergartens, and early elementary classrooms in the years after television was first introduced as a mass medium.

Early childhood classrooms are, in their way, natural laboratories for observing children's play. Over a number of years trained teachers can perceive patterns of behavior among their young students that may not be evident to parents or professionals who work with individual children rather than children in groups. It was in these "natural" laboratories that teachers began to observe changes in children's play patterns as a non-television population was transformed into a television-viewing one, almost within a single decade.

During the early 1970s when the first interviews for this book were conducted, teachers who bridged the gap between the pre-TV generation and the television generation were still teaching in schools throughout the country. These veteran teachers, all of whom had taught for more than two decades (and all of whom have now passed retirement age), were a unique group of witnesses to one of the greatest technological changes in our society. Their keenly observed comparisons of these two populations of children—those who came into their classroom before television entered the home, and those who arrived having watched significant amounts of television throughout their early childhood—are particularly noteworthy today:

The principal of a private elementary school in New York and former nursery school teacher with more than thirty years of teaching experience relates:

> Children do not play the way they used to. I don't mean outdoor play particularly. Outdoors they're still vigorous. They still climb and run and use bikes and wagons. It's inside play that has changed. You don't get as much dramatic play as you used to. Children are more interested in sitting down with so-called educational materials at a very young age. They don't seem to have as much imagination, either in verbal expression or in the ways they play or in the things they make.

Another teacher with thirty-five years of kindergarten experience notes:

> There's a greater passivity about their play. They'll get interested in something, but then if it means that they have to do something themselves, they'll lose interest.

A Denver teacher with twenty-nine years of teaching experience says:

> There's been a movement from active, impulsive kids who were just very eager to get their hands on things to do, to more cautious, passive kids with attitudes of wanting to be entertained or instructed. They don't want to just go ahead and explore by themselves.

Another elementary school teacher who goes back to pre-television days says:

> Children expect entertainment in school. And they manage pretty well when the school work's entertaining. But their attitude is: Is this going to be fun or is it going to be boring? And if it's boring, they feel, well, you just switch the channel. Only it makes it a bit difficult in school because you can't always switch the channel.

A Riverdale, New York, nursery-school teacher says:

> I find I'm having to sell things that are great activities that I never had to sell in the past, because some kids won't stick around long enough to find out if it's going to be fun if the first moments don't catch them. So I find I have to introduce things somewhat differently. Some children simply tune out very, very quickly.

Another kindergarten teacher whose experience spans both eras reports:

*I've had to change my style of teaching greatly over the past
years. I used to feel free to initiate a great many activities
because children then were quite capable of initiating their own
activities, too. Now I get the feeling that children want me to do
all the initiating. They'll go along with the activities I initiate,
and when I don't initiate anything, they'll just wait patiently
until I do. It's a kind of withdrawal on the part of the kids.
Now I try to encourage kids to get involved. I try to wait and be
patient while the enriched environment of the classroom comes
through to the child and he accepts the invitation to make his
own structure rather than to accept one made for him. But it's
hard sometimes—one has to be very patient. And it's tempting
to simply do all the initiating, because the kids will always go
along so cheerfully.*

Another teacher adds:

*Nowadays I really feel the need to encourage children to be more
active. I never felt that way twenty years ago. My word,
children were too active then!*

Might the testimony of these teachers merely reflect a prejudice
against a new technology, or a things-were-better-in-the-old-days
way of looking at the world? Probably not, because a pattern becomes evident in these reports, a pattern that does not differ from
school to school or area to area. That pattern reflects well-known aspects of the television experience—its essential passivity and capacity
for instant gratification—making it likely that these teachers are reporting real rather than fancied changes in children's play.

There's one way to demonstrate that these changes in play patterns are connected with television watching: They may be reversed
by the removal of television from a young child's daily life. As a publication of the Group for the Advancement of Psychiatry notes: "We
suspect that television deters the development of imaginative capac-

ity insofar as it preempts time for spontaneous play. Experience has shown that children who cease watching television do play in ways clearly suggesting the use of an active imaginary world. Resuming their viewing, the children decrease this kind of play."

Today's teachers, having taught only television-bred children, are unable to see these changes. As far as they know, the children they teach represent the realities of childhood, and the idea that television has affected young children's play behavior seems farfetched to them. Why, they themselves were brought up watching television!

Play Deprivation

Since play is clearly a vehicle for many of children's most important learnings and the means whereby they are able to practice and develop behaviors necessary to their success as social beings, what might be the consequences of the loss of playtime among today's children?

A classic experiment by psychologist Harry Harlow undertook to assess the general function of play among monkeys whose play behavior exhibits many similarities to the play of human children. The findings that emerged from this and similar studies of play deprivation carry implications about the possible effects of play deprivation upon individuals of species for whom playing is a normal activity—humans in particular.

Harlow observed that monkeys who are offered normal play opportunities during their early months follow a certain pattern of behavior. During the first months of life, they cling tenaciously and exclusively to their mothers. Their first play experiences involve a variety of manipulations from the cozy safety of their mothers' backs. In their second or third month they begin to make sorties away from their mothers in order to play with other baby monkeys. The mothers aid them in their burgeoning independence, encouraging them to stop clinging by pushing them away more and more often. By four months of age the young monkeys spend much of their waking time in a variety of rough-and-tumble games with other monkeys, including wrestling and a kind of "tag" game.

Then Harlow observed a group of monkeys brought up normally in every respect but one: they were denied all opportunities to play with other monkeys. After eight months of play deprivation, when these monkeys were exposed to normally reared monkeys of their own age, Harlow discovered that a singular behavior deviation had developed: the play-deprived monkeys were significantly more aggressive in their social behavior than monkeys brought up with adequate play opportunities. Though the deprived monkeys ignored the efforts of the normal monkeys to bring them into their play activities and though they withdrew from most of the rough games that characterize normal monkey play, the play-deprived monkeys initiated biting attacks on other monkeys at inappropriate times. They showed no fear of other monkeys and displayed very little control of their aggressive instincts.

It was not a matter of an increase in aggressive instincts among the play-deprived monkeys, for all normal monkeys manifest aggressive impulses from an early age. But the monkeys who had enjoyed regular opportunities to play from an early age had learned to mitigate those aggressive instincts during the course of their daily play. Little actual violence was ever inflicted by one monkey on another among the normally reared group. In contrast, the play-deprived monkeys allowed their aggressive impulses to emerge unchecked, with unfortunate consequences for others and especially for themselves, since they often attacked monkeys much stronger than they.

Ever since television became a mass medium, much attention has been devoted to the relationship between violence on television and childhood aggression. Could it be that the sizable reduction in children's playtime, not the violent content of the programs children watch, has helped bring about an increase in children's aggressive behavior, behavior that might once have been mitigated and socialized through play experiences? "Pity the monkeys who are not permitted to play," Harry Harlow wrote in a discussion of his experimental work. What about the children who have spent their childhood *watching* instead of playing?

PART III

Television and the School Years

9

A Defense of Reading

Television's impact is undoubtedly greater on preschoolers and pre-readers than on any other group. Until television, never in human history had very young children been able to enter and spend sizable portions of their waking time in a secondary world of incorporeal people and intangible things, unaccompanied by an adult guide or comforter. School-age children fall into a different category. Because they can read, they have other opportunities to leave reality behind. For these children television is merely *another* imaginary world.

But are these imaginary worlds equivalent? Since reading, once the school child's major imaginative experience, has now been seriously eclipsed by television, the television experience must be compared with the reading experience in order to discover whether they are, indeed, similar activities fulfilling similar needs in a child's life.

What Happens When You Read

It is not enough to compare television watching and reading from the viewpoint of quality. Although the quality of the material available in each medium varies enormously, from junky books and shoddy programs to literary masterpieces and fine, thoughtful television shows, the nature of each experience is different, and that difference significantly affects the impact of the material taken in.

Few people besides linguistics students and teachers of reading are aware of the complex mental manipulations involved in the reading process. Shortly after learning to read, a person assimilates the process so completely that the words in books seem to acquire an existence almost equal to the objects or acts they represent. It requires a fresh look at a printed page to recognize that those symbols we call letters of the alphabet are completely abstract shapes bearing no inherent "meaning" of their own.

Look at an "o," for instance, or a "k." The "o" is a curved figure; the "k" is an intersection of three straight lines. Yet it is hard to divorce their familiar figures from their sounds, though there is nothing "o-ish" about an "o" or "k-ish" about a "k." Even when trying to consider "k" as an abstract symbol, we cannot see it without the feeling of a "k" sound somewhere between the throat and the ears, a silent pronunciation of "k" that occurs the instant we see the letter. A reader unfamiliar with the Russian alphabet will find it easy to look at the symbol "щ" and see it as an abstract shape; a Russian reader will find it harder to detach that symbol from its sound, *shch*.

That is the beginning of reading: as the mind transforms the abstract symbols into sounds and the sounds into words, it "hears" the words, as it were, and thereby invests them with meanings previously learned in the spoken language. Invariably, as the skill of reading develops, the meaning of each word begins to seem to dwell within those symbols that make up the word. The word "dog," for instance, comes to bear some relationship with the real animal. Indeed, the word "dog" seems to actually possess some of the qualities of a dog. But it is only as a result of a swift and complex series of mental activities that the word "dog" is transformed from a series of meaningless squiggles into an idea of something real. This process goes on smoothly and continuously as we read, and yet it becomes no less complex. The brain must carry out all the steps of decoding and investing with meaning each time we read. But it becomes more adept at it as the skill develops, so that we lose the sense of struggling with symbols and meanings that children have when they first learn to read.

But the mind does not merely *hear* words in the process of reading; it also creates images. For when the reader sees the word "dog" and understands the idea of "dog," an image representing a dog is conjured up as well. The precise nature of this "reading image" is little understood, and it is unclear what relation it bears to visual images taken in directly by the eyes. Nevertheless images necessarily color our reading, else we would perceive no meaning, merely empty words.

The great difference between the "reading images" and the images we take in when viewing television is this: We create our own images when reading, based on our own experiences and reflecting our own individual needs. When we read, in fact, it is almost as if we were creating our own, small, inner television program. The result is a nourishing experience for the imagination. As psychologist and writer Bruno Bettelheim once noted, "Television captures the imagination but does not liberate it. A good book at once stimulates and frees the mind."

Television images do not go through a complex symbolic transformation. The mind does not have to decode and manipulate during the television experience. Perhaps this is why the visual images received directly from a television set are strong, stronger, it appears, than the images conjured up mentally while reading. But ultimately they satisfy less.

The perfect demonstration that a book image is more fulfilling than a television image is available to any parent whose child has read a book before its television version appears. Though the child will tune in to the TV program eagerly, hoping to recreate the delightful experience the book provided, he or she invariably ends up disappointed, if not indignant. "That's not the way the mother looked," the child will complain, or "The farmer didn't have a mustache!" Having created personalized images to accompany the story, images that are never random but serve to fulfill some emotional need, the child feels cheated by the manufactured images on the screen.

A ten-year-old child reports on the effects of seeing television dramatizations of books he has previously read:

> *The TV people leave a stronger impression. Once you've seen a character on TV, he'll always look like that in your mind, even if you made a different picture of him in your mind before, when you read the book yourself. The thing about a book is that you have so much freedom. You can make each character look exactly the way you want him to look. You're more in control of things when you read a book than when you see something on TV.*

It may be that television-bred children's reduced opportunities for "inner picture-making" accounts for the curious inability of so many children today to adjust to nonvisual experiences. Twenty years ago, a first-grade teacher who bridged the gap between the pre-television and the television eras reported:

> *When I read them a story without showing them pictures, the children always complain "I can't see." Their attention flags. They'll begin to talk or wander off. I have to really work to develop their visualizing skills. . . . They get better at [it], with practice. But children never needed to learn how to visualize before television, it seems to me.*

Today reading specialists have begun to examine the phenomenon of "aliteracy," a condition that seems to be increasing among American schoolchildren. One of their findings about this large cohort of kids who have mastered the skills of reading yet do not choose to read for pleasure is relevant to a discussion of television's impact on reading: aliterate readers "need help visualizing what they are reading."

Losing the Thread

A comparison between reading and viewing may be made in respect to the pace of each experience and the relative control we have over it. When reading, we can proceed as slowly or as rapidly as we wish. If we don't understand something, we may stop and reread it. If what we read is affecting, we may put down the book for a few moments and cope with our emotions.

It's much harder to control the pace of television. The program moves inexorably forward, and what is lost or misunderstood remains so. Even with devices like a VCR, though a program can be stopped and recorded, viewers find it hard to stop watching. They want to keep watching, so as not to lose the thread of the program.

Not to lose the thread . . . it is this need, occasioned by the relentless velocity and the hypnotic fascination of the television image, that causes television to intrude into human affairs far more than reading experiences can ever do. If someone enters the room while we're watching television—perhaps someone we have not seen for some time—we feel compelled to continue to watch or else we'll lose the thread. The greetings must wait, for the television program will not. A book, of course, can be set aside, reluctantly, perhaps, but with no sense of permanent loss.

A grandparent describes a situation that is, by all reports, not uncommon:

> Sometimes when I come to visit the girls, I'll walk into their room and they're watching a TV program. Well, I know they love me, but it makes me feel bad when I tell them hello, and they say, without even looking up, "Wait a minute . . . we have to see the end of this program." It hurts me to have them care more about that machine and those little pictures than about being glad to see me. I know that they probably can't help it, but still. . . ."

Can they help it? Ultimately, when we watch television, our power to release ourselves from viewing in order to attend to imperative human demands is not altogether a function of the program's pace. After all, we might choose to operate according to human priorities, rather than yielding to an electronic dictatorship. We might quickly decide "to hell with this program" and simply stop watching when a friend enters the room or a child needs attention.

We might . . . but the hypnotic power of television makes it difficult to shift our attention away.

The Basic Building Blocks

At the same time that children learn to read written words they begin to acquire the rudiments of writing. Thus they come to understand that a word is something they can write themselves. That they wield such power over the very words they are struggling to decipher makes the reading experience a satisfying one right from the start.

A young child watching television enters a realm of materials completely beyond his or her understanding. Though the images on the screen may be reflections of familiar people and things, they appear as if by magic. Children cannot create similar images or even begin to understand how those flickering electronic shapes and forms come into being. They take on a far more powerless and ignorant role in front of the television set than in front of a book.

There's little doubt that many young children have a confused relationship to the television medium. When a group of preschool children were asked, "How do kids get to be on your TV?" only 22 percent of them showed any real comprehension of the nature of the television images. When asked, "Where do the people and kids and things go when your TV is turned off?" only 20 percent of the three-year-olds showed the smallest glimmer of understanding. Although there was an increase in comprehension among the four-year-olds, the authors of the study note that "even among the older children the vast majority still did not grasp the nature of television pictures."

Children's feelings of power and competence are nourished by another feature of the reading experience: the non-mechanical, easily accessible, and easily transportable nature of reading matter. Children can always count on a book for pleasure, though the television set may break down at a crucial moment. They can take a book with them wherever they go, to their room, to the park, to their friend's house, to school to read under the desk: they can *control* their use of books and reading materials.

A Preference for Watching

There'd be little purpose in comparing the experiences of reading and television viewing if it were not for the incontrovertible fact that children's television experiences influence their reading in critical ways, affecting how much they read, what they read, how they feel about reading, and, since writing skills are closely related to reading experiences, what they write and how well they write.

Children read fewer books when television is available to them, as reports from so many TV Turnoffs make clear (see chapter 18). A child is more likely to turn on the television set when there's "nothing to do" than to pick up a book to read—it simply requires less effort. In a survey of more than 500 fourth- and fifth-graders, all subjects showed a preference for watching over reading any kinds of content. Nearly 70 percent of 233,000 sixth-graders polled by the California Department of Education in 1980 reported that they rarely read for pleasure. Meanwhile, in the same poll, an identical percentage of students admitted to watching four or more hours of TV a day.

In 1992 a government report made headlines by stating that

one-third of all students *never* read in their spare time and that one-third of all eighth- and tenth-graders read fewer than five pages a day for school or homework. At the same time, the report noted, while two-thirds of the eighth-graders who had been tested for reading skills and comprehension watched more than three hours a day, those students who watched two hours or less proved to get higher grades on the exam.

Children are often candid about their preference for watching over reading. The twelve-year-old daughter of a college English teacher explains:

> I mean television, you don't have to worry about getting really bored because it's happening and you don't have to do any work to see it, to have it happen. But you have to work to read, and that's no fun. I mean, it's fun when it's a good book, but how can you tell if the book will be good? Anyhow, I'd rather see it as a television program.

The mother of boys aged twelve and ten and a girl aged nine reports:

> My children have trouble finding books they like in the library. They seem to have some sort of resistance to books, even though my husband and I are avid readers. I think if they didn't have television available they'd calmly spend more time looking for something good in the library. They'd have to, to avoid boredom. But now they don't really look in the library, whenever I take them. They don't zero in on anything. It's not the ultimate entertainment for them, reading. There's always something better and easier to do. So they don't have to look hard at the library. They just zip through quickly and hardly ever find more than one or two books that interest them enough to take out.

Understandably those children who have difficulty with reading are more likely to combat boredom by turning to television than successful readers are. Television plays a profoundly negative role in such children's intellectual development, since only by extensive reading can they hope to overcome their reading problems. This point is frequently raised by teachers and reading specialists: Television compounds the problems of children with reading disabilities because it offers them a pleasurable nonverbal alternative, thus reducing their willingness to work extra hard at acquiring reading skills.

It's easy to demonstrate that the availability of television reduces the amount of reading children do. When the set is temporarily broken, when a family participates in a TV Turnoff, or when a family decides to eliminate television entirely, there's always an increase in reading, both by parents and by children. When the less taxing mental activity is unavailable, children turn to reading for entertainment, more willing now to put up with the "work" involved.

Home Attitudes

The role of the home environment was the subject of one of many studies looking into television and its relation to children's reading achievement. The researchers centered attention on the various stages of reading development and compared the impact of television viewing at each stage—from a pre-reading stage, through the initial decoding stage, into the stage of increasing fluency, and finally, to the stage in which children can read for knowledge and information.

The authors noted: "If the home environment encourages and enhances reading activities, the child has a better chance of progressing trouble-free through the first three stages. On the other hand, if the home environment has few facilitating mechanisms for reading development, and if it stresses television as the means for entertainment, activity, interaction and information acquisition, then the child's reading development may be impeded." The authors conclude by noting that "age is an important variable in the study of televiewing and reading, and the younger the children included in the study, the higher the probability that effects of the home environment and television viewing on reading behavior will appear.

Lazy Readers

Besides reducing children's need and willingness to read, television may subtly affect the actual ways in which children read, what might be called their reading style. For while children of the television era can and do still read, something about their reading has changed.

Reading specialists sometimes refer to certain children as "lazy readers." They define them as intelligent children from educated families who have never made the transition from learning *how* to read to being able to absorb what they read. They read well enough, but not with the degree of involvement and concentration required for full comprehension.

Critic George Steiner referred to this sort of reader when he noted: "A large majority of those who have passed through the primary and secondary school system can 'read' but not *read*."

Similarly, educator Donald Barr once observed: "Children may pick up and leaf through more books, but what they do looks to me less like reading every year." He, too, connected the deterioration in meaningful reading with children's television experiences. "TV stimulates casting your eye over the page, and that is a far different thing from reading."

Many teachers speculate about a connection between this style of reading and children's television involvement. Concentration, after all, is a skill that requires practice to develop. The television child has fewer opportunities for learning to sustain concentration than the "book" child of the past. Indeed, the mental diffuseness demanded by the television experience may influence children's attention patterns, causing them to enter the reading world more superficially, more impatiently, more vaguely.

Nonbooks

Parents often assuage anxieties about their children's television involvement by maintaining that their children still read. But the reading reported by parents often falls into a category that might be called the "nonbook." The headmaster of a selective boys' school in New York reports:

> *For as much television as our boys watch I have found no substantial correlation between the amount of television watching and the circulation of books from the library. The important change is in the kinds of books the boys read. . . . [W]hat is really a new trend, it seems to me, is the great interest children have in reading the 'nonbook' kind of thing. The most conspicuous example of a 'nonbook' is the* Guinness Book of Records. *A great deal of the reading the boys seem to be doing these days falls into that category.*

The nonbook seems designed to accommodate a new reading style. It is not the kind of book with a sustained story or a carefully developed argument that is read from beginning to end. It's a book to be scanned, read in fits and starts, skimmed, requiring little concentration, focused thinking, or inner visualization. Yet it provides enough information and visually pleasing material to divert the child who does not feel comfortable with the old sequential style of reading.

For the television-bred child, an important aspect of the nonbook is its instant accessibility. Reading a "real" book can be hard at the outset, as the scene is verbally set and new names and places and characters are introduced. But a nonbook, like television, makes no stretching demands at the start. Composed of tiny facts and snippets of interesting material, it does not change in any way during the course of a child's involvement in it. It does not get easier, or harder, or more exciting, or more suspenseful; it remains the same. Thus there is no need to "get into" a nonbook as there is with a book, because there are no further stages to progress to. But while the reader of a nonbook is spared the trouble of difficult entry into a vicarious world, he is also denied the deep satisfactions that reading *real* books may provide.

Parents and teachers suggest that boys are more likely to turn to nonbooks than girls. Indeed, boys have long been known to be more resistant than girls to any form of narrative fiction. Then, in 1998 a literary phenomenon arrived from across the Atlantic that grabbed girls and boys alike: a mild, bespectacled boy with magic powers named Harry Potter.

What about Harry Potter?

Just when the cause of reading seemed hopeless, something happened to show that all was not lost. Suddenly tens of thousands of kids all over the United States (and the world) found themselves entranced by a series of books that had no tie-ins with any TV programs or movies whatsoever, books that simply stood on their own as a good, old-fashioned read. Harry Potter had taken the country by storm.

Children from the third grade on up through high school (and adults too) became so involved with Harry Potter that they skipped their regular television programs in order to continue reading. Parents and educators were amazed . . . and delighted. Reading for pleasure among children had been in a long, long decline. Was it possible that today's children were suddenly becoming the sorts of passionate readers once common before television came into the home?

The Harry Potter books are everything children's literature ought to be: superbly written, filled with suspense and excitement, containing adult characters both exotic and somewhat familiar from the real world, and one of the most appealing cast of child characters ever gathered in a single work. There's an inspiring and yet not too goody-goody boy hero, several girl heroines any feminist would applaud, a couple of deliciously hateable kid villains, as well as a host of imaginary creatures—dragons, hippogrifs, phoenixes, manticores, glumbumbles, basilisks, and more.

In no way is Harry Potter a nonbook. Each volume contains long, complex narratives that require sustained attention to follow. Moreover, there are almost no illustrations, thus requiring much inner visualizing in order to bring the people and fantastic creatures to life.

That a population of video-weaned children were able to fall for the charms of this marvelous, marvel-filled series of books has been one of the most hopeful omens of the television era. It is an indication that skills and abilities like inner-visualizing and following a narrative have not disappeared; they have just gone underground. Under the right circumstances—a great book combined with an international craze—these skills can once again be activated.

As I write, however, the movie version of the first Harry Potter book has just been released. Though the film was criticized (by adult critics, to be sure) for hewing too closely to J. K. Rowling's book, it was a huge success with children throughout the country, who were delighted that the film was so faithful to the story they loved. The movie broke box office records, and will surely continue to attract a large audience for years to come. Film versions of the next two Harry Potter books are already in production.

For most of the Harry Potter fans who flocked to see the movie, it was a fine recreation of their reading experience. But from now on great numbers of children will see the movies before reading the books. For them, things will be different. Having seen the film, a boy who then chooses to read the book will never be able to transform the main character into himself as he reads—a deeply satisfying part of the reading experience. Thereafter he will visualize only the movie's version of the bespectacled boy wizard. Similarly a girl reader who admires Harry's friend Hermione will never have the pure pleasure of creating the adorable though sharp-tongued little witch in her own image. Hermione will now resemble the Hollywood version.

Radio and Reading

Before television, children listened with pleasure to radio programs. Now that television has captured the child audience almost in its entirely, people tend to think of radio as simply an inferior version of TV—television without the pictures. But is this indeed the way to look at radio?

During the early days of video technology, psychologist and art theorist Rudolph Arnheim spoke out in favor of "blind broadcasting," suggesting that radio listening provides similar gratifications to reading: "The words of the storyteller or the poet, the voices of dialogue, the complex sounds of music conjure up worlds of experience and thought that are easily disturbed by the undue addition of visual things."

Among the thousands of studies of the various media's effects on children, there is little research directed toward the effects of radio listening. But the few studies available go far in confirming Arnheim's hunch that a visual medium like television will have deleterious effects on a viewer's powers of imagination, while the radio experience will not.

A study at the University of California compared children's responses to a radio story and a television version of the same story. The researcher found that children were able to provide far more creative endings to the audio version than the video one, provoking the inescapable conclusion that radio stimulates children's imagination significantly more than television does.

An example of radio's power to stimulate the imagination appeared in a recent review of a book about the baseball player Joe DiMaggio:

> The beauty of radio is that, unlike television, it puts the
> listener in the mix. There are no highlight shows, instant
> replays, or let's-go-to-the-videotape features to show us what
> happened. Visual images speak to the visceral, while voices

heard but not seen allow free play in the cineplex of the mind . . ."

Many educators believe that radio, an exclusively linguistic medium, has far more in common with reading than with television, a medium relying to a great extent on the visual. Indeed, while television has long been associated with a decline in academic achievement among its heaviest viewers, radio listening may prove to reinforce verbal skills almost as well as reading can. Certainly there is circumstantial evidence supporting such a view, notably, the long decline in SAT scores that began when the first television generation sat down at the test tables (see *Mystery of the Declining SATs,* page 283). During the heyday of children's radio, on the other hand, when there were great numbers of national radio broadcasts and American children invested almost as much time listening to the radio as they now spend watching TV, there was no equivalent decline; indeed, scores went steadily upward.

While television has displaced radio as an entertainment medium for children (with the exception of teenagers who listen to the radio almost exclusively for popular music), Books on Tape and other companies offer similar opportunities for listening experiences without pictures. The growing popularity of taped books as a source of entertainment for children may be a sign that parents are seeking to loosen television's bondage on their lives. Or, since Books on Tape are mainly used on car trips, it may simply mean that television has not yet penetrated the car market as it has the minivan market (see A Wonderful Addition to the Family, page 189). Time will tell.

If You Can't Beat 'Em, Join 'Em

A somewhat desperate attempt to stem the decline in children's free-time reading is seen in the if-you-can't-beat-'em-join-'em approach that enlists television itself as a spur to encourage children to read more.

Over the years a spate of television programs have appeared, some sponsored by public funds, others by television networks themselves, all with the much-applauded aim of promoting reading among children. Programs such as *Reading Rainbow* enlist a chirpy, magazine-style format and a TV-star host to stimulate an enthusiasm for reading among children clearly in need of such stimulation—after all, they *are* watching the program, not reading a book.

Other efforts of the past have included the Read More About It project, initiated by CBS with the cooperation of the Library of Congress, which had the stars of a number of TV shows based on books step out of their roles at the close of the dramatization to exhort the TV viewers to go out and read the book now that they have seen the program. NBC too did not fail to plug reading: "When you turn off your set, turn on a book" was the message flashed at the end of a popular late-afternoon children's series. Similarly, ABC joined the reading bandwagon by ending certain children's specials adapted from books with the words "Watch the Program—Read the Book."

No one, however, either on public or commercial television, has gone so far as to suggest: "Don't watch the program—read the book instead." And yet, as it happens, that would be a far more effective message. While there is no evidence whatsoever that television exhortations lead to a greater love of reading, there is the considerable evidence from TV Turnoffs organized by schools and libraries throughout the country, as well as from the annual National TV-Turnoff Week, run by the TV-Turnoff Network, demonstrating that when competition from the TV set is eliminated, children simply and easily turn to reading instead.

While efforts to encourage reading via TV programs may be well intentioned, they represent a misguided hope that there is an easy out from a difficult state of affairs. Indeed, the ways to encourage reading are well known, and require time and effort on the part of the parent. An education writer expressed it well:

Future readers are made by mothers and fathers who read to their children from infancy, read to them during quiet moments of the day and read them to sleep at night. Only then does the book become an essential element of life.

Why Books?

Well, what of it? Isn't there something a bit old-fashioned about a defense of reading in the electronic era? The arguments for reading are powerful:

Reading is the single most important factor in children's education. Reading trains the mind in concentration skills, develops the powers of imagination and inner visualization, lends itself to a better and deeper comprehension of the material communicated. Reading engrosses, but it does not hypnotize or seduce a reader away from human responsibilities. Books are ever available, ever controllable. Television controls.

In reading, people utilize their most unique human ability—verbal thinking—by transforming the symbols on the page into a form dictated by their deepest wishes, fears, and fantasies. As novelist Jerzy Kosinski once noted:

> [Reading] offers unexpected, unchannelled associations, new insights into the tides and drifts of one's own life. The reader is tempted to venture beyond a text, to contemplate his own life in light of the book's personalized meanings.

In the television experience, on the other hand, viewers are carried along by the exigencies of a mechanical device, unable to bring into play their most highly developed mental abilities or to fulfill their particular emotional needs. They are entertained by television, but the essential passivity of the experience leaves them basically unchanged. For while television provides distraction, reading supports growth.

10

Television and School

A Negative Relationship

Evidence that the more television children view, the worse they do in school has been accumulating since research on television's impact on children began. Twenty years ago, in a summary of television research organized by the National Institute of Mental Health (NIMH) all but one of the numerous studies cited in the section on educational achievement showed a negative relationship between television viewing and school achievement. During recent decades further evidence has continued to come in. The crucial question, of course, is whether the relationship is causal—whether, in other words, television itself is the cause of this decrease in achievement, and not some other concurrent factor.

One of the clearest indications of a causal relationship between television viewing and a decline in school achievement may be found in the unique Canadian study cited earlier which documented the effects of television's arrival in the small Canadian town without television the researchers called Notel.

Before TV's arrival, children in Notel scored higher on a reading exam than kids in two similar but television-viewing communities. While a strong negative relationship was thus determined, it was not necessarily evidence that the absence of television was responsible for the Notel children's higher scores. After all, some other variables might be at work. Perhaps the teachers in Notel were better, or perhaps some socioeconomic factors had not been taken into consideration that might explain the score differences.

Then television arrived in Notel. If something besides the absence of TV had caused the higher scores in Notel, then even after the establishment of television in every Notel home, the reading scores there should have remained higher than those in the other towns. But this was not the case. When the children in Notel were retested two years after television had come to their town, their scores had gone down to the level of the other two towns.

This negative relationship has been demonstrated by other researchers during the past twenty-five years. In 1997 a large-scale study conducted in the Netherlands concluded that television viewing had a negative impact on children's development of reading comprehension. The researchers attributed the impact, at least in part, to television's displacement of reading as a leisure time activity.

Three other studies included in the NIMH roundup of research provide "relatively strong negative associations between viewing and achievement":

1. Children who had been allowed to watch many hours of daily television in the years before they started school proved to have lower scores on reading and language tests at the end of first grade than children who had watched little TV during their preschool years.

2. To eliminate IQ as a variable, a survey of 625 students in the sixth through ninth grades attending a suburban-rural public school compared high-IQ students who were heavy TV watchers with equally bright students who watched little TV. The light viewers had significantly higher scores on a reading comprehension text.

3. A large-scale California survey examined TV habits and school grades of more than 500,000 public school students in the sixth and the twelfth grades. The results showed a

strong statistical relationship between TV viewing and low school achievement. The California Superintendent of Schools noted that such variables as intelligence, parental income, or numbers of hours of homework assignments did not alter the negative relationship between television viewing and school achievement. For him the evidence was strong enough to elicit the comment: "Television is not an asset and ought to be turned off."

More recently, a National Assessment of Educational Progress report assessing long-term trends in school achievement noted a strong negative relationship between time spent watching television and students' scores on the NAEP mathematics test. In all three age groups tested, the heaviest watchers scored lower than their peers who watched less. Meanwhile, among two groups, the lightest viewers, those who watched two hours daily or less, had the highest math scores.

A 1999 survey that looked at children's use of all media, not only television, provides especially valuable confirmation of the negative link between school achievement and viewing activities. Children who got good grades in school spent 4 hours and 34 minutes per day at various screen activities such as TV, video, video games, movies, and taped TV shows, while those who got fair to poor grades spent 5 hours and 27 minutes.

Establishing a negative link between television viewing and educational achievement may be far more important than trying to understand why, in fact, such a connection exists. Yet speculation about why television viewing has negative consequences on children's schoolwork is inevitable. The possibilities cover a wide range, from actual physiological changes in thinking patterns during the early years of life, to a widespread displacement of reading as a free-time activity, thus eliminating practice with verbal material.

Then there's the deceptively simple fact that television causes children to stay up later than they did in pre-TV days, as statistics demonstrate. By causing children to be less attentive in school, this reduction in sleep may be far more consequential than people think. As an elementary-school teacher in France commented in the era when there were still numbers of children without television: "I can tell children with TV at home from those who haven't because those without are far more receptive in the morning.

A Stepping Stone out of a Stumbling Block (Media Literacy)

One of the indisputable ways in which television has changed the face of education in America today has been the appearance of a new and increasingly popular addition to the traditional school curriculum—the study of television itself. Variously called "Media Literacy," "Critical Awareness," "Viewing Skills," and other names, these courses offer a tantalizing possibility: making a stepping-stone out of a stumbling block by using television itself to transform a classroom of "vidiots" into selective, critical viewers.

The reasoning behind the media literacy movement goes like this: Children already watch a great deal of television and nothing much can be done about it. Let's help them get more out of their viewing by teaching them to be more critical about what they view. An administrator of the New York State Department of Education offers a typical rationalization: "It's unrealistic to expect that children—or parents—are going to turn off television and devote themselves to books instead." Knocking television isn't the answer, she insists. Schools should simply help children become better viewers.

And thus children, to their delight, are finding that in place of arduous studies requiring reading and writing and concentrated effort, they can settle back in their seats, chat about TV, and watch programs in school relating to those they enjoy at home.

One such program that made its way into second-, third-, and fourth-grade classrooms a number of years ago was called *Getting the*

Most out of TV. Emanating from the Yale Family Television Research and Consultation Center and funded, not surprisingly, by a major TV network, the program's goal was to help young children distinguish what is real and what is unreal on television. It went about this goal by comparing cartoon characters like the Incredible Hulk with real people that the kids on the show had met, as well as by asking children to compare their own families with TV families. It also pointed out that TV commercials often exaggerate the value and appeal of various products.

Children may indeed learn to watch television more critically and may even be helped to understand the difference between television's unrealities and life's realities by means of media literacy courses—though it's hard to believe that second graders need help in distinguishing the Incredible Hulk from ordinary people. Nevertheless, even if a well-designed course has the capacity to make children's television experiences richer and more meaningful, the question remains: In an era of declining literacy when children are growing up with diminished abilities to read and write well, at a time when children are known to spend 4,000 more hours watching television in the course of their school careers than they actually spend in the classroom, is it not the responsibility of schools to redress this imbalance? Shouldn't teachers devote all their energies to the preservation of literacy and the development of those cognitive skills that will give children access to the heritage of the past—history, science, literature—and help them understand and deal with the increasing complexities of life in today's society?

The television critic Walter Goodman once inquired: "Can a course labeled visual literacy enhance anyone's appreciation of the English language?" Noting that the gains such a course might offer children "seem trivial beside the need to give them some defense against the tube's relentless attack on language and thought," he concluded: "The best way to protect children from being misled by television or newspapers or politicians or corporations is to broaden their knowledge. As a start they might be taught to read well enough to recognize the ignorance behind a phrase like 'visual literacy.'"

Television for Homework

Faced with large numbers of students who simply do not complete their homework assignments, often as a result of home television viewing, many teachers today are nevertheless reluctant to give up on homework entirely. Today's common compromise solution: television programs for homework. Teachers either assign openly educational shows such as *National Geographic* specials, hoping at least that the kids will turn from their regular TV programs to more "worthwhile" subject matter, or, as is far from uncommon, they assign the regular programs themselves for whatever educational value they might provide. One teacher, for example, assigned the once-popular *Lou Grant* show for homework. "It's the only assignment I know they'll do," he wearily admitted.

For most teachers, assigning TV viewing for homework is not a maneuver taken to lighten their workload; it is an act of true desperation. Facing a classroom of children with poor verbal skills and a disinclination to read and write, these teachers hope against hope that by engaging their students in the study of their favorite medium they might manage to sneak in some lessons of a more traditional sort along the way.

A high-school teacher whose English class is entirely devoted to the making of video programs and the study of existing shows on television explains:

> One of my prime goals in this class is to use TV video as a
> motivational tool for reading and for writing. We write scripts
> and we read about television. And when I assign them to watch

*TV they are aware of the content as well as the technical aspects.
They know they are related in the same way as the form of a
book is related to its content.*

It's not hard to understand why there's a waiting list to get into
this teacher's class, or why more and more teachers are turning to television to make their classes more attractive to children of the television generation. Making video films in the classroom and watching
situation comedies for homework is fun! Struggling with the complexities of a sonnet, striving to uncover subtle meanings, ironies, or
patterns, can be work, no matter how gratifying the final experience
of reading might ultimately prove to be.

The trouble with using television as a motivational device arises
when students must make the shift from the TV-related reading and
writing that seems so much fun in the classroom to those forms of
reading and writing that lead to clear thinking and a better understanding of the world of people and events—that is, to the reading of
literature and history, or the writing of well-presented, logical ideas
and arguments. As one of the students in a television-centered English class explained, when asked why he chose the class in place of
the customary, book-centered course: "A regular English class gets
boring, where you just sit around and read books."

Social critic and media observer Joel Meyrowitz speaks wryly of
such efforts: "Attempts by some teachers to adjust school curricula to
incorporate programs that children watch on television suggest a
new means of 'leading' children by running after them as quickly as
possible."

Unfortunately, that style of "leading" rarely advances children
toward literacy. In a published interview about the use of television
in schools, a high-school journalism teacher demonstrates an un-
friendly attitude toward books (and a shaky sense of grammar):

Using television makes for a nice change of pace in the
routine. It's much more effective than getting it out of a

book because these kids are of the television generation and what they see they believe more than what they read.

By assigning programs for children to watch at home and by adopting a "with-it," television-centered approach in their teaching programs, teachers often subtly reinforce parents' fatalistic attitudes toward their children's television viewing: since they're going to watch a great deal of television anyway, they might as well be forced to watch something good.

Indeed, the schools' habit of assigning programs for homework frequently deters parents struggling with serious television control problems from setting firm rules about viewing hours, such as "No TV on school days," or getting rid of the television set entirely. "We can't manage without television," such parents say. "The children *have* to watch certain programs assigned at school." Clearly the schools' generally acquiescent or enthusiastic attitude toward television does not offer such parents the sort of help they badly need.

Commercials in the Classroom

In 1989 a company named Channel One struck a Faustian bargain with a number of school districts across the country: it would provide at no cost the high-tech equipment that schools, predominantly less advantaged ones, believed they needed to pull them out of their educational slump: satellite dishes, wiring, videocassette recorders, and television sets, one for every classroom in the school. In exchange, the schools would show a 12-minute program provided by the company to every child in the school. Not once a month or once a week, but every day.

For parents struggling to control TV at home, adding a daily TV program into the school day was bad enough. But that was not the whole bargain. The program would be accompanied by two minutes of commercial advertisements. Unlike the commercials on home TV screens, however, these could not be zapped with a remote-control device. The captive audience in the classroom had to watch them in their entirety. That was the deal. It was a notable first in American education, the first breach in the educational stronghold by commercial interests.

The introduction of commercials into the classroom provoked a storm of outrage. Almost every national educational group, including the National PTA and the National Educational Association, took a strong stand against Channel One and other commercial broadcasts in the classroom. The American Academy of Pediatrics published an angry broadside against the program, noting that the specific commercials chosen to air in classrooms "encourage materialism and market products that in many cases can contribute to eating disorders, obesity, poor nutrition, inappropriate behaviors and poor self esteem."

Small wonder educators and doctors were indignant. The commercials promoted candy, junk food, and video games—the very things schools and doctors strive to de-emphasize. As one parent complained bitterly to a reporter, "We have an obesity crisis in this country and here we have government schools telling children to eat Snickers and drink Pepsi." Meanwhile advertisers signed on in droves. They know that reaching consumers early in life and imprinting a brand name on their consciousness is good business.

The 10-minute "educational" program that accompanies the two minutes of commercials is itself a cause for widespread anxiety. A current events round-up with a "hip" spin, it is aired to students without any scrutiny by parents, teachers, or the local school board. Indeed, it is virtually impossible for school administrators to review the programming before airing it, since it is broadcast into a locked box in each school every morning before being aired in classrooms. Moreover, Channel One has long refused public access to its tapes and programs.

When a group of researchers finally managed to get their hands on tapes of the program, they found that only 20 percent of its air-time is spent on coverage of the "current events" the Channel One producers claim the show is all about. The rest was devoted to advertising, sports, weather, features, and star profiles. Professor William Hoynes of Vassar College, one of the researchers, concluded: "It is dubious whether such news provides educational or civic benefits to either students or educators." Other research confirms that Channel One's primary purpose is advertising, not education.

The Center for Commercial-Free Public Education is one of the organizations most vocal in its opposition to Channel One. It points out that Channel One's claim that they "give" schools the TV sets and video equipment is deceitful. They merely lease the machines to schools for as long as they're willing to air the programs.

Losing the equipment, however, might be a blessing in disguise for the schools that subscribe to Channel One. Haven't the decades of declining educational achievement in the midst of proliferating technology in classrooms demonstrated that anything distancing kids from the vital activities of reading and writing is counterproductive? The idea that by signing off Channel One a school can get rid of not only the show and its commercials, but all the TV sets, satellite dishes, and VCRs too, sounds like the best bargain of all.

A Primary Factor

Surely television can't be entirely to blame, people often assert. While allowing that television has had *some* effect on children's school achievement patterns, parents and educators often bring up other important factors. And yet television, it may be seen, is significantly intertwined with each of these factors.

A panel of experts, for example, when asked to interpret the NAEP findings showing a decline in inferential reasoning among American high-school students, came up with a number of other possible explanations for the downturn besides television viewing habits: less reading for pleasure was one explanation and a lack of rigor in secondary-school curriculums was another. In fact, television is deeply involved in both these changes as well.

Why less reading for pleasure? One might suggest that the relaxed attention style habitually devoted to television material may make meaningful reading seem more like hard work than pleasure.

As for changes in secondary-school courses of study, to a great extent they are epitomized by the various media-oriented programs and strategies previously described. These have arisen in schools precisely as an accommodation to a new breed of students used to being entertained by the fast pace of television and accustomed to the discipline of focused, sustained attention to a subject at hand. Children who have watched TV in their nursery years instead of pasting pictures in scrapbooks or building castles with blocks, children who can always turn quickly to another program if the one they are watching grows tedious, children who are used to the quick visual exposition of a scene on television and are unfamiliar with the mental effort of having a scene slowly unfold in the mind through a verbal description—such children are not likely to adapt easily to the old-style school curriculums, the ones that help produce good readers and writers.

And thus necessity has driven schools to change. They try this and that new strategy, hoping against hope that *something* will work—media-literacy programs, TV production workshops, "educational" TV programs for homework, and finally regular television programs in the classroom, accompanied by commercials just like on the home TV. The final capitulation to the "televisionized" child may be seen in the current push for computers in the classroom (see chapter 15).

PART IV

How Parents Use Television

"Don't you understand? This is life, *this is what is happening. We* can't *switch to another channel."*

11

Before Television

Small children have not changed over the centuries. They have always shown the same indefatigable energy, curiosity, irrationality, persistence, emotional instability, and unpredictability during their first five years of life that they exhaust us with today. It is mainly how parents deal with these difficult though normal aspects of development that has changed.

How did parents of the past deal with the normal problems of rearing small children? Were their methods any better than using the "plug-in drug"? Looking back at the long-ago past, the answer is a resounding No. But revisiting some parents of the more recent past, particularly those raising kids during the decades just before television's arrival—the 1930s, 1940s, and 1950s—brings to light some strategies today's parents might find surprisingly useful, particularly those who feel they could not survive parenthood without a television in the home.

The Bad Old Days

"The history of childhood," wrote psychoanalyst Lloyd de Mause, "is a nightmare from which we have only recently begun to awake." That nightmare, in which neglect and brutality characterized the ways adults dealt with young children, describes most of recorded history. The biblical injunction "spare the rod and spoil the child" was once followed with an awesome zeal, as children were beaten regularly and savagely, sometimes to within an inch of their lives. Nor was child beating performed secretly. Children were beaten publicly and deliberately, in classrooms, in family parlors, before audiences of relatives and friends, wherever and whenever the need arose.

Terrorizing children was once a common practice. Seventeenth-century parents, for example, commonly brought their small sons and daughters to witness public hangings and executions in order to frighten them into compliant behavior. And from the earliest known times, children were scared out of their wits with stories of witches and monsters waiting to pounce on them if they misbehaved. Although vestiges of this practice remain today in certain folk tales and legends, the horror stories these have evolved from were once presented so graphically and dramatically that histories record incidents of young children being literally frightened to death.

Starvation and food deprivation were yet other common means of controlling children's behavior (surviving mainly in vestigial versions such as "No dessert if you don't behave"). Moreover, a wide variety of sedatives and depressants for children, labeled with names such as "The Mother's Helper" or "Mothers' Blessing," were once freely available to parents seeking relief from the normal behavior of young children. Containing enough laudanum or cocaine or opium to render a small child passive if not altogether comatose, these potions were effective in eliminating the troubles children's natural activity level might cause a parent or caretaker.

All these practices, universally held to be reprehensible today, were regarded as normal and acceptable well into the nineteenth century. How could parents of the past have treated their children so reprehensibly, yet without guilt or remorse? Surely nothing short of a universal change in consciousness about the nature of children and childhood could have led to a reversal in thinking so great that behavior once common and acceptable has come to seem wicked and even pathological.

The crucial catalyst for this change in thinking lay in a new awareness of the special needs of the young child. Without such an awareness parents were free to use child-rearing methods purely because they worked, with no regard for how they might affect the child. Not until parents came to understand children's developmental needs and how they were different from their own could they be constrained to modify their behavior toward children so as to prevent the child's suffering.

A New Light on Childhood

Beginning with Jean-Jacques Rousseau's writings in the eighteenth century, new ideas about childhood began to spread and filter through all levels of society, starting with the educated classes and gradually making their way to those ranks of society most resistant to change. Over the next two centuries a newly empathetic view of children began to prevail. Not only did this transform how parents dealt with children's behavior; it also changed children's own ways of behaving and adapting.

During the early decades of the twentieth century parents began to turn to more "psychological" methods of discipline—reasoning, cajoling, distracting, withdrawing approval, and the like in place of corporal punishment, food deprivation, terrorization, and other powerful behavior modifiers. By mid-century the new style was the norm.

But while such strategies reflected a more sympathetic understanding of child development and promoted the child's basic needs, there was a big problem from the parent's point of view: These methods were not always effective. Reasoning with a young child rarely works as well as a quick whack, and never as swiftly. As a result, parents found it far more difficult to manage their kids and still do the things that had to be done in the household.

One difficulty facing parents in the new empathetic childrearing era stemmed from the dawning awareness that it was not necessarily "good" for a child to be good. In the old, unenlightened days, the emphasis in child rearing was on character development. Since a "good" child is an untroublesome one, and since being good requires the child to behave in ways that do not conflict with adult needs, this worked well for parents.

As the ideal of "goodness" was replaced by the new goal of "emotional security," the parent's lot became harder. In the new era parents had to deal with normal behaviors like grabbing, throwing, interrupting, whining, and demanding—conduct that was once considered "bad" and was swiftly punished out of existence—in new ways that required more time and effort.

Parents' difficulties were further increased by a new awareness that those very years when children make the most demands on parents' time and energies and when they are the most difficult to handle—the years, that is, of early childhood—are of critical importance to the child's acquisition of that much desired emotional security. Not only did parents now have to be more tolerant of child behavior that interfered with their adult life, but they also felt obliged to spend *more* time with their children, difficult as that might be, having come to understand that this helped build the crucial foundations for the child's emotional and intellectual future.

The new era's careful attention to children's needs worked well from the child's point of view, far better than previous methods. Children developed physical, emotional, and intellectual strengths that allowed them to surpass, in many ways, children of the past. But a natural by-product of increased parental attentiveness appeared: children also became more demanding. This, it must be understood, did not represent a change in the child's basic nature; young children continued to follow the same developmental patterns they had always followed. Their increased demands were an adaptation to the new permissiveness in child rearing, just as docility and submission had once been an adaptation to life-threatening brutality. The very fact that the parents had given them so much of what they desired made children demand even more.

How Modern Parents Survived Before Television

Children's new self-assertiveness, coupled with a vigor and precocity that stemmed from the optimal satisfaction of their early needs, contributed to the mid-twentieth-century parental dilemma: how to deal with these powerful kids without resorting to the old, effective strategies. Beating was out. Starvation was out. Drugging the kids with Mother's Helper was out. Even mild shaming and the gentlest of terrorizing (Santa Clause won't bring you any presents if you don't behave) were frowned upon.

In this child-centered era with its increased burdens of child care, necessity occasionally impelled parents to resort to certain parent-centered strategies that bought them some respite from child care. Though some of these went against the modern grain, yet they proved to be of value to children themselves by counterbalancing some of the excesses of a permissive upbringing.

• *Firmness*

Parents were firmer before the television era, not because they believed this was a better way to raise kids, but simply because firmness was necessary for parents' survival. The child-rearing style so prevalent today, characterized by questions parents steadily ask their small children, such as "Do you want to have your dinner now?" or "Do you want to go shopping with Daddy?" was unthinkable in that era. Parents couldn't afford to ask such questions and have their children say "No, I don't want to" (as they are so likely to do). Four-year-old Nancy *had* to go shopping with Daddy, so Mom could nurse the baby or help Buddy with his homework, and she was simply told that's what was about to happen in a nice firm voice. Not knowing that she had a say in such affairs, the small child was more likely to comply than kids are today.

• *Observing with an Eagle Eye*

Before television, training children to play alone for periods of time was a vital part of parenthood. Once again, this was not because parents thought this was particularly good for the child's development, but because they desperately needed those chunks of time for their own purposes. Yet accomplishing this goal without resorting to the punitive ways of the past was never a simple matter.

Observing children with an eagle eye to obtain a subtle picture of their changing development was the pathway to success in getting children to entertain themselves successfully and reliably. A mother (the usual caretaker of small children in pre-television days) might take pains to discover, for instance, if her three-year-old was capable of learning to cut with a pair of blunted scissors. If this activity amused the child, it would be worth the mother's while to work on it a bit, to help the child learn how to cut properly, to provide a supply of colored papers or old magazines, a jar of paste perhaps, because once the skill was acquired her reward would be a self-entertaining child. For similar reasons the mother might provide buttons or beans for sorting, or dough for molding, or blocks for building, spurred not entirely by devotion to her child's happiness, but also by a certain amount of healthy self-interest.

Capturing her child's nascent interests and utilizing them to serve her own needs was once an important element for success as a mother. But as it happens, the intimate knowledge of her child gained through sharp observation of developmental progress also led the mother to a more satisfying relationship with her child, with greater opportunities for shared pleasures as well as a reduced likelihood of misunderstandings and inadvertently inflicted suffering.

From the child's point of view, the period of solitary play, augmented by the mother's efforts to get things started, led to the development of important skills and to actual, tangible accomplishments—constructions, drawings, sculptures, collages, and the like. These skills and accomplishments, in turn, gave the child a sense of competence, and thereby helped to counteract those feelings of helplessness and dependence that dominate early childhood.

Indeed, the heightened attentiveness to children's needs and interests that parents once displayed affected the entire family in a beneficial way. Parents became experts on their children, and the information inevitably enabled them to raise their children more humanely and more effectively.

The availability of television as a child-rearing tool has reduced parents' immediate need to know their children well. Though affection or a sense of duty still inspires them to observe their children and communicate with them in a variety of ways, parents are no longer compelled by necessity to make great efforts to discover their children's special interests.

• *The Nap*

The most dependable survival aid for parents of the past was the nap. Not too long ago children took naps regularly during their early childhood, often until they began school. It wasn't necessarily that they needed to nap, nor that they wanted to nap: quite simply, they *had* to nap. The nap was as inevitable and accepted a part of life as going to bed at night or getting dressed or brushing teeth or doing any of those many things that children don't particularly want to do but simply have to do in the course of their childhood.

Babies needed their hours of sleep, and parents needed those hours of peace. They saved up their telephone calls, their letter writing, reading, or sustained thinking for that interval of the day when an eye or an ear didn't have to be cocked in the direction of a small child.

Then came the inevitable moment during the second or third year when the child no longer fell asleep automatically at nap time.

This was a crucial transition point for parents of the past. Though the child may have stopped physically needing the nap, and had begun to fuss and resist it, the parent hadn't stopped needing it—far from it. As children grew older and needed more attention and care, parents needed that daily hiatus more than ever.

This is why parents of the past persevered in their efforts to retain the nap in spite of the child's initial resistance. Through firmness based on a certain desperation as well as a strong sense that the period of quiet rest was still good for the child, parents succeeded in gradually turning the sleep nap into a quiet-play nap, during which time children were required to remain in their room, playing or listening to music or dreaming or puttering about quietly. In this way, once upon a time, parents kept the nap as a regular part of their daily routine until school brought them the opportunity of a new daily break.

That fairy tale time is over. Babies still spend the greatest part of their day sleeping, and children during their first two years continue to sleep for certain intervals during the day. But today's parents do not "work" to keep the nap as their kids outgrow the need to sleep. Instead, with relief in sight second only to the relief they feel when their child is asleep at night, parents encourage their young children to watch television for reliable periods of time. Perhaps some of children's deep affection for television in their later years is rooted in their earliest experiences with the medium when their parents, seeing television as a survival aid, made special and seductive efforts to "plug them in."

Finally It "Took"

A young, well-educated mother in need of relief from the hardships of life with a small child describes her efforts to establish her child on a television-watching routine:

Last spring, when Jeremy was one and a half, he gave up his morning nap. It was a difficult time, for him and for us. At that point I first started to try Sesame Street. I made an effort to interest him in the program. I'd turn the set on and say, "Look! There's a car!" or whatever. But he showed absolutely no interest. It really didn't seem worth working at then.

Then, in the fall, when he was two, he gave up his nap entirely. The day loomed so long that I began to make another effort to interest him in Sesame Street. He was more verbal then, and I thought there was a better chance that he'd understand it. I'd turn it on, and he'd show an initial interest in the first moments. It was an event. He'd look at it briefly, and then go on to other things. I'd leave it on and he'd pass by and look at it on his way to somewhere else. I might sit in front of it myself for a while, to try to make it more inviting, to try to coax him to watch. If he asked for a bottle, I'd certainly let him have it there, in front of the television set. Sometimes I'd even suggest a bottle.

Anytime we were home and Sesame Street was on, around four o'clock, I'd turn it on and try to interest him by commenting about things on the screen. "Oh, look at the snow!" and things like that. Then I bought a book on Sesame Street and we looked at it together. I think that helped get him interested. It took from about October to Christmas. Finally it "took." It was quite gradual. But now he watches every day, with a bottle, always, in the morning and in the afternoon. And Mister Rogers, too, most of the time, and it's really a great breathing spell for me.

I know television probably isn't great for kids, but a few hours a day can't really be so bad. I suppose if I hadn't had a TV set I would have tried to establish some quiet-time routine in his room, a play-nap sort of thing. But it would have been hard. He's a very determined little boy. He probably wouldn't have stayed there.

In choosing television over the nap, today's parent is following a simple, perfectly normal imperative of human nature: always choose the easier of two possible courses of action. Pre-television parents who persevered in enforcing a regular nap were operating on the same principle—in their case the harder alternative was to have a child underfoot all day. But there is an essential difference between these two "easier" courses, the nap and television watching.

When children who take regular daily naps outgrow the need for actually sleeping, the nap period begins to serve a new function: it provides them with their first regular opportunity to experience free time. An understanding of the importance of free time in a child's life reveals how great a deprivation its loss may be.

12

Free Time and Resourcefulness

Not so long ago, children were regularly faced with periods of time they were required to deal with on their own. Today not merely are children's lives packed with more meetings, lessons, and other structured activities than ever before, but all the possible chinks of empty time cropping up between these activities are filled in with the mortar of television. That curiously unvalued commodity called free time has been eliminated almost entirely from children's lives.

No Free Time

James Harrison is three years old. He wakes up in the morning at seven o'clock, gets dressed with a little help, and watches *Sesame Street* until breakfast. He spends the morning at nursery school. After arriving home from school, he eats lunch, and has a long nap until three. On various afternoons he goes to gymnastics class, music class, swimming class, and dancing class. When he comes home he "unwinds" by watching cartoons or a video while his mother prepares dinner. After dinner he half-watches a comedy program with his older sister, has a bath, and goes to bed.

Margo Brown is seven. She gets up in the morning at seven-thirty, dresses, watches cartoons on TV, has breakfast, and leaves for school. She goes to an after-school program after regular school. On Friday afternoons she leaves school at three, and the baby-sitter takes her to a piano lesson. On other days the baby-sitter picks her up at five o'clock and takes her home, where she usually watches cartoons until her mother comes home after six. While her mother prepares dinner she often watches her favorite programs: *The Cosby Show,* if she's home early enough, followed by *The Waltons, Sabrina,* or a video from her large collection. Her older sister usually watches with her. After dinner she does her homework, practices the piano if there's time, has a bath and usually watches another television program before her bedtime at eight-thirty or nine.

Danny Evans, an eighth-grader, is going on fourteen. He gets up at seven, dresses, eats breakfast, looks at the sports page of the morning paper, and leaves for school at eight o'clock. He returns at four-thirty, grabs something to eat, and heads for the park where he's part of a kids' baseball league. If it rains or if it's too cold, they play in a basement playroom in Danny's apartment house. When he comes home in the late afternoon, around five-thirty or six, he collapses in front of the television set and watches whatever his younger brother is watching, or he'll pay Nintendo until dinnertime. He has dinner in the kitchen with his brother and little sister while watching television, since his parents eat later. After dinner he does homework, usually missing one of the programs the younger children watch. He uses his computer for some of the homework, and will alternate the work with electronic chats with friends via instant messaging. He often watches one more television program with his parents after the younger kids have gone to bed, a movie or Masterpiece Theatre. His bedtime is around ten-thirty.

There is something these three children have in common with one another and with a great number of children in America: they have no free time.

Attachment and Separation

Television appears to have been instrumental in greatly diminishing, if not completely wiping out, free time in children's lives.

Why does this matter? It matters because learning to use free time serves a valuable role in the growing-up process.

Infants have no clearly defined self; they are still in the thrall of an almost physical attachment and dependence on their primary caretakers. Consequently most parents operate with an instinctive understanding of their child's need for a certain kind of time-filling during the first years of life. That is to say, they cuddle their babies, dandle them, sing little songs to them, play This Little Piggy Went to Market with their toes, rather than leaving them to their own devices. Clearly, the ability to communicate with language, to exercise control over their own bodies, to operate, in short, with some degree of independence, must be developed before children can make use of time in their own way.

But as they approach the age of three there's a distinct decline in the intensity of children's attachments. They no longer grieve loudly and passionately when their parent or caretaker leaves. They no longer cling to her for security in new situations. The emotional foundations have been laid, as it were, and a new developmental stage sets in. Now the drive of curiosity begins to overtake the drive for security and dependence, as children begin to explore their environment with increased interest and tenacity. Of course, the attachment behavior does not altogether disappear. Young children swiftly return to their familiar haven of security when frightened or hurt. But they've taken their first steps toward independence.

There's an evolutionary purpose to this behavior progression from a parent-centered, passive, receptive orientation to an environment-centered, active, learning style of life: the individual's survival in society is necessarily a function of active, adaptive behavior. It is precisely at this point in a child's development, somewhere between the ages of two and three, that parents are most likely to begin turning on the television set for their young children.

While watching television, young children are once again as safe, secure, and receptive as they were in their mother's arms. They need offer nothing of themselves while watching, as they must do, for instance, when they play with another child. They run none of the small risks that normal play entails: they won't get hurt, they won't get into trouble, they won't incur parental anger. Just as they're beginning to emerge from their infant helplessness, the television set temporarily but inexorably returns them to a state of attachment and dependence.

Why Kids Can't Amuse Themselves (Gresham's Law of Child Activity)

It's all very well to sing the praises of free time for children and exhort parents to turn off their television sets. It's the *reality* of free time that makes it so difficult for parents to stick to their resolve of limiting their kids' television consumption.

After expecting their offspring to suddenly metamorphose into old-fashioned children who pursue hobbies and wholesome adventures once the set is turned off, it's depressing to see them hanging around doing nothing. In a variety of rude ways the kids reject those fine, creative activities with which they are supposed to fill the vacuum, challenging the parents to either amuse them themselves or relent and let them watch television.

Is it partly or wholly because of their early television experiences that children today seem less capable of dealing with free time? Do kids in the twenty-first century have greater difficulties in combating boredom than children did in the pre-television era?

Along the lines of Gresham's Law in economics stating that lower-valued currency will drive out more valuable coin, a sort of Gresham's Law of Child Activity seems to operate here: passive amusements will drive out active ones. It's based on an aspect of human nature that holds for adults and children alike: all other things being equal, doing something easy is preferable to doing something hard. This is not to say that choosing the easier path makes people happier. Perhaps human nature did not evolve with happiness as a goal.

Observe a girl playing with a simple wooden truck who is presented with a complicated mechanical locomotive. Until then she had been obliged to amuse herself by pushing the symbolic vehicle around the floor, devising an imaginary route in and out and under furniture (providing her own sound effects). Now she watches the new toy with fascination, amazed by the smoke spouting from the stack, charmed by the rhythmic toot-toot of the engine, delighted by its ability to propel itself backward and forward.

But after a while the child's pleasure in the new toy begins to diminish. The fascinating toy, after all, has a limited repertory of actions: it moves, blows smoke, and goes toot-toot. The child wrings a terminal bit of amusement from the toy by taking it apart to see how it works. And it is finished.

The child's play with the simple wooden truck does not lead to a similar habituation because its range of activities is limited only by her own imagination.

But now the troublesome aspect of Gresham's Law of Child Activity becomes apparent: for though the attraction of the mechanical plaything is brief, there is something so compelling about the passive pleasure it affords the child that the appeal of another toy requiring active participation is diminished. When the mechanical toy breaks down, the child is not likely to go back to her wooden truck. That sort of play seems a bit dull and tame, a bit difficult now. How silly it seems to push a truck around the house and pretend that it's real when a locomotive that moves on its own is so much *more* real!

Not only will the child choose this particular mechanical toy over the more effort-demanding symbolic toy it was meant to replace, but in the future she will be a bit more likely to choose a passive occupation over an active one. Passive play experiences inevitably make active play less appealing, and therefore less likely to occur spontaneously.

The television set is the one mechanical toy that does not lead easily to habituation and boredom, though children's involvement with it is as passive as with any other mechanical toy. It chugs and toots and produces movements, while the child watches with wonder. But its actions and sounds are far less repetitive than the toy train's, so the watching child can maintain wonder and fascination almost indefinitely.

But just as mechanical toys change children's relationship to symbolic toys, so do the passive pleasures of television watching transform children's relationship to their own time. The strong pleasures of that safe, effortless, ever-amusing experience make the pleasures afforded by active entertainments seem too much like work.

This is not to say that normal children will stay huddled before the television all day in preference to playing baseball or helping to bake a chocolate cake or engaging in some other appealing activity. Certain activities will always confound Gresham's Law of Child Activity by dint of their exceptional attractions: special trips and activities, particularly with parents, beloved sports and games, activities that dovetail with the child's special interests. But those activities have got to be *pretty good*. Otherwise there's always television.

A mother relates:

> *TV is a killer of time for my children. I think they'd almost rather do* anything *than watch TV. If I find them something they like to do and do it with them, they're perfectly happy. They'd prefer that to watching TV. It's just so much less effort to watch TV than to have to think of something to do. So if they don't have something* special *to do, like getting a Halloween costume ready or even going to a friend's house, their first thought is to watch TV.*

Another mother says:

> *What I find with my seven-year-old is that it's the excuse of television, the very* presence *of the television set when he doesn't know what to do with himself, or when he has a day when*

another child isn't coming over to play, that keeps him from looking to himself for something to do. Instead, he'll want to sit in front of the television set just to let something come out at him. That's been the hardest thing about television for me. If the television were not there, if it didn't exist, he wouldn't have that problem.

A mother of a five-year-old boy observes:

My child is not the kind of child who will make a scene or have a temper tantrum. He'll just mope around and be bored. And I find it very hard to take that. It bothers me to think that he can't do anything with his time. The presence of the television is the excuse. He knows in the back of his mind that when he really hits rock bottom he can go to that television set.

An educator and authority on early childhood with forty years of experience as teacher and principal has noted a change in children's behavior since the advent of television:

Young children today have a sophistication that comes from all their contacts with the outside world via television, but sophistication and maturity are not the same thing. Children today are often less *mature in their ability to endure small frustrations, or to realize that something takes a longer time to do, that it isn't instant. They're less tolerant of letting themselves become absorbed in something that seems a little hard at first, or in something that is not immediately interesting. I spend a lot of time at school telling children that they have to participate in activities and try things even if something doesn't seem all that interesting right at the start.*

Other teachers observe that young children today find it harder to work by themselves than children did in the pre-television era, that there is a constant need for adult supervision or entertainment.

Whether children are so used to immediate gratification via the television set that their abilities have atrophied, or whether a simple lack of experience with free time has left them with undeveloped abilities, it nevertheless seems clear that children today have greater difficulty dealing with free time than children of past eras.

For when those favorite, special activities are not available (as often is the case, which is what makes them so special), then today's children are not likely to enlarge their interests by trying something new. They will not take the same desperate measures to combat boredom that children of the past resorted to: inventing games, playing make-believe, reading, rereading, writing to pen pals, pursuing hobbies—activities that grow on a child and foster growth. With the presence of a source of passive amusement in every home, readily available at the first sign of boredom, a child's time becomes more and more dominated by this single time-suspending activity.

"Nothing to Do"

What exactly is the function of free time in a child's life? Wouldn't it be just as well if the child's life were so full of things to do that the whole question of having "nothing to do" would be eliminated?

There's a picture book by Russell Hoban called *Nothing to Do* that illuminates the value of free time for children, and the importance of helping them learn how to deal with it. Hoban's book deals with little Walter Possum, a member of an endearing family of humanoid possums, who bothers his parents because he has "nothing to do." Father Possum tells Walter to "play with your toys." But Walter doesn't feel like it. The father assigns him a job—to rake the leaves. But Walter soon loses interest. The only activity that seems to relieve the tedium is quarreling with his sister Charlotte, a terrible pest.

When Mother Possum needs to clean the house, Father gives Walter a smooth brown stone and instructs him to rub it when he has nothing to do. It is a magic stone, Father tells him. "You have to look around and think while you're rubbing it, and then the stone gives you something to do."

Naturally, belief in the magic of the stone leads Walter to discover all manner of things to do. He finds a long-lost ball, he visits a friend, he dreams up a buried treasure game. He even devises a clever way to keep his irksome little sister from interrupting his game by presenting her with a stick that is also invested with putative magic powers. Besides having fun, he stays out of his parents' hair all afternoon.

Hoban's book, as is the case with so many fine books for young children, contains guidance for parents as well as entertainment for children. Children need help, suggests Hoban, in gaining access to their inner resources. The clever possum-parent, discovering that straightforward rejection of the "go find something to do on your own and don't bother me" variety only serves to exacerbate his child's dependent, clingy tendencies, encourages the possum-child to find pleasure in his own inventiveness by making a game out of the very idea of thinking up things to do.

The possum-child is not really fooled—that's a crucial point. He proves it by using the same stratagem to get his sister to amuse herself. But still the magic stone works, even though the child clearly understands that it contains no thoughts and that he himself is providing the good ideas.

What is that magic stone Father Possum gave Walter? It's a necessary release, an embodiment of the idea that it's all right to be less dependent, that his parents are permitting him to act on his own, to use his time in his own way. That's what Walter required in order to be able to deal with his free time.

If Father Possum had given his son a different sort of magic device, a box, for instance, with ever-changing pictures to keep him amused, the parental purpose might have been equally served (to keep Walter out of the way). But were it the most entrancing source of entertainment, it would still have been an extension of the parent.

Though fascinated by it, the child would have found in it no release from helplessness, no source of growth or confidence.

That, finally, is the primary function of free time in children's lives: to provide the necessary opportunities for reducing their dependence and developing their separate selves. This cannot happen in one or two or even twenty grand epiphanies, but only through a gradual, day-after-day, year-after-year accumulation of free-time experiences, each providing a revelation so tiny, perhaps, that neither the child nor the parent recognizes it. Only through those self-propelled activities in which games are invented and dreams dreamed will children discover a self dependable enough to sustain them in place of those people and things they have been dependent on for so long.

Competing with TV

Some conscientious parents, wishing to reduce their kids' TV time, expend huge amounts of energy presenting alternative activities. They're afraid that if they don't do something pretty special, the kids will turn to the television set.

A mother of three young children reports:

The thing I notice is that I have to spend a lot of my time and mental energy avoiding television. I have to keep thinking up things to do to keep the kids from watching TV. Their normal inclination is to watch television when they have no scheduled activity, and only if I make some sort of effort can I keep them from doing it.

A mother of two boys aged seven and five tells an interviewer:

I can't stand the idea of families where the kids come home from school and turn on the TV. You never get to talk to your kids. But it's complicated, you see. I don't need the TV as a baby-sitter at three-thirty when the kids come home from school, so I don't want them to watch then. I do need it between five and seven when I'm making dinner. That's when I want them to watch. And they do watch television then. It certainly makes life a lot easier for me. The trouble is they want to watch at three-thirty also. And unless I dream up something terrific for them to do then, they don't just want to play. They pester and pester me to let them watch.

A Brooklyn mother reports:

I spend the weekends driving the children around to places just to keep them from the TV. Two weeks ago I drove from Brooklyn to Hershey, Pennsylvania, just to get the kids away from the television set. That's an eight-hour drive!"

A New York grandmother gives another example of television's powerful competition:

A few weeks ago I went to a hospital to visit a little boy with a broken arm. There was a television set at the foot of his bed and he had the controls at hand. His mother had told me that he was really looking forward to my visit, and yet the whole visit was dominated by the presence of the television set. I arrived with a couple of good storybooks and I proceeded to read him a story but I quickly realized that the moment I or the story wasn't quite interesting enough, he was going to turn on that television set. And in fact every so often he did turn it on, just to see what was on. I went on desperately, reading stories, playing cards, and hangman and tic-tac-toe, telling jokes, because I was determined not to let that damn set win. I was definitely competing against that television set the whole hour I was there. I practically had to stand on my head, but I think I did win, but not a complete victory, only about seventy-five, twenty-five in my favor.

For some parents, competition with the television set reflects an underlying lack of trust in their children's capacity to amuse themselves.

> *I tell the kids, "Get out of my hair and go watch television,"*
> *because I can't imagine their being on their own without*
> *something to stimulate them—I think that's why television is*
> *such a problem in our house.*

A mother of two young children began to limit her children's television consumption to an hour a day. She tells an interviewer:

> *I began to realize that the message I was giving him every time*
> *I broke down and said, "Yes, you can watch one more program"*
> *was "No, you're not able to do anything else with your head*
> *besides watch television." The message was that I didn't think he*
> *had the capacity to do anything else with his time himself and*
> *so I was giving him an out with the television.*

In many families, of course, children fill their free time themselves by turning on the television set. But even in those families that limit television watching, the competition parents engage in with the television set effectively eliminates free time in their children's lives. If either the television set or some competing activity is always available, there is never a time during the day when a child has "nothing to do."

The Half-Busy Syndrome

An illustration of the counterproductive consequences of relying on television to fill the empty chinks in a child's day is seen in that combination of circumstances that might be called the *half-busy syndrome*. This describes a cycle in which the parent or caretaker, let's say the mother, is *half*-busy *all* the time. She goes about her various duties and occasional leisure-time activities in bits and spurts, stopping whatever she is doing to take care of this or that, answering the child's persistent questions, taking make-believe tastes of endless mudpies, admiring drawings. She is busy, but never too busy to look up from her book or stop her work to attend to the child's needs or wishes.

She becomes hardened to the half-busy way of life and finds a certain satisfaction in the idea that she's a good mother. But occasionally she feels she must have some relief from being constantly on tap. Suddenly the television set seems the only solution.

She feels a bit guilty about using the television set as a baby-sitter, but what else is she to do? She has tended, minded, soothed, coaxed, and displayed the patience of a saint. She must get away somehow. After all, children are children and it's their nature to seek attention. She doesn't know that there's something about her state of "half-busy-ness" and perpetual availability that actually works against her own needs, making her child *more* demanding and creating the necessity of turning to the television set for relief.

Parents intuitively understand that children's demands for attention bear an inverse relation to parental availability: the less available the parent, the more demanding the child. For instance, it is universally observed that children are particularly troublesome when their parents are on the telephone. But parents who feel they devote great quantities of attention to a child in the course of each day do not generally understand that the nature of that attention is a crucial factor.

Research findings suggest that the quality of a parent's attention matters considerably. In one experiment a selected group of preschool children was left for a period of time with a consistently available and attentive adult, while a second group spent a similar period of time with an adult who pretended to be busy with her own work. The children in the "low availability" condition proved to be considerably more demanding of the adult's attention than the group whose caretaker was consistently available. The quality of the available caretaker's attention seemed to allow the children to play more independently and make fewer demands on her. The caretaker who seemed to be busy was far more beleaguered.

A later research study observed nursery-age children with their mothers, some of whom were instructed to be busy and some to be wholly attentive. The results showed that many more bids for maternal attention were made when the mother was busy than when she was completely available to the playing child.

Clearly children whose mother or caretaker is half-busy all the time are never more than half-free themselves. They are never presented with the real necessity of confronting time in their own way. Meanwhile, the parent is deprived of any truly free time for herself. A reverse process may sometimes begin to operate: a parent deprived of free time grows dependent upon the child for emotional gratification that might better come from other sources.

The experiences of parents who have changed the quality of their attentiveness confirm the likelihood that being half-busy throughout the day makes children more demanding and dependent. When periods of complete attention are alternated with periods of nonavailability to the child, both parent and child begin to enjoy truly free time.

A mother of two preschool children provides a good battle plan for ending the half-busy syndrome:

> One day I realized that I had fallen into the habit of caring for
> the children in a halfway sort of manner all the time. I'd get
> half a letter written and then have to stop because a child
> needed something. It went on that way most of the day and I'd
> never get away completely except when I plopped them in front
> of the television. I hated doing that, but I just couldn't help it. I
> needed to get away. Then I began to realize that I was in a sort
> of vicious circle, not really doing my own things, and not really
> enjoying the children very much either. Meanwhile I had a
> sinking feeling that time was passing, that there were only so
> many years when the children would be small, and that

somehow I was never really completely committed to them, nor was I ever completely free of them.

I was late coming to this realization and I actually had to work hard to make a change. It might have been easier if I had started right from the start. But of course when they were babies they needed a different sort of attention, didn't they? What I wanted to do now was to really be with them *when I was with them, not just give them half of my attention. I'd drop everything for a while and really play with them,* down on the floor *much of the time. I wouldn't keep trying to get back to my letter or doing something else.*

But the other part of it was that I worked on getting away just as completely, without plugging them into the TV. It seemed somehow fair that if I gave them my time completely, they could also give me some time completely to myself. I didn't even think then that they would profit from having time entirely to themselves. But in fact I began to realize that often that was the case. I'd tell them that I was going to do something for a while and they could not interrupt me, and that when I was finished I'd do something with them. And then I stuck to my guns!

I started out little by little, because they wouldn't let go at first. I'd say, "I'm going to sit here and read to the bottom of the page." And then I'd persist, no matter what they did, even though it meant ignoring things like falling down or a fight. It never got to a life-or-death situation—I suppose I would have intervened then. Gradually I increased the time I was unavailable to them, slowly, page by page.

It worked. In fact, it was pretty easy. Now they will really give me time, without demanding attention or getting attention in devious ways—by getting hurt, for instance, or by making a horrible mess. Somehow, my giving them honest-to-goodness attention really seems to make a difference. It seems to fill them up, in a way, almost as if they've had enough to eat. They

become calmer, less clingy. They seem to be more capable of
being on their own for long periods of time.

Waiting on Children

When television is used to fill in children's free time, parents are often led to compensate for the lost opportunities of becoming close to their children by waiting on them more than they might ordinarily do. It might surprise them to learn that the many little services they provide children who could easily help themselves may be debilitating to the children. Parents might be even more surprised to realize that their compulsion to wait on their children is related to the role television plays in their family life.

There have always been parents who like to "baby" their children unnecessarily. Literature is full of such parents, usually mothers, who perform ridiculous services for their perfectly capable (and ungrateful) offspring and openly struggle to hold on to their children by keeping them mentally and physically dependent.

But those parents who fetch drinks and snacks for their television-watching children, who release them from their chores to watch favorite programs, are not all overanxious mothers. Their motives for waiting on their children are frequently related to their use of television as a surrogate parent.

An illustration of the relationship between children's television-watching and parents' waiting on children is given by Caroline L., a musician and mother of two children aged seven and ten:

> *I've scheduled my life and my work in such a way that I can be*
> *there when the children come home from school. I want to be of*
> *some help to them, to greet them, to make them feel good in*
> *some way. Well . . . [she laughs with embarrassment] I regret to*
> *say that they plunk themselves in front of the television as soon*
> *as they come home, and sometimes I can barely get two sentences*

out of them before they're involved in their program. Then I
can't get another word out of them. And so I bring them some
carrot sticks or Triscuits and cheese for a snack, feeling a little
ridiculous about it, because they're certainly old enough to peel
their own carrots and make their own snacks. But somehow I
allow myself to do it. I mean, if they love those television
programs so much . . .

Caroline L. brings her children snacks because she can think of
no other way to maintain communication with them as they watch
television. She feels rejected, cut off from normal human contact
with her kids. Moreover, she feels guilty that she set up this situation
herself, by using television regularly for her own convenience when
the children were smaller.

She is aware of her dependence on the television set but fears
that the alternatives would be too burdensome:

The funny thing is, when they come home from school I really
have a desire to sit down and talk to them about what they're
doing in school. I'd love to hear about that. But they don't want
to talk about it. I'm sure if I were willing to do something with
them in the afternoon, something they really like, at least there
would be a chance they'd be willing to do that instead of watch
TV. Maybe not. But I'd have to completely devote my time to
entertaining them, even to the extent of not answering the
phone. And that's really hard for me. I've tried.

In this way countless parents who are regularly "turned off" by
their children in favor of the television set (just as they "plugged them
in" when they were younger), now perform unnecessary little services
to manifest their love and devotion, to show their kids in deed rather
than word that they care for them and want them to be happy. That
is the only possibility left to them, they feel, since their words have
been preempted by television's electronic words.

A child psychotherapist and consultant for a New York private school comments on the effects of waiting on children:

> It's a very infantilizing thing for mothers to wait on children, clear away their dishes, bring them drinks and little snacks while the children sit there watching television. Long after children reach an age when they ought to begin to develop self-reliance, they can't help but continue to regard their parents as servicing people. Of course, babies don't see their parents as servicing people—they need to be taken care of. But when seven- or eight-year-old children habitually ask their parents to fetch them a glass of water because they're watching a television program, and the parents meekly comply, then there's something unwholesome going on.
>
> The parents rarely bring this up as an issue, however. I just pick it up as they're talking. They'll be describing a certain situation and they'll mention that so-and-so called them to bring him a sandwich—that he's watching TV—and so-and-so is ten years old!

There is a certain amount of wonder in the therapist's voice as she relates this incident. She continues:

> The parents feel guilty about allowing their children to watch so much television, and so they try to compensate by waiting on their children. It's not that they are trying to keep them dependent, as parents sometimes do. But these parents just don't seem to know what else to offer. Somehow they have come to think that they have to do all the offering. That's what astonishes me.

Sickness as a Special Event

Before television there were occasions in almost all children's lives when they were faced with a great deal of unexpected free time:

the inevitable days when they were removed from their normal schedule of activities by sickness.

The diminishing cohort of adults today who grew up before television have strong memories of their childhood illnesses.

A mother thinks back:

> My mother worked when I was a child, but when I was sick she stayed home for at least a few days. So I remember those times very well. I remember the endless card games and cutting out pictures from magazines with her. I remember lying in bed and calling her to come and bring me this or that, again and again and again. And I remember how wonderful it felt, that she always came! I suppose I ran her ragged, but that's a very important memory for me, to this day.

It is remarkable how often the actual physical discomforts of sickness are absent from these childhood memories, although in reality a child's sickness is dominated by symptoms and the mental changes that accompany them. Parents, on the other hand, remember their children's sicknesses as difficult, wearisome times. Yet parents in those bygone days swallowed their impatience and suspended their weariness when the kids were sick. It wasn't that they were better parents than today's. It was because they had no alternative.

Television has transformed the experience of children's sickness for parents and children alike. Gone are the onerous requirements of time and patience on the parent's part—the endless story readings, the tedious card games ("I thought I'd go mad if I had to play one more game of War"), the listening to whiny complaints, the steady need to restrain impatience, to maintain sympathy, to act more lovingly than ever.

Gone too is a special opportunity for children. For before the television era, sickness was more of a special event. That's when kids got to do special things and were able to enjoy special relationships with their parents and siblings. Indeed, the opportunities for more time together frequently exposed both parents and kids to new aspects of each other's personality.

Best of all, from the child's viewpoint, the usual sibling battle was suspended when illness struck. Parents no longer had to take pains to be "fair" about their allocation of time or affection: sickness was special, and parents were able to bestow on the sick child giant doses of time and affection without fear of provoking mutinous jealousy among siblings.

Today's parents often rationalize their use of television by invoking the child's need of distraction from pain. It must be said that if television is available to distract a child from real pain or discomfort it may serve a valuable purpose. But in reality, much of the time children spend at home because of sickness does not involve pain but rather restlessness and boredom. The earache or flu or stomach virus is over in a day or two, and then comes a time of recuperation, regaining of strength. Still parents feel that television is a necessary part of the process.

Today what makes sickness special for children is mainly that they are allowed to watch more television than ever.

A mother who normally limits her children's television viewing says:

When the children are sick I'm likely to let them watch all they want. Otherwise I'd have to read to them all day. Also, it's slightly making up to them for the miserable time they're having.

Another mother observes:

When the kids are sick it's permissive time so far as the television is concerned. Usually we're pretty strict about television, but when they're sick I feel they ought to have a special treat somehow. Although it's a little odd to make a treat of something I normally disapprove of. But it's too tempting not to let them watch.

That law of human nature dictating the choice of something easy over something hard makes it almost irresistible for parents not to avail themselves of TV when a child is sick. But for today's children, whose opportunities for shared experiences with their busy parents are already so limited, those stories not read, those card games not played, those quiet times not spent together when the television is turned on during an illness are a particular loss.

Back to the Past

When television appeared, parents did not fail to recognize the amazing opportunity it offered them: a flick of the switch could transform their child completely though temporarily, from an energetic, noisy, intrusive creature craving activity and experience and requiring constant supervision and attention, into a docile, quiet, undemanding presence. And this marvelous transformation is achieved with the child's cooperation! The child *wants* to watch television, *loves* to watch, can't seem to have enough of it!

Perhaps it is children's unprecedented complicity in their own pacification by television that allows parents to employ it so relentlessly. Perhaps because encouraging children to watch television is so easy and pleasant when compared to the disagreeable strategies of the distant past or even the moderate strategies of the more recent past, it allows today's parents to overlook a crucial fact: those very things kids do that cause parents trouble, those explorations, manipulations, and endless experiments in cause and effect, are profitable, indeed necessary activities for a small child. It might give parents pause to consider that dealing with their children's difficult behaviors by eliminating them entirely via television is not all that different from suppressing a child's natural behavior by threats of physical punishment. It is surprisingly similar to drugging a child into inactivity with laudanum or gin.

13

Family Life

Not much more than fifty years after the introduction of television into American society, the medium has become so deeply ingrained in daily life that in many states the TV set has attained the rank of a legal necessity, safe from repossession in case of debt along with clothes and cooking utensils. Only in the early years after television's introduction did writers and commentators have sufficient perspective to separate the activity of watching television from the actual content it offers the viewer. In those days writers frequently discussed the effects of television on family life. However, a curious myopia afflicted those first observers: almost without exception they regarded television as a favorable, beneficial, indeed, wondrous influence upon the family.

"Television is going to be a real asset in every home where there are children," predicted a writer in 1949.

"Television will take over your way of living and change your children's habits, but this change can be a wonderful improvement," claimed another commentator.

"No survey's needed, of course, to establish that television has brought the family together in one room," wrote *The New York Times*'s television critic in 1949.

The early articles about television were almost invariably accompanied by a photograph or illustration showing a family cozily sitting together before the television set, Sis on Mom's lap, Buddy perched on the arm of Dad's chair, Dad with his arm around Mom's shoulder.

Who could have guessed that twenty or so years later Mom would be watching a drama in the kitchen, the kids would be looking at cartoons in their room, while Dad would be taking in the ball game in the living room?

Of course television sets were enormously expensive when they first came on the market. The idea that by the year 2000 more than three quarters of all American families would own two or more sets would have seemed preposterous. The splintering of the multiple-set family was something the early writers did not foresee. Nor did anyone imagine the number of hours children would eventually devote to television, the changes television would effect upon child-rearing methods, the increasing domination of family schedules by children's viewing requirements—in short, the power of television to dominate family life.

As children's consumption of the new medium increased together with parental concern about the possible effects of so much television viewing, a steady refrain helped soothe and reassure anxious parents. "Television always enters a pattern of influences that already exist: the home, the peer group, the school, the church and culture generally," wrote the authors of an early and influential study of television's effects on children. In other words, if the child's home life is all right, parents need not worry about the effects of too much television watching.

But television did not merely influence the child; it deeply influenced that "pattern of influences" everyone hoped would ameliorate the new medium's effects. Home and family life have changed in important ways since the advent of television. The peer group has become television-oriented, and much of the time children spend together is occupied by television viewing. Culture generally has been transformed by television. Participation in church and community activities has diminished, with television a primary cause of this change (see Television and the Social Chill, page 291). Therefore it is improper to assign to television the subsidiary role its many apologists insist it plays. Television is not merely one of a number of important influences upon today's child. Through the changes it has made in family life, television emerges as *the* important influence in children's lives today.

The Quality of Life

Television's contribution to family life has been an equivocal one. For while it has, indeed, kept the members of the family from dispersing, it has not served to bring them together. By its domination of the time families spend together, it destroys the special quality that distinguishes one family from another, a quality that depends to a great extent on what a family does, what special rituals, games, recurrent jokes, familiar songs, and shared activities it accumulates.

Yet parents have accepted a television-dominated family life so completely that they cannot see how the medium is involved in whatever problems they might be having. A first-grade teacher reports:

> *I have one child in the group who's an only child. I wanted to find out more about her family life because this little girl was quite isolated from the group, didn't make friends, so I talked to her mother. Well, they don't have time to do anything in the evening, the mother said. The parents come home after picking up the child at the baby-sitter's. Then the mother fixes dinner while the child watches TV. Then they have dinner and the child goes to bed. I said to this mother, "Well, couldn't she help you fix dinner? That would be a nice time for the two of you to talk," and the mother said, "Oh, but I'd hate to have her miss Zoom. It's such a good program!"*

Several decades ago a writer and mother of two boys aged three and seven described her family's television schedule in a newspaper article. Though some of the programs her kids watched then have changed, the situation she describes remains the same for great numbers of families today:

> We were in the midst of a full-scale War. Every day was a new battle and every program was a major skirmish. We agreed it was a bad scene all around and were ready to enter diplomatic negotiations. . . . In principle we have agreed on 2½ hours of TV a day, *Sesame Street, Electric Company* (with dinner gobbled up in between) and two half-hour shows between 7 and 8:30 which enables the grown-ups to eat in peace and prevents the two boys from destroying one another. Their pre-bedtime choice is dreadful, because, as Josh recently admitted, "There's nothing much on I really like," So . . . it's *What's My Line* or *To Tell the Truth*. . . . Clearly there is a need for first-rate children's shows at this time. . . .

Consider the "family life" described here: Presumably the father comes home from work during the *Sesame Street–Electric Company* stint. The children are either watching television, gobbling their dinner, or both. While the parents eat their dinner in peaceful privacy, the children watch another hour of television. Then there is only a half-hour left before bedtime, just enough time for baths, getting pajamas on, brushing teeth, and so on. The children's evening is regimented with an almost military precision. They watch their favorite programs, and when there is "nothing much on I really like," they watch whatever else is on—because *watching* is the important thing. Their mother does not see anything amiss with watching programs just for the sake of watching; she only wishes there were some first-rate children's shows on at those times.

Without conjuring up fantasies of bygone eras with family games and long, leisurely meals, the question arises: isn't there a better family life available than this dismal, mechanized arrangement of children watching television for however long is allowed them, evening after evening?

Of course, families today still do things together at times: go camping in the summer, go to the zoo on a nice Sunday, take various trips and expeditions. But their ordinary daily life together is diminished—those hours of sitting around at the dinner table, the spontaneous taking up of an activity, the little games invented by children on the spur of the moment when there is nothing else to do, the scribbling, the chatting, and even the quarreling, all the things that form the fabric of a family, that define a childhood. Instead, the children have their regular schedule of television programs and bedtime, and the parents have their peaceful dinner together.

The author of the quoted newspaper article notes that "keeping a family sane means mediating between the needs of both children and adults." But surely the needs of the adults in that family were being better met than the needs of the children. The kids were effectively shunted away and rendered untroublesome, while their parents enjoyed a life as undemanding as that of any childless couple. In reality, it is those very demands that young children make upon a family that lead to growth, and it is the way parents respond to those demands that builds the relationships upon which the future of the family depends. If the family does not accumulate its backlog of shared experiences, shared everyday experiences that occur and recur and change and develop, then it is not likely to survive as anything other than a caretaking institution.

Family Rituals

Ritual is defined by sociologists as "that part of family life that the family likes about itself, is proud of and wants formally to continue." Another text notes that "the development of a ritual by a family is an index of the common interest of its members in the family as a group."

What has happened to family rituals, those regular, dependable, recurrent happenings that give members of a family a feeling of belonging to a home rather than living in it merely for the sake of convenience, those experiences that act as the adhesive of family unity far more than any material advantages?

Mealtime rituals, going-to-bed rituals, illness rituals, holiday rituals—how many of these have survived the inroads of the television set?

A young woman who grew up near Chicago reminisces about her childhood and gives an idea of the effects of television upon family rituals:

> As a child I had millions of relatives around—my parents both come from relatively large families. My father had nine brothers and sisters. And so every holiday there was this great swoop-down of aunts, uncles, and millions of cousins. I just remember how wonderful it used to be. The cousins would come and everyone would play and ultimately, after dinner, all the women would be in the front of the house, drinking coffee and talking, all the men would be in the back of the house, drinking and smoking, and all the kids would be all over the place, playing hide and seek. Christmas time was particularly nice because everyone always brought all their toys and games. Our house had a couple of rooms with go-through closets, so there were always kids running in a great circle route. I remember it was just wonderful.
>
> And then all of a sudden one year I remember becoming suddenly aware of how different everything had become. The kids were no longer playing Monopoly or Clue or the other games we used to play together. It was because we had a television set which had been turned on for a football game. All of that socializing that had gone on previously had ended. Now everyone was sitting in front of the television set, on a holiday, at a family party! I remember being stunned by how awful that was. Somehow the television had become more attractive.

As families have come to spend more and more of their time together engaged in the single activity of television watching, those rituals and pastimes that once gave family life its special quality have become more and more uncommon. Not since prehistoric times, when cave families hunted, gathered, ate, and slept, with little time remaining to accumulate a culture of any significance, have families been reduced to such a sameness.

Real People

The relationships of family members to each other are affected by television's powerful competition in both obvious and subtle ways. For surely the hours that children spend in a one-way relationship with television people, an involvement that allows for no communication or interaction, must have some effect on their relationships with real-life people.

Studies show the importance of eye-to-eye contact, for instance, in real-life relationships, and indicate that the nature of one's eye-contact patterns, whether one looks another squarely in the eye or looks to the side or shifts one's gaze from side to side, may play a significant role in one's success or failure in human relationships. But no eye contact is possible in the child-television relationship, although in certain children's programs people purport to speak directly to the child and the camera fosters this illusion by focusing directly upon the person being filmed. How might such a distortion affect a child's development of trust, of openness, of an ability to relate well to *real* people?

Bruno Bettelheim suggested an answer:

Children who have been taught, or conditioned, to listen
passively most of the day to the warm verbal communications
coming from the TV screen, to the deep emotional appeal of
the so-called TV personality, are often unable to respond to

real persons because they arouse so much less feeling than
the skilled actor. Worse, they lose the ability to learn from
reality because life experiences are much more complicated
than the ones they see on the screen. . . .

A teacher makes a similar observation about her personal viewing experiences:

*I have trouble mobilizing myself and dealing with real people
after watching a few hours of television. It's just hard to make
that transition from watching television to a real relationship. I
suppose it's because there was no effort necessary while I was
watching, and dealing with real people always requires a bit of
effort. Imagine, then, how much harder it might be to do the
same thing for a small child, particularly one who watches a lot
of television every day.*

But more obviously damaging to family relationships is the elimination of opportunities to talk and converse, or to argue, to air grievances between parents and children and brothers and sisters. Families
frequently use television to avoid confronting their problems, problems that will not go away if they are ignored but will only fester and
become less easily resolvable as time goes on.

A mother reports:

*I find myself, with three children, wanting to turn on the TV
set when they're fighting. I really have to struggle not to do it
because I feel that's telling them this is the solution to the
quarrel—but it's so tempting that I often do it.*

A family therapist discusses the use of television as an avoidance
mechanism:

*In a family I know the father comes home from work and turns
on the television set. The children come and watch with him
and the wife serves them their meal in front of the set. He then*

*goes and takes a shower, or works on the car or something. She
then goes and has her own dinner in front of the television set.
It's a symptom of a deeper-rooted problem, sure. But it would
help them all to get rid of the set. It would be far easier to work
on what the symptom really means without the television. The
television simply encourages a double avoidance of each other.
They'd find out more quickly what was going on if they weren't
able to hide behind the TV. Things wouldn't necessarily be
better, of course, but they wouldn't be anesthetized."*

A number of research studies done when television was a relatively new medium demonstrated that television interfered with family activities and the formation of family relationships. One survey showed that 78 percent of the respondents indicated no conversation taking place during viewing except at specified times such as commercials. The study noted: "The television atmosphere in most households is one of quiet absorption on the part of family members who are present. The nature of the family social life during a program could be described as 'parallel' rather than interactive, and the set does seem to dominate family life when it is on." Thirty-six percent of the respondents in another study indicated that television viewing was the only family activity participated in during the week.

The situation has only worsened during the intervening decades. When the studies were made, the great majority of American families had only one television set. Though the family may have spent more time watching TV in those early days, at least they were all together while they watched. Today the vast majority of all families have two or more sets, and nearly a third of all children live in homes with four or more TVs. The most telling statistic: almost 60 percent of all families watch television during meals, and not necessarily at the same TV set. When do they talk about what they did that day? When do they make plans, exchange views, share jokes, tell about their triumphs or little disasters? When do they get to be a real family?

Undermining the Family

Of course television has not been the only factor in the decline of family life in America. The steadily rising divorce rate, the increase in the number of working mothers, the trends towards people moving far away from home, the breakdown of neighborhoods and communities—all these have seriously affected the family.

Obviously the sources of family breakdown do not necessarily come from the family itself, but from the circumstances in which the family finds itself and the way of life imposed upon it by those circumstances. As Urie Bronfenbrenner has suggested:

> When those circumstances and the way of life they generate
> undermine relationships of trust and emotional security
> between family members, when they make it difficult for
> parents to care for, educate and enjoy their children, when
> there is no support or recognition from the outside world
> for one's role as a parent and when time spent with one's
> family means frustration of career, personal fulfillment and
> peace of mind, then the development of the child is
> adversely affected.

Certainly television is not the single destroyer of American family life. But the medium's dominant role in the family serves to anesthetize parents into accepting their family's diminished state and prevents them from struggling to regain some of the richness the family once possessed.

One research study alone seems to contradict the idea that television has a negative impact on family life. In their important book *Television and the Quality of Life,* sociologists Robert Kubey and Mihaly Csikszentmihalyi observe that the heaviest viewers of TV among their subjects were "no less likely to spend time with their families" than the lightest viewers. Moreover, those heavy viewers reported feeling happier, more relaxed, and satisfied when watching TV with their families than light viewers did. Based on these reports, the researchers reached the conclusion that "television viewing harmonizes with family life."

Using the same data, however, the researchers made another observation about the heavy and light viewers: ". . . families that spend substantial portions of their time together watching television are likely to experience greater percentages of their family time feeling relatively passive and unchallenged compared with families who spend small proportions of their time watching TV."

At first glance the two observations seem at odds: the heavier viewers feel happy and satisfied, yet their family time is more passive and unchallenging—less satisfying in reality. But when one considers the nature of the television experience, the contradiction vanishes. Surely it stands to reason that the television experience is instrumental in preventing viewers from recognizing its dulling effects, much as a mind-altering drug might do.

In spite of everything, the American family muddles on, dimly aware that something is amiss but distracted from an understanding of its plight by an endless stream of television images. As family ties grow weaker and vaguer, as children's lives become more separate from their parents', as parents' educational role in their children's lives is taken over by the media, the school, and the peer group, family life becomes increasingly more unsatisfying for both parents and children. All that seems to be left is love, an abstraction that family members know is necessary but find great difficulty giving to each other since the traditional opportunities for expressing it within the family have been reduced or eliminated.

PART V

New Technologies

© David Suter 2000

14

Computers in the Classroom

In less than twenty years, computers have become a conspicuous part of American education, and each year children spend increasing amounts of time pursuing education via machine. For children who already spend 20 to 30 hours each week watching television at home, the advent of computers into the school has meant that school time, which once added some balance to their screen-dominated lives, now helps to tip the scale even further into unreality on the real life/ virtual life scale.

Billions upon billions of dollars have been spent and continue to be spent on bringing high-tech equipment into every classroom, from kindergarten through high school, and as time goes by, parents and teachers in every community throughout the nation, rich or poor, liberal or conservative, white or black or brown, push for more, hoping against hope that technology will pull American children out of a long-term educational slump. Yet no real evidence exists that computer use in the classroom leads to any significant gains in achievement, while evidence of a negative impact, especially in early childhood and elementary education, is beginning to trickle in. Even in high schools and colleges, where the computer has obvious promise as a writing and research tool, the presence of computers in classrooms and dorms often seems to impede the educational process as much as it assists it.

For children of all ages the computer seems to be just one more machine playing an important role in their lives at times when human interactions might serve their purposes and needs better. As Dr. Stanley Greenspan, former director of the Clinical Infant Development Program at NIMH, observed: "So-called interactive computer-based instruction does not provide true interaction, but merely a mechanistic response to the student's efforts." He issued a serious warning that as children grow up with fewer opportunities for human relationships, "we can expect to see increasing levels of violence and extremism and less collaboration and empathy." With horrendous incidents of school violence still vivid in our national memory, Dr. Greenspan's warning should not be ignored.

Do They Help?

What is the evidence that computers are *not* helping to boost students' academic achievement? According to tests and surveys by the government's National Assessment of Educational Progress, little change occurred in long-term trends in students' reading performance between 1971 and 1996, the years when computers streamed into American schools in ever-increasing numbers. Student writing performance remained mainly unchanged from 1984 to 1996, with the exception of eleventh-graders', whose scores declined during that period.

A recent survey by the NAEP of students' use of computers in writing added more negative evidence: fourth-grade students and eighth-grade students who reported using computers infrequently for writing stories or reports (only once or twice a month) achieved higher scores than those who used computers for this purpose more often (at least once a week). If computers were helping children write well, surely the reverse would be true.

While the levels in mathematics ability for all age-groups in America rose somewhat between 1982 and 1996, there is little reason to believe that the use of computers contributed to this rise, and some evidence that it did not. In the latest NAEP math assessment, students who spent more time on computers in school didn't score any higher than their peers; in fact their performance was slightly worse. One further piece of evidence that diminishes faith in classroom computers, at least for teaching elementary school math: teachers of fourth-graders in five of the seven nations that outscored the United States on the Third International Mathematics and Science Study [TIMSS], the most rigorous international study of student achievement ever conducted, reported that they never, or almost never have students use computers in mathematics lessons.

In the year 2000 the Heritage Foundation, a conservative think tank in Washington, D.C., undertook a statistical analysis of the data from the 1998 NAEP exams to determine whether the use of computers in classrooms had a direct and positive effect on academic achievement. The conclusion of the foundation's report reads:

> As this analysis shows, the use of computers in the
> classroom may not play a significant role in explaining
> reading ability. Thus dedicating large amounts of federal tax
> dollars to the purchase of computer hardware, software and
> teacher training could crowd out other worthwhile
> education expenditures on, for example, new textbooks,
> music programs, vocational education, and the arts. This
> report does not suggest there is no place for computers in
> the classroom. It does, however, demonstrate that computers
> may not have the effect on academic achievement in reading
> that some might expect, even when they are used by
> well-trained instructors.

Big Bucks

Though there is little hard evidence that computers are the educational panacea many claim them to be, or that they even help the least little bit, nevertheless almost everyone has jumped on the computer bandwagon. A survey indicated that 90 percent of all parents believe that schools with computers can better prepare students for jobs than those without. Of these believers, 61 percent would even support a Federal tax increase of $100 a year to speed technology into schools. Poor schools decry the "digital divide" and believe that if they had as many computers as the rich schools, their kids wouldn't be so far behind. And while taxpayers often grouse loudly about how their precious tax dollars are spent on this or that item they don't deem worthy, nobody seems to mind the billions of tax dollars spent each year on computers and related equipment for American classrooms.

What's powering this aggressive push for computers in education? The profit motive, for one thing. The high-tech industry's effective promotional efforts and advertisements, with full-page ads in newspapers and magazines and well-placed commercials on television singing the praises of computers, have done a great job in spreading the message that computers are the pathway to success. Thanks to public demand (prompted largely by all that promotion), and thanks to the industry's vigorous lobbying activities and generous campaign donations, the government, state, and local communities continue to allocate large portions of the education budget for high-tech equipment. In 1999, for example, schools spent an estimated $6.9 billion on computers, servers, Internet access, software, and related equipment.

While the real benefits to students remain unclear, one thing is crystal clear: computerizing schools means big bucks for Intel, Microsoft, Apple, IBM, and other technology companies. It is not irrelevant to note that one of the two chairs of the task force that produced former President Clinton's 1997 "Report to the President on the Use of Technology to strengthen K–12 Education in the United States," the report that inspired his famous "computer for every classroom" initiative, was the former CEO of Hewlett-Packard.

Will American taxpayers or their children ever receive an adequate return on their vast investment in electronic technology for the classroom? The enthusiasts insist that in spite of the dismal state of affairs at present—teachers inadequately trained to teach with computers, malfunctioning equipment, inadequate software, and the like—the future will be bright once the various glitches are worked out. In April 1999, research scientist Glenn Kleiman of the Harvard Graduate School of Education noted that the enormous investment in technology for schools was comparable to the enormous investment in dot-com stocks on Wall Street, both being based on the *potential* of new technologies rather than on any visible profits. As everyone knows, the dot-com bubble burst spectacularly later that year. Will the school technology investment follow the example of the dot-coms—reaping pennies for the dollars invested?

Computers in Early Childhood

Any useful discussion of the role of computers in education must assess their value for different age groups with differing pedagogical requirements. In making decisions about computer use in classrooms, it is particularly important to consider early childhood separately from the later school years.

Early childhood is a developmental stage with very different thinking and learning styles, many of them based on the young child's neurological immaturity. For this reason the foundations of early childhood education are built on sensory experiences—touching, smelling, listening, tasting, manipulating. You really can't effectively teach little kids any other way. As the technology director of the Bank Street College once stated:

> Our lower school teachers feel the computer is a distraction. Kids need more concrete experiences. They can do spreadsheets, with the help of an adult, and hypercard, but they'd be better off fooling around with a piano.

Yet much of the public discussion about computers in education fails to make distinctions between early childhood and the later school years. Clinton's "computer for every classroom" initiative, for example, mandated a computer for *every* classroom, from kindergarten to twelfth grade—or K–12, as it is known in education circles. By ignoring early childhood education as a special category requiring different understandings, different teaching methods, and, obviously, different technologies in the classroom, the report becomes virtually useless. Yet it resulted in the outlay of billions of dollars of public funds.

What about the common belief that in order to succeed in the Computer Era children must learn computer skills early? "I don't want our kids to be left behind!" said the president of a suburban school board as he justified the purchase of computers for every classroom—K–12—in his district. Similar statements have been made by hundreds, perhaps thousands of other school administrators as they push for more and more classroom computers.

Yet no one demands that children begin Driver's Ed in kindergarten or even fifth grade, though learning to drive a car is also a vital skill in today's society. It's easy to see that there's time enough to begin teaching kids to be good drivers in high school. Yet the thought prevails that children's future in a high-tech society requires them to start learning computer skills in kindergarten or earlier.

A computer programmer addressed this issue a few years ago in a letter printed in *The New York Times*. As he explained:

> I became a computer programmer at the age of thirty-six in the mid-1970s. I learned programming on my own and on the job. The only prerequisite to learning computing is interest and general literacy.
>
> The education I received in the late 1940s through the early 1960s better prepared me for the computer revolution

than today's kids are being prepared. I never spent one minute in front of a computer. If kids are taught reading, writing, mathematics and thinking, they'll have no trouble picking up computer skills they'll need later on.

Why Computers Are Not the Answer

When 180,000 eighth-graders in thirty-eight nations took an international test of science and math a few years ago, the American students scored significantly lower than their counterparts in the majority of industrialized nations. Yet four years earlier, when those kids were in the fourth grade, they had come out near the top. What had caused their standing to decline so markedly?

Certainly it was not because they had fewer computers in their classrooms. On the contrary, during those four years, American schools had invested far more on high technology than any other nation in the world. Rather, the educators analyzing the results focused on differences between American teachers and those in the higher-scoring nations. It appears that 71 percent of students in higher-scoring nations learned math from teachers who majored in mathematics in college, but only 41 percent of American students did.

The analysts suggested two additional explanations for why American kids score lower than British, French, and other students: curriculum differences. Most of the nations with higher rankings begin teaching subjects like geometry, chemistry, and physics well before high school, giving students more time to absorb the concepts. Moreover, teachers in those nations tend to spend more time on professional development—that is, they take courses to improve skills in their various subjects.

It costs money to hire teachers with degrees in the subjects they teach, more money than employing teachers with general education degrees who can be assigned to any classroom that needs a teacher. Allowing teachers to take courses that advance them in the subjects they teach also costs money. Yet that's not where our education dollars are going these days. Obviously, if the money is spent on technology, there will be less of it for all the other things that can make a greater difference: teacher salaries, teacher training, smaller classes, and lower-cost low-tech equipment, notably books, the most cost effective educational resource available.

What Are They Replacing?

Propelled by federal, state, and local initiatives, schools are spending huge sums on the acquisition of computers and software for the classroom. From the government's, the schools', and the parents' point of view it may seem to be a good deal, a quick fix for an education system that has been going downhill for decades on every level of the academic ladder.

Meanwhile, the computer juggernaut leaves many valuable programs destroyed in its wake. After all, the huge sums of money used for purchasing high-tech equipment and software are rarely an extra item in the budget. Something has been eliminated in their stead. Too often it turns out to be funds for music and arts programs, as in a California school that killed its music program to hire a technology coordinator, or funds for new library books, for remedial-reading teachers or math specialists. A district in Massachusetts eliminated art, music, and gym teachers to spend $300,000 on computers.

In many districts the funds spent on technology equipment might have been used to hire more teachers, thereby achieving the lower student-teacher ratio known to be an important factor in improving the academic achievement of a school's population. The funds might have been used for repairing old school buildings, for rehabilitating crumbling walls or roofs, or school facilities.

Technology critic Clifford Stoll visited a number of schools' computer labs, and always asked the question: "What did this room used to be?" The answers he received were telling: an art room, a machine shop, a music studio. Further questions revealed that the schools had variously dropped their art programs, sold their musical instruments, dropped their music instruction programs, and eliminated their shop programs in their zeal to computerize.

Writer and education scholar Diane Ravitch has often spoken of the poor trade-off schools make between computers and other budget items that are cut in their place, musical instruments and instruction, for example. To learn a musical instrument takes time and effort, she emphasizes. "You have to practice, and you need concentration. That's what American kids don't get enough of."

The Computer-Television Connection

In the mid 1970s I interviewed a large number of experienced early-childhood and elementary-school teachers who bridged the gap between the pre-television generation and the television generation. The testimony of these master teachers, almost without exception, was highly critical of television's influence as reflected in new kinds of behavior in their classrooms (see "An Experiment of Nature," page 82).

Twenty-five years later I interviewed a similar group of experienced teachers, this time ones who bridged the computer gap. Based on my experience of the past, I fully expected these teachers to be equally negative about computers. I couldn't have been more mistaken. Most of the teachers I interviewed were extremely enthusiastic about the new machines in their classrooms.

A partial explanation for the computer's appeal to teachers has to do with that hot issue in education today, accountability. As teachers face an ever-increasing demand for evidence that the children in their classrooms are really learning, a computerized program that keeps track of a child's progress from level to level becomes very attractive as a form of documentation. The computer provides something in hand to show parents, whether, in fact, the progress demonstrated is as substantial as the less measurable kind achieved through more old-fashioned methods. In interviews with teachers, this feature of various computer programs was mentioned enthusiastically. Understandably, parents are more likely to accept a report that their child is backward in math skills from an impersonal computer than from a teacher who might be picking on the kid for some reason.

But that was not the main reason these teachers were so gung-ho about computers. When I questioned them further and visited some of their classrooms, I came to see that these teachers' hopefulness and relief at the arrival of computers in their classroom bore a connection to the negative reactions to television of those teachers who had bridged the television gap twenty-five years earlier.

The teachers in the 1970s perceived a new technology—television—as a *cause* of certain problems: children with short attention spans, children with difficulty concentrating, children who lose interest in a lesson if the teacher isn't entertaining, children unwilling to put in the slogging effort required for the acquisition of anything beyond the most basic reading and writing skills. Now a new generation of teachers was pouncing on another new technology—the computer—as a potential *cure* for those same problems.

But these teachers no longer make a clear connection between children's learning problems and television. They don't necessarily recognize that children have ever been different, that they were once more attentive, more focused. All they know is that getting kids to learn is an uphill struggle.

Enter the computer. A machine with a screen! At last the kids don't have to be coaxed or entertained or motivated. They already have a deep and pleasurable relationship with screens. No wonder these hard-working, dedicated men and women greet computers so fervently. Here at last might be a way to get their students to learn.

Teachers' descriptions of students' attitudes toward computers confirms the connection between children's television experiences and their receptiveness to classroom computers. "It's the best thing we've ever done," a teacher in San Francisco exulted about her school's new acquisition of computers. "Every single child will do more work for you and better work with a computer. Just because it's on a monitor, kids pay more attention. There's this magic to the screen."

Yet the teachers can't fail to observe that while their students are far more easily motivated to work with the classroom computer, they don't necessarily acquire those all-important basic skills. A teacher in California describes Hilda, a fifth-grader so enthusiastic about computers that she spends most of her free time in the school's computer lab, surfing the Internet and writing E-mails—surely a good way to practice reading and writing skills. She is indeed proficient on the computer, and even helps her less experienced classmates to acquire computer skills. But her grades and test scores are poor and show no signs of improving. When she writes an essay on the computer, it is riddled with errors.

The head of a Palo Alto organization aimed at promoting school technology and funded, in part, by software manufacturers, countered any negative views about the value of computers in classrooms by saying, "It makes children enjoy learning, and that's worth a lot. We hear 'Is this going to improve children's reading and writing and arithmetic?' That's almost irrelevant. It's the tool of our children's day."

Fortunately, not all teachers will agree that efforts to improve basic skills like reading and writing and computing are irrelevant. But faced with the difficulties of teaching verbal and logical skills requiring concentration and perseverance to children whose lives have been dominated by visual experiences requiring little concentration and no perseverance, they can't help but be gratified to see them show real enjoyment at learning computer skills—at least they're learning *something!*

Not Making the Connection

"I love computers, I really do," declared a master teacher with thirty years' experience of classroom teaching in a school district near Albany, New York. She praised a number of programs she's used during the last decade: Oregon Trail, Third-Grade Mysteries, Math Blasters. She's teaching her students to use search engines like "Ask Jeeves" on the Internet. Last week she coordinated a CD-ROM on the rain forest with a unit her class is doing on rain forests. Yet even this enthusiastic proponent of computers in the classroom couldn't help citing numerous problems she is encountering in trying to teach third-graders via computers:

> One problem always comes up with a new program. When the computer says, "Do you need help? Do you need information?" They'll say, "No!" and go right into the program. Because certain things they do play, in terms of the games, it's instant gratification—bing, bang, boom—fast! They like stimulation. They like change.
>
> So when you give them something that's a three-step situation, you lose them. They don't want to read. They don't want to read instructions or directions. They'll just hit the Enter button and go on. Because they want to get to the game. After the work they get to the game.
>
> Another problem: when you're up there teaching and some of the children are on computers, if someone has a problem on the computer—and they always do—what are you supposed to do with the lesson you're teaching the rest of the class? You go help one child, put out that little forest fire, and then other kids need help!

Sometimes she almost seemed surprised to hear her own answers when asked to compare teaching before computers became available as a teaching tool and after:

*Did my kids end up with poorer basic skills during all the years
I was teaching before computers? No, absolutely not! Are they
going to be better readers because of computers? Or better
writers? No, in some cases they were better writers years ago. I
think they're worse writers now. But now that we have
computers, it's enhancing their learning. But of course before we
had computers we did it differently and that worked too.*

*One of the problems these days is that children don't listen
the way they used to. If you teach them by repeating something
over and over, you're teaching them not to listen—that's what
their parents do. What I say to them is "Once." I say: "You
didn't hear it? Fine, go ask someone else."*

When she came to the subject of television, however, her enthusiasm for technology went into reverse gear. And once again she seemed almost surprised to hear herself comparing the two technologies:

*Does the computer have anything to do with their not listening?
Well, I think their TV watching has something to do with it. So
maybe it's connected. The computer is a lot like TV!*

*And the kids are absolutely couch potatoes. Today in
Physical Education they had to run a mile and walk a mile
and some of them were dying after two minutes, they're totally
not physically fit. Actually, some of them are computer potatoes
because they go home and work on the computer for 4 hours.
And some of them are addicted to video games.*

*But you know something? The parents have allowed this to
happen. Like TV, the video games and computer are babysitters.
And for some families, rewards. "You've been good, so you can
go on the computer." Or "Go watch an extra hour of TV." Mom
is cooking dinner so "Let's not have a conversation. I don't want
to know about your day." It's easier to put them in front of the
TV or computer instead of arguing with them. I think kids
have lost a lot of social skills.*

> *Children need time, they need care, they need you to sit*
> *there and help with their problems, to listen to them once in a*
> *while. But parents aren't doing it. They say, "If you leave me*
> *alone you can go on the computer."*
>   *"Still I love computers," this teacher reiterated. "They really*
> *motivate the kids to learn."*

Why Not Get Rid of Them?

Even as the educational value of computers in classrooms remains unproven, the most frequently heard argument for their continued use is some variation on the theme that progress lies in ever more complex technology. The idea of eliminating computers from classrooms has become unthinkable, almost like the idea of removing television sets from homes.

William L. Rukeyser, a former Education Department official, likens the unthinking acceptance of computers' various virtues to a religious belief. Presently the coordinator of Learning in the Real World, a nonprofit organization that challenges the use of computers in schools, Rukeyser stated, "The nearest thing I can draw a parallel to is a theological discussion. There's so much of an element of faith [in the educational value of computers] that demanding evidence is a sign of heresy."

But there's a more practical explanation for the continuing and expanding presence of computers and technology in the classroom. Since billions of dollars have already been spent on computers for the classroom, nobody's going to say: Oh well, we made a mistake. Let's get rid of them. Admitting a mistake on that kind of scale would be political suicide.

If you question the use of computers in the elementary-school classroom, you are almost certainly going to hear some version of the response Andy Carvin, an associate at the Benton Foundation, gave to such a question: "We have to move beyond that debate and think about what we can do to take advantage of this technology."

Now that they're in every classroom, the argument goes, we must do the best we can with them. But shouldn't someone have figured out if they were a good thing *first*, before spending all those billions?

The Problems of Bucking the Tide

Even when enlightened schools resist the rush to computerize, they are often faced with a parent backlash that is hard to deal with. In an article entitled "Honey I Wired the Kids," the writer complains that "Technology is looked down upon" in the "academically superior school" he and his wife chose for their three kids. He describes with considerable indignation the "condescending" anticomputer attitude he has to "endure" at this school:

> My middle-school daughter has recently come home to
> report that every time she goes back to an interesting kid site
> or game site at a school computer, a blocking sign appears,
> saying DO YOUR HOMEWORK!

Furthermore, he recounts, that "gallingly, we recently endured the great E-mail ban in our academically superior school," a ban that made it an offense to send or receive personal E-mail from a school computer.

The writer's well-written, entertaining article reveals that he is the recipient of a fine education himself. His complaint that his kids' school won't let them play computer games during schooltime, or send personal E-mail on school computers, gives an idea of what well-intentioned educators, striving to provide a similar education to his children, are up against these days.

In addition to subtle pressures from sophisticated, "with-it" parents, there is another, more serious difficulty facing school administrators who might want to keep their schools low-tech: Parents demand computers and make decisions about school choice based on the numbers of computers in the classroom. Even those schools whose educational philosophy might make them hold back on using computers, at least in the lower grades, are compelled to introduce computers into their classrooms as a matter of self-preservation. But nothing compels them to use them, and often they don't. The "academically superior" school with the "condescending anticomputer attitude" attended by the kids of the magazine writer cited above is probably such a school. And perhaps the fact that it is superior academically is not unrelated to this attitude.

Computers to Enhance Reading

Those making the case for computers as a valuable educational adjunct often propose that they are useful as motivational tools.

"If your child is captivated by certain writers," a supporter argues, he or she "can learn more about the authors and their books at their personal Web sites. . . . Many of these sites are rich with information."

But how does the child get captivated by a writer in the first place? The child gets hooked by reading the book. Only after that will the information about the author provided on the Web site be meaningful to the child. It won't work the other way—the additional information is unlikely to make the child want to read the book. In other words, this is an example of reading as a tool for developing interest in the computer, not the other way around.

Other suggested ways to foster interest in reading, such as providing a site where children's book authors conduct online discussions with children, may be seen in the same light: enrichment activities for children who are already readers.

A more direct approach for creating readers is offered by the Sylvan Learning Centers, who have developed a computer-mediated reward system to entice children into reading: BookAdventure.com. This site offers a multiple-choice quiz that kids can take after reading a selected book. If they score well, they are eligible for prizes such as a free meal at TGI Friday's [one of the sponsors of the Web site]. It's a bit depressing to think that in the future children will be reading books not for the sheer pleasure of being transported into new worlds, or for the excitement and wonder that books offer, but in order to get a free meal at a chain restaurant.

Much of the software now available for teaching kids reading skills on the computer is appealing to kids. But will it teach reading? Perhaps these programs will work to help kids incorporate decoding skills. But so far the only known way to acquire advanced reading skills—the ones that allow readers to absorb complex ideas and gain insight into their own lives—is by reading, reading, and more reading.

Computer vs. Workbook

Most of the computer programs that teachers are enthusiastic about, the ones they feel are most useful and educationally effective, turn out to be those that provide children drill and practice in various verbal and mathematical skills. But in spite of these programs' "glitzy" nature, often taking the form of little animated games with sound effects and built-in positive reinforcement ("You're right! You're a star!!"), a comparison may be made with a far more humble teaching device that has long been the mainstay of elementary classroom teachers around the world: the workbook. In each case standardized material is provided to fill a student's time in what is hoped will be a profitable way, without the need of a teacher's intervention. Thus the teacher is freed for individual work with one or a small number of children.

There's no doubt that a good teacher working individually with a student, a teacher able to recognize a child's particular needs, a teacher able to explain, discuss, and, perhaps, inspire, will always provide a more valuable educational experience than a computer program or a workbook. Good teachers being a rare commodity, however, and small classes the asset of an advantaged minority, there is always a need for attractive, time-filling teaching aids.

But the comparison between computerized drill-and-practice programs and workbooks might serve to remind a hopeful public that while such mechanical devices may help to consolidate certain specific skills, nevertheless the important goals of education—to be able to adapt these skills for human purposes, to be able to think clearly, to be able to assimilate the complex thoughts of others, to be able to make reasoned judgments—such goals are unlikely to be achieved without a human guide: a teacher able to offer the quirky, unpredictable, flexible, and rich resources of her or his own amazing computer, the human brain.

On the High School and College Front

Though the value of computers in high school and college cannot be denied, yet unrealistic expectations about computers as some sort of magic cure for American students' academic deficits are widespread, fueled as usual by politicians and countless entrepreneurs.

A case in point may be seen in the experience of Trinity High, an impoverished high school in a remote logging town in northern California. The school had long dreamed of offering college-level Advanced Placement courses to its students; these courses help kids get into the most competitive colleges. But the school couldn't afford to hire even a single special teacher needed for such a course.

When a private company began offering college-level courses online, conducted entirely through electronic text and animated short films, Trinity leaped at the chance. After all, the company charged only $400 per student, while hiring an AP teacher would have cost more than $50,000 a year.

Two Trinity students signed up for Advanced Placement Government and Politics. One dropped out midway. Without an actual teacher's guidance he was unable to summon up the self-discipline needed to complete the rigorous weekly writing requirements. "I didn't feel like doing any work," he admitted, a not uncommon attitude for an adolescent. The other managed to complete the course, but because of technical difficulties in signing onto the company's Web site, he finished several weeks behind schedule. It doesn't seem likely that online AP courses are going to equalize the discrepancies between rich and poor schools anytime in the near future.

Meanwhile, on the college front, it is equally short-sighted to suppose that a computer connection and Internet access in every college dormitory room will lead to a nation of better educated graduates. An illuminating look at the realities of computer use on campus is offered in the following excerpt from a newspaper op-ed piece written by a Swarthmore College sophomore:

> Take a walk through the residence halls of any college in the country, and you'll find students seated at their desks, eyes transfixed on their computer monitors. What are they doing with their top-of-the-line PC's and high-speed T-1 Internet connections?
>
> They are playing Tomb Raider instead of going to chemistry class, tweaking the configurations of their machines instead of writing the paper due tomorrow, collecting mostly useless information from the World Wide Web instead of doing a math problem set—a host of other activity that has little or nothing to do with traditional academic work.

From the college teacher's point of view, the situation looks no rosier. A law professor at Yale reported that students in his classroom use their laptops for a variety of other purposes besides taking notes: playing solitaire, surfing the Web, sending E-mails, and trading stock. Making a point reminiscent of the myriad elementary-school teachers who complain that TV-conditioned kids tune out when a lesson is not entertaining, he wrote:

> They toggle between windows during any part of the class they deem to be boring—often when their fellow students are asking questions or answering them. Admittedly students can mentally check out of class in other ways—for instance by daydreaming or doodling. But not all activities are equally addictive.

He reported that when he finally asked his students to refrain from using their computers in class for anything besides note-taking, they "went ballistic."

Many college faculty members, particularly those in the humanities where clear thinking and good writing are critical skills, feel less than sanguine about the promise of computers in higher education. They place their bets on the traditional student-teacher relationship, on teachers' ability to pass along enthusiasm and even passion for their subject to students in their classroom. Education via computer, at a remove from the inspiring mentor, will not lead to that sort of bond.

A Matter of Balance

As with television, it's obvious that computers are here to stay. As with television, the problems computers present often depend on how they are used, and how much time their use occupies. Though younger children in the most crucial stages of development require experiences that computers cannot provide, and though the introduction of computers into their lives may displace those more valuable experiences, nevertheless, computers can be fun, and will do them no harm if used in a limited way. It's a matter of balance.

For exceptional children, learning disabled children, sight-impaired, dyslexic, and other children with special needs, computers can be a godsend. While very gifted children obviously also need much personal attention, computers can serve them as a source of enrichment and advancement at times when other children might need more help and a more hands-on experience for learning.

For older children—junior high, high school, and college students—computers are indeed a valuable tool. By the time they've reached their teens, the time has come for them to learn some of the computer's complexities. But without the proper educational foundation, these children, too, will founder on the shoals of high technology. Without the ability to read well, write clearly, compute accurately and think logically, without curiosity and creativeness, without an ability to concentrate, to work hard without immediate rewards—no amount of computer know-how will turn them into educated men and women.

15

Home Electronics

During the last decades of the twentieth century, as personal computers began proliferating throughout America, parents welcomed a number of other bright new electronic devices into their homes—notably the VCR and a variety of video-game consoles or terminals. Uneasy about the passivity of their children's television watching, parents hoped that computer programs for kids as well as video game play would provide a better, more mentally active experience than the tube offered. With the VCR, parents hoped at least to have more control over the quality of programs their kids were exposed to. All in all, parents hoped these new technologies would help to wean their children from television, and restore a little balance in their lives.

But rather than displacing television, as many had predicted they would do, the new machines supplemented it. To the 2¾ hours per day the average child was spending with television, ½ hour to 45 minutes of video viewing was added. And on top of that came 20 more minutes a day of computer- and video-game play. The more video technology that's available, it turns out, the most time kids spend in front of screens.

But is it time better spent? Not really. Parents can't help observing that their children's various activities at home computers and video game terminals often appear as unprofitable and addictive as television viewing, as likely to displace outdoor play, practice of musical instruments, hobbies, and leisure-time reading.

This is not to say that there aren't worthwhile videos available from the local video shop, or computer programs or electronic games for children that are challenging or entertaining, just as there are programs on television that teach and delight children. Once again, as with television, it is a matter of an electronic medium's inordinate fascination, and its ability to displace other important childhood experiences. Once again, as with television, the gravest concerns arise about the use of these new technologies by very young children, those developmentally most in need of different kinds of experiences.

The VCR

Before VCRs became almost as common in American households as television sets, conscientious parents who monitored their children's television consumption faced a certain number of hours each day when there was nothing suitable for viewing on any channel. Those were the times when parents hardened their hearts and said "No!" to television. In place of viewing they brought out the blocks, the puzzles, the modeling clay, and their small kids played. Parents steered their older kids to books, to hobbies. They sent them off to practice their musical instruments, or let them just daydream and do nothing. And if the kids got cranky or bothersome, those were the times parents had to be firm, not because they enjoyed laying down the law, but out of necessity.

Once a VCR is available, this natural check on screen viewing is removed. Now, whenever an empty hour looms and there's nothing to do—when a kid is sick, for example, or when it's raining, or when a parent needs to make a call, or finish some work—at any time at all, even in the middle of the night when *Sesame Street* couldn't possibly be on the air, the carefully chosen video is popped into the VCR, and the kids are plugged in.

In conversations with dozens of families throughout the country, it became evident that the very parents who once carefully controlled their kids' TV consumption were now using well-chosen video programs to buy peace and quiet from their kids.

Invariably these parents extolled the advantages of VCRs over broadcast television. "It gives my daughter the freedom to fast-forward something if it gets scary," one mother noted. Another said, "It enabled my son to explore things that wouldn't have been available via TV. He's fascinated by sharks, but how many times a week do you find a shark show on television?"

But most of these parents admitted that it wasn't because of the worthwhile programs that they turn on the VCR, but because it's an effective child sedative. An exceptionally candid upstate New York mother of two preschool children reported:

> I use the VCR because it makes me feel slightly less guilty about plunking the kids in front of the television. Sometimes, when they're driving me crazy I'll let them watch a short tape while I'm fixing dinner. Or if it's pouring rain or on cold winter afternoons. I do it out of desperation. At least there are no commercials on a tape . . .

A Dallas homemaker ordinarily limits her children's regular TV viewing to one hour of PBS on school days. But she has no limits on their viewing of her carefully selected tapes:

> I'm more comfortable with a VCR. The kids can watch just about anything we have on tape. Walt Disney cartoons, Abbott and Costello films, and sweet stories and fairy tales—Mary Poppins and the like—that we've been given as gifts by grandparents.

The unavailability of children's programming was once one of the most important forms of "natural television control" available to parents (see Natural Control, page 230). With the introduction of the VCR into virtually every American home, parents gained another break from the difficulties of life with little kids. Children, meanwhile, lost one of their last remaining opportunities for play and for living *real life* as compared to watching it.

A Wonderful Addition to the Family

Once upon a time, long car trips provided unforgettable opportunities for unifying the family. As the car set off for the vacation home or the camping trip or the visit to Grandpa and Grandma, everyone was confined to the close quarters of a car, unable to wander off and "do their own thing."

Kids being kids, they would often take advantage of the circumstances in ways that did not necessarily conform to their parents' dreams of family togetherness—that is, they'd fight, whine for various services, beg to stop at every junk-food concession along the way. This is why parents collected good car games to play along the way (License Plate Bingo or In My Grandfather's Trunk). They'd organize sing-alongs of time-consuming cumulative songs ("There's a Hole in the Bucket" or "Ninety-nine Bottles of Beer on the Wall"). Having nothing better to do, the kids often resorted to looking out the window, noting various features of the landscape that would become familiar landmarks on all future trips.

Perhaps for the very reason that long car trips were so tough on parents, they were memorable for the kids. Nobody is likely to forget the time everyone was rough-housing in the back seat, and Dad pulled over at the side of a field and ordered: "Out! Right this minute," whereupon he directed the three kids in ten minutes of rousing calisthenics. Or the time Mom burst into tears in the front seat, sobbing, "I can't take this for one more second. I'm losing my mind!" at which point the kids stopped fighting and pretended to search for it.

For better or worse, these were experiences everyone would

laugh about at family reunions twenty-five years later: the games, the songs, the scenery, the sobs and threats. It was all part of the richness of family life.

Now parents can find peace and quiet on family trips in a new way. These days Chevrolet's Venture Minivan includes a built-in videocassette player in the backseat.

It has proved to be a highly popular car accessory. As of December, 2000, one out of five GM minivans sold included the backseat VCR. According to a GM executive, the biggest purchasers of the VCR option have been families, including grandparents. And if parents hesitate, feeling guilty about adding more screen time, the company reminds them of the safety benefits—by keeping the kids from distracting the driver, the VCR prevents accidents.

Today "the kids can't wait to hit the road," said a proud owner of such a van. She described the scene on a recent trip: the kids sat in the back with headphones, giggling as they watched their favorite movie while she and her husband peacefully listened to CDs up front. "It's been a wonderful addition to the family," she declared. It seems only fair to ask: Family? What family?

Lapware

Just as the dot-com and high-tech stock bubble was bursting towards the end of the millennium, one computer product succeeded beyond anyone's expectations—computer games for very, *very* young children. Since some of the prospective players of these games were actually too young to sit unassisted, the product became known as "lapware." Between July 1999 and July 2000, sales of lapware rose by 20 percent.

The success was partly fueled by canny marketing. The manufacturers' advertisements preyed on parental anxieties about their kids' development (My baby isn't talking yet. Is something wrong?) and their desires to give their offspring an educational jumpstart. One of these programs is actually called *JumpStart Baby,* and its package declares that it "breaks new ground by offering important developmental skills."

In addition, the marketers capitalized on the pervasive belief that children must be introduced to computers early if they're to succeed in the brave new world of high technology, or conversely, the fear that if kids don't jump on the cyber-bandwagon as early as possible, they'll be out of luck later on. A San Diego farther of a five-month-old child whose developmental skills were being "enhanced" by a lapware program called "Baby Wow" called the game a perfect "initial introduction to the keyboard and mouse" for his child. In addition to making babies computer-savvy, "Baby Wow" also offers to introduce babies to eight foreign languages and bring them up to snuff on the laws of cause and effect.

Of course education is not the only reason parents have been rushing out to buy lapware for their babies. As anyone who has ever lived with toddlers knows, just about anything that will keep a small child entertained for a few moments is fairly irresistible for a parent or caretaker, especially during the years before the child is ready to watch TV for any real period of time. If the experience is also going to help them get smarter, so much the better.

The vast majority of parents would avoid giving their child something actually harmful just to keep them quiet. The days of dosing kids with laudanum or phenobarbitol just to achieve a little peace are over. But while today's child development experts believe that exposing babies to large doses of computer stimulation is inappropriate and perhaps damaging, their opinions are not promoted as aggressively as those of manufacturers and marketers touting their products' marvelous virtues.

Among the experts' opinions: "A computer is a wonderful tool but it doesn't make any sense for infants when their visual systems and motor skills aren't well developed." So says David Elkind, professor of child development at Tufts University and author of *The*

Hurried Child. About software for toddlers, educational psychologist and author Jane Healy says, "There's no evidence that you're helping your child and it could hurt." Almost all early childhood specialists agree that babies and small children need hands-on, sensory-rich experiences in order to thrive, and human interaction, with eye contact, to develop socially.

But whatever the ill effects of computer games on babies, they will be subtle, as hard to pin down as television's adverse effects on children have always been. The great difference here is the child's age. Before this development, most children enjoyed at least two or two-and-a-half years of real-life experience before they began to watch television. Here, on the cozy lap of Mom or Dad, the child can begin a relationship with an electronic machine shortly after birth, before he or she can talk, or walk, or even sit up. That this loss of time spent with real things will have *some* effect is beyond doubt. The question only remains: what will this effect be? When dealing with a resource as precious and irreplaceable as our children, it seems short-sighted to take a chance that the effect will be harmful in even the smallest way.

Computer Toys

In the beginning there were Tamagotchis, odd little creatures that came to be called "virtual reality toys." Resembling a chick or a dog or a little dinosaur, the Tamagotchi needed virtual care—make-believe feeding and attention of various sorts—in order to be "happy." You couldn't turn it off. Then there was Furby—a robotic stuffed toy that performed certain actions and reacted to certain manipulations by its owner. You couldn't turn this one off either.

Soon other computer-driven "smart" toys began to fill the toy stores of America, toys such as the Tonka Dig 'N Rigs Playset, a gizmo parents could strap over the keyboard of their computer. Now a toddler was able to pilot a virtual front-loader on screen without setting a chubby finger on a real toy.

Even more popular were robotic dolls such as "My Real Baby" that closely mimic human emotions and responses. Some of these dolls are programmed to behave so realistically that small children, whose concepts of the world are still in formation, come to believe they're real, or, at least, that they fall into some new category between real and unreal.

In one sense computer toys are simply fancier versions of that time-honored staple of the toy armamentarium, the mechanical toy. Wind-up or battery-operated gadgets have always beguiled children, though parents know that they don't have the staying power of simple playthings like blocks and wooden trains and trucks. The child is dazzled for a few days and then completely loses interest. After all, the mechanical toy only does one thing while the simple toys that depend on a child's imagination and ingenuity to move and do things have endless possibilities for play (see Why Kids Can't Amuse Themselves, page 134).

But a computerized toy's highly successful representation of the real thing sets up even greater obstacles to the playing child than a mechanical toy. The baby doll that talks pre-programmed words, or the telephone that answers as if it were different people, require even less imagination than the battery-operated doll that crawls backward and forward at the push of a switch. The electronic element of these toys may keep the child fascinated for a while. But you can hardly call it "play": the toy says and does things, while the child watches and listens. A little like television.

While computerized toys proved to be a marketing success, a growing phalanx of child experts and child-advocacy organizations have begun raising questions about their appropriateness as they had done for other computer applications earmarked for young children.

Diane Levin, a professor of education at Wheelock College,

notes: "The main point of these electronic toys becomes figuring out and controlling the technology, not using the toy in the service of issues you need to work on."

"What are we doing to children when we encourage them to attach emotionally to machines and objects rather than real, loving people?" asks author and social commentator Mary Pipher. "We know that attachment in childhood is everything. It's kind of a dangerous thing when you teach your child to become attached to machines, especially when the machines are programmed to act like they are emotionally attached to your child."

Dorothy Singer, senior research scientist in psychology at Yale University, calls programmed electronic dolls "very limiting." A much better toy, she maintains, would be a simple doll for which the children themselves may do the talking. She and her husband, Yale psychologist Jerome Singer, are advocates of simple make-believe play using the simplest of accessories—boxes, paper bags, socks and the like—and have written a book demonstrating the value of such play, with ideas of how to encourage it.

The Alliance for Childhood, a partnership of educators, health professionals, parents and other child advocates, agrees. "These [computerized] toys are the opposite of what children need," said Joan Almon, the U.S. coordinator of the Alliance. "They need simple, open ended toys that leave room for the child's own imagination." She called the latest robotic toy, My Dream Baby, "the worst toy idea of the year."

Video Games

Here's the good news: video games *do* allow more leeway for mental activity and even the discharge of fantasy than simply staring at a TV set. Kids get to *do* something, and something happens as a result. Nevertheless, as a form of play these games fall short of many older and simpler pastimes of childhood. Among these are activities that develop manual skills (making model planes, for instance) or foster interests the child might carry into adulthood. Preferable are forms of play that allow for conversation and discussion and the acquisition of social skills (playing cards or board games) or team play that involves cooperation.

As psychologist Eugene Provenzo has written: ". . . compared to the worlds of imagination provided by play with dolls and blocks, [video games] ultimately represent impoverished cultural and sensory environments for the child." Parents, however, remain eternally hopeful. Observing their children's fascination with computer and video games, and their willingness to spend many hours with this single medium, parents hope that at least it will improve their kids' eye-hand coordination. This might transfer to some useful skill later in life—mastering a musical instrument, for example, or playing tennis.

Unfortunately, children accustomed to the quick gratifications of video games may not be willing to make the long, arduous efforts necessary to play an instrument well or to excel at a sport. It's pretty quick and pleasurable to become a whiz at video games. How is the video child to know that it will take far more time and effort, some of it not particularly pleasurable, to become good at tennis or the violin?

Parents have long suspected that there's something hypnotic and addictive about their kids' video-game play. Now at least one scientific study has found a solid cause for concern. In a study at Hammersmith Hospital in London, researchers used Positron Emission Tomography (PET) scans, to monitor the brains of volunteers playing video games. When comparing the players' brain activity with that of a control group monitored while staring at a blank screen, the researchers found that production of the neurotransmitter dopamine doubled in the course of video-game play, an increase as large as that seen when subjects are injected with powerful and highly addictive stimulants such as amphetamines or Ritalin.

One small but hopeful indication of the human organism's marvelous facility for self-regulation may be seen in the new popularity among teenagers of an old, low-tech game—Skee-Ball. The surprising renaissance of this simple, non-electronic bowling-type game in video arcades across the country was easily explained by its enthusiastic players: It's an antidote for video fatigue, they asserted.

Computer Games

What about computer games? Do they fall into the same category as video games? In part it's a semantic distinction: video games include arcade games, games for systems like Sega and Nintendo, and stand-alone games like the well-known Game Boy. Computer games are played on a personal computer. Otherwise the play in both is similar, with the action occurring on a screen, while the child uses a keyboard of some sort to manipulate electronic images. Play is often accompanied by a noisy sound track of some sort.

There are differences in content, however. Computer games often include arts and crafts and educational activities. Video games are rarely educational. More often than not their narrative framework is violent—for instance, the figures moving on the screen are aliens the player must destroy. As the narrative progresses, it is usually accompanied by loud and exciting background sounds. Studies confirm what most parents already know: boys are three times as likely to play video games as girls, and violent video games are far more popular than the few educational ones. One survey found that only 2 percent of the children studied preferred games with an educational content. Not surprisingly, video games are considerably more popular than computer games.

Screen Time

Today sensible parents tend to lump the various electronic technologies into one category. They talk about "screen activities" and "screen time," and end up making the same rules for all these technologies, particularly trying to limit the total amount of time children can devote to them. Issues of control have become the same for VCRs, family computers, and video games as for family television sets. Indeed, the arrival of the new devices has compounded parents' control problems. As one parent wrote in a magazine article, "We were protecting ourselves against the television screen, but the computer screen caught us unawares. Because of our desire for them to stay ahead of a fast-moving technology that will define their lives, we basically failed to set limits." Consequently the next section of this book, "Controlling Television," applies equally to all screen activities, not only television.

PART VI

Controlling Television

"And now an important message from your sponsor: *GO OUTSIDE AND PLAY!*"

16

Out of Control

Parents often complain bitterly about the television programs available for their children to watch. They write letters to their local papers, boycott advertisers, join organizations that lobby for better children's programming. There is, of course, a simpler way to deal with such problems: turn the set off. But that is precisely what parents cannot seem to do.

Why is it so hard to control television in the home? Some of the difficulties lie in widespread parental attitudes about television, as well as in well-established child-rearing trends. But many problems of television control are inherent in the medium itself.

How Parents Get Hooked

Television arrived on the scene as a *deus ex machina* to help the beleaguered parent survive the rigors of modern child-rearing. But as television replaced other strategies, parents found themselves increasingly unable to bring up their children without resorting to its use. As a mother of three children admits:

> *I'm afraid not to have a television set even though I know the kids would probably be a lot better off without it. What would I do when I needed it? I'd just go to pieces. I'm hooked on using it.*

Interviews with parents reveal a pattern of growing dependence upon television as a child-rearing tool. This occurs even when the parent does not start off using television to suit her own purposes but introduces it for the child's sake alone. *Sesame Street* is frequently mentioned by parents when describing "the way it all began."

A Denver mother of two preschool girls relates:

When I first started turning on the television for the children, it wasn't out of need, but because I thought it was a good thing to offer. I'd turn on the television set and say, "It's time for Sesame Street, *even if it meant interrupting the girls in the middle of play. They didn't need to be coaxed to watch television. They enjoyed watching, and I often watched with them.*

But after a time television took on a different aspect in our household. The change was subtle, but looking back now, it's clear that a real change did take place. I suppose it was because I discovered how dependable an amusement television was, more dependable than any other. After a time whenever things came up, tiny domestic emergencies—when I had to talk to somebody on the phone, or when somebody dropped in, or when Marty called to say that he was bringing somebody home for dinner— that sort of thing—then I would turn to television for help.

Suddenly I realized that I was no longer using television as an experience to offer the children, but as something with value for me. But by now it was hard to change my operating procedure. Now I no longer had to remind the children that it was time for their programs, or interrupt them in their play. They really *wanted to watch and were quite unwilling to find other amusements when I wasn't able to play with them myself.*

Another mother reveals a similar pattern:

When Robby first started watching Sesame Street, *I was the one who started it. He went to school in the afternoons, and I'd put* Sesame *on in the mornings, from nine to ten, I guess it was. I wanted him to watch it. I thought it was a good program,*

*that he'd learn his numbers—you know, an educational kind of
thing. Then, once I stopped working and I was home mornings,
it was a lovely hour for me to have him watching television.
That was absolutely a relief for me, to have that time. That was
definitely how I saw it. I mean, it was good, there were numbers
and all those other things there, too, but . . .*

While some mothers first set their children before the television
primarily for the child's benefit, the majority of parents begin using
television in an open quest for relief. They look forward to those
hours of peace so eagerly that sometimes they actually push the child
into watching.

The mother of Ian, age six, and Emma, age four, recalls such a
beginning:

*Ian first started watching television when he was two but he
didn't get really addicted until he was three. At first many of the
programs frightened him. Even* Sesame Street *was too violent
for him and he refused to watch it. But he was willing to watch*
Captain Kangaroo *and I guess I did encourage him to watch it.
I loathed the mornings and it was a way to allow myself some
time to feed the baby and to be quiet myself while he watched*
Captain. *I couldn't resist doing it.*

Whatever her reservations, Ian's mother was as unlikely to spurn
the advantages offered by television as she was to go scrub her laun-
dry at the nearest stream because the washing machine is bad for the
environment.

A Terrible Saga

Helen S., a part-time musician and mother, began using television as a handy child sedative while she prepared dinner. She describes the evolution of a serious television problem:

There was a time when Kitty and John were both little when they watched nothing but Mister Rogers. *Our whole dinner schedule was geared to that program, and I'd have dinner ready for them exactly at five-thirty when* Rogers *was over. That was a nice useful time to have them salted away watching TV. I was the one who turned on the set at that time, and I didn't turn it on any other time. But that program was very convenient.*

Then there was a time when they watched Sesame Street *and* Mister Rogers. *That didn't seem too much television to me. But pretty soon a time came when* Mister Rogers *became too tame for John. When he was four he discovered* Batman. *So now there was* Sesame Street *and* Batman. *And sometimes* Underdog, *which both of them liked a lot. And then they developed a great fondness for* The Flintstones. *I don't know where they got interested in all those other programs, maybe from baby-sitters, who always let them watch TV.*

Now I began to feel a bit uneasy about television. You see, I had been in such complete control at first. But then, slowly, all these other programs infiltrated, and they seemed to want to watch so many things! So I decided to limit the time they spent watching.

But what began to bother me was that John often refused to go out and ride his bike in the afternoon because he preferred to stay at home and watch TV. Well, I fought that tooth and nail! I'd explode and have a tantrum and say, "We're not going to watch any *television if it has that sort of a hold on you." I'd make a scene about it and declare that we were going to have some new rules about television! But those never lasted very long. Also, I talked to the school psychologist about the television problem and she told me not to worry, that if John wanted to watch two or three hours of television, it was probably the best thing for him to do. Well, that went against all my instincts, but it was the easiest thing to do, to just let him watch.*

When they were six and seven they discovered the Saturday morning cartoons. They adored them and would watch them all morning. I can't deny that this was great for us, because we'd be able to lie in bed nice and late while they watched their programs.

Then last year they discovered I Dream of Jeannie. *[Groan.] The combined message of* Jeannie *and* The Flintstones *is so sexist that it makes me furious. But the school psychologist assured me that TV is just TV and that kids know it isn't real.*

Last year our pattern was a terrible one. Jeannie *was on from five-thirty to six-thirty, but our dinnertime was six o'clock. I'd tell the kids that if they insisted on watching* Jeannie *they'd have to turn it off when dinner was ready. They'd say, "Yeah, sure, we'll turn it off." Then I'd come and warn them that dinner would be ready in five minutes. Then I'd come in and tell them to turn it off at the next commercial. Of course, they didn't turn it off. I'd always have to come in and turn it off and they'd be very angry about this. They'd say, "I hate you," and come in to dinner shoving and kicking each other, angry and pouty, very, very angry. So dinnertime would be very unpleasant for all of us.*

They'd stay grumpy for the whole meal. It was the worst time of the day, really! And this went on all year. Every once in a while I'd get fed up and make threats like "We won't watch TV anymore if this is what happens when you watch!" I don't think I ever made good on those fancy threats.

At this point in the narrative the mother stopped, and then said in a changed voice,

This is really a terrible saga, isn't it?

Undisciplined, Grumpy Children

What emerges from talks about television in the family is a picture of the parents' steady loss of control as they gradually withdraw from an active role in the children's upbringing. Growing less powerful, parents discover themselves less and less capable of coping with their strong but undisciplined, grumpy children. Common sense suggests that without television parents couldn't have survived under such circumstances; they'd have *had* to socialize their children more persistently, *had* to work a little harder at making them speak more agreeably or behave more considerately.

But television, as the parents' testimonies indicate, abolishes the need to establish those sorts of disciplines. There is no longer the impetus to ensure the sort of behavior that would allow a mother to cook dinner or talk on the telephone or assert herself as a parent in any way without being eaten alive, in a manner of speaking, by her children.

To be sure, the poor socialization of children today is not entirely due to television's presence in the home. Since television arrived as a mass medium the family has undergone other changes that have affected children's outcome. Fewer stay-at-home mothers, higher divorce rates, and changing, less protective attitudes toward children have all have played a role. But in its widespread use during the early-childhood years, precisely when behavior patterns are established, television has undoubtedly had the deepest influence—not through the programs children watch, but indirectly, through the hours of steady, day-after-day, year-after-year socialization that television viewing has displaced.

By allowing parents to bring up undisciplined children, television may even have contributed to the exodus of mothers from the home. Though many mothers go to work out of economic necessity, and many others because of new career opportunities, there are more than a few who choose to work at any available job, though they don't need the money for family survival. It may be that the prospect of spending many hours with their difficult children makes staying at home seem less appealing to mothers than the dreariest office job.

Parental flight, in turn, may exacerbate a family's television problems. For parents know that a full-time nanny or baby-sitter is an inadequate substitute for a loving parent, and this makes them feel guilty. Their guilt is compounded by anxiety about the treatment the child might be receiving in their absence. The parental burden of guilt and anxiety is considerably relieved by the knowledge that while they are gone, the child can spend his time sitting peacefully in front of the television set instead of driving the care-giver up the wall. The parents can leave with an easy mind.

Parents often declare that baby-sitters insist on using television and that their children's overuse of television is a result of the baby-sitter's reliance on television to make her life easier. There is some truth to this. But parents rarely admit that their own peace of mind depends upon the knowledge that their children are temporarily socialized and civilized, in their absence, by the television set. A mother who normally limits her children's viewing time to an hour a day says:

> When I have a baby-sitter and I realize that the sitter has to control them, then I let them watch the TV whenever they want. One time I came home and realized that the kids had been watching TV from about two to eight. But I don't know if the sitter would have managed without TV.

Television's possible role in encouraging mothers to join the workforce takes on additional significance in light of new findings about the effects of child care on children's behavior. The largest long-term study of child care in the United States, conducted under the aegis of the National Institute of Child Health and Human Development, recently reported a stunning finding: children who spend more than 30 hours a week in child care—whether in a day-care center, or with a relative or nanny—are three times as likely to have behavior problems in kindergarten as those who are cared for primarily by their mothers. Those in child care are more aggressive, more demanding, less compliant.

Of course the study did not prove that the increase in aggression was caused by being cared for away from home. Other factors that differentiate kids in child care from kids at home might be the cause. For example here is one possibility relevant to the subject of this book: perhaps children in child care watch more television than children tended by their mothers. Then the increased aggressiveness could be attributed to their viewing, not to the fact that they are in child care. It would make sense. After all, there is good evidence (see the Stanford study on page 50) that children who cut down on TV become *less* aggressive.

How many preschool children today are cared for primarily by a parent? Roughly one fourth of the total, according to the study. Of the rest, nearly 30 percent are in day-care centers, 15 percent are with family child-care providers, and 5 percent are with in-home caregivers, that is, nannies or baby-sitters. Another 25 percent are cared for by relatives. So far there are no statistics about how much television kids in child care watch compared to children cared for by parents or nannies.

Ten Reasons Why Parents Can't Control TV

1. Fear of Saying No

The particular difficulty latter-day parents have in saying "no" to their children is often implicated in a family's problems with television control. A child psychiatrist considers the possible sources of parents' fearful permissiveness:

I don't tell people what they should or shouldn't do. But I find among so many parents, not only of patients but of children I meet in schools, a lot of conflict about being able to raise their

*children according to their own lights. . . . They seem to be
fearful of getting angry at their own children, fearful of telling
them to turn the television set off. These parents feel that a child
has to do what he likes. But in fact they are fearful of having a
direct and personal relationship with their children.*

*I work with parents to help them understand their fears
and to understand their children's needs. And when they begin
to understand, they stop having doubts about turning a
television set off. When parents get to feel a connection of some
kind with their children, they invariably begin to turn the
television set off. Sometimes they even get rid of it.*

2. The Parents' Own Viewing Habits

Frequently the parents' own viewing habits nullify their attempts
to reduce their children's dependence on television. Parents who
themselves have come to depend on television for amusement, relaxation, or escape find it hard to set limits on their children's viewing.
It makes them feel hypocritical to set up a "do as I say, not as I do"
policy in their household, and their canny children will be quick to
take advantage of their parents' insecurity.

A mother describes this dilemma:

*I try to limit the kids' TV watching, but Alfred [her husband]
likes to watch quite a bit. Limiting the kids means he'd have to
limit himself, and he doesn't really want to do that.*

A New York mother relates:

*When the kids were younger, up until the youngest was about
eight, I was really terribly worried about their television
watching. There were times when I was tempted to just throw
the set out. But I didn't because I myself like to watch the
movies and Carol Burnett. . . .*

Another mother notes:

*I'd probably miss it more than the kids. And feeling like that
makes it very hard for me to say, "No, you can't watch TV. It's
not good for you." Just as I can't say with any real conviction,
"Peter, it's bad to suck your thumb," when I smoke!*

It's undoubtedly easier to control children's television viewing if
the parents don't spend much time watching television themselves
while the children are awake. Still, there's no reason why parents who
set strict rules about their children's television time should have to be
furtive about the programs they want to watch themselves. Their
own lives, after all, are different in many ways: they work, they have
adult responsibilities, and they engage in a number of adult activities
they would not dream of including their children in. Television viewing may be seen as one of those adult activities.

3. Will my child be a social outcast?

Great numbers of parents who really believe television is having
a bad effect on their kids and family life nevertheless don't get rid of
their sets or set firm limits because they're afraid that watching less
TV or none at all will turn their kids into social outcasts. This pervasive anxiety is one of the strongest deterrents to effective television
control in American families.

A mother of two school-age children explains:

*That's all kids talk about, this TV program and that one. If I
got rid of the set—and believe me I'd love to do it—my kids
would really be out of it. How would they make friends?*

Even parents of very young children are anxious that if they limit
television they are blighting their children's social future. A mother
of a two-year-old boy says:

*I really believe small children are better off watching no TV at
all, but I'm worried about what will happen when Roger starts*

nursery school next year and all the other kids talk about
Sesame Street. *I'm thinking I'd better let him start watching.*

Parents also worry that if television is not available freely in their homes, other children won't want to come over and play with their kids. Or worse, that their children will prefer to spend their free time away from home, watching TV with kids who have no limits on their watching.

There's little evidence that the absence of television in the home or strict limits on its use creates social difficulties for children; indeed, there's some reason to believe that it works in quite an opposite way.

The mother of a third-grader whose television viewing is restricted to weekends reports:

> *At first when kids came over to play with Katie after school, they'd ask, "Where's the TV?" But when I simply said there's no TV on schooldays in our house and suggested that they might bake cookies or steered them to the dress-up box, or brought out some games, they seemed perfectly happy to do something else. This house is always full of kids and I honestly think they like to come over here* because *they have more fun than watching TV.*

A bright sixth-grader whose family has chosen to live without TV answered a question about the effects of no TV on his social life in this way:

> *Well, my friends do talk a lot about TV programs. You know, "Did you see so-and-so last night?" and I just say, "No, I missed it," or something like that. I don't make a bid deal about not having TV at home, and nobody seems to care anyhow. The funny part is that I've seen most of the shows everybody talks about at least once, say at my grandparents' house or at friends', and so I know the names of the characters. And those programs are pretty much the same most of the time, so I can keep up with those conversations perfectly well.*

A father of two pre-teenagers expressed an attitude that might help allay other parents' anxieties about television control and its effect on children's social life:

> I used to say to my kids, "Your friends are going to like you because of the way you behave—whether you're generous or friendly or fun to be with, and not because you've watched the same TV shows they watch. It's who you are that matters." My sons seem to have as many friends as any other kids, in spite of the fact that their TV viewing is limited to two hours a week.

4. Ambivalence

Parents' difficulties are compounded by a lack of certainty about what role they wish television to play in their family life, and a basic ambivalence about television. A mother of two small children says:

> When they say they want to watch TV and it's a nice sunny day, I get really mad at them. I'll tell them that I'll go out to the park and play soccer with them and they'll say no, they'd rather watch a TV program. Well, it's terribly galling when that happens, but what I do all depends on my mood, because I'm very ambivalent about it. So sometimes I'll tell them, "I think you're very stupid to stay indoors on a beautiful day, but that's your own decision," and then other times I'll just slam it off and scream and march everybody out of the house.

Another mother describes similar feelings:

> I've always been in conflict with myself about television. The kids keep begging to watch, "Oh, Mom, please!" even when there's something better to do, and I want to say, "Absolutely not! I'm throwing it out the window!" But I don't really want it to become a great big thing that we fight over all the time. So I've been very inconsistent about it. . . . Some days I feel that I

*have to fight, and other days . . . I just don't. Which I guess is
not very good for them, but I'm so conflicted about it.*

5. Lack of Conviction

A well-known child psychiatrist and author suggests that parents
are deceiving themselves when they say they cannot control television, that it is "too much of a hassle" or "not worth the agony." She
believes that for a number of reasons they don't really *want* to control
their children's viewing.

When parents tell me that they can't *make a child do this or
that, it's very easy to demonstrate that they haven't tried. I'll ask
them, "Do you allow your three-year-old to walk around with a
sharp knife? Do you allow her to cross the street by herself?"
They'll immediately describe how they keep their child from
running into the street or playing with sharp objects. So I say
that obviously the child gets the message when they feel firmly
about something. What's the difference, I ask them, about this
particular thing that they say they can't control? They'll answer,
"Well, it's not so important," or "It's only a matter of my
convenience." Obviously they haven't given the child the message
that they mean it, because within themselves they* don't really
feel it firmly. *If parents want to control their children's
television watching, they have to make it clear that it's as
important as not playing with sharp knives or running into a
busy street.*

6. Lack of Confidence

The diminishing authority of the family in general has made
parents less likely to rely on common sense and their private assessment of what is right or wrong when confronted with a problem
such as how to limit their children's television viewing. Instead, they

tend to wait for the government or the school or a psychiatrist to tell them what to do.

A mother of three children who is anxious about the number of hours her children spend watching television and yet who cannot seem to set limits, casts some light upon the crisis of confidence that afflicts American parents today:

> *What's wrong with me is that I don't know what's right and what's wrong and neither do my children. Now my mother, to this day, believes in right and wrong, and she believes she knows what's right and what's wrong. But I absolutely don't. Outside of a very few moral issues, I don't know what's right or wrong about a lot of things. And the TV brings that to a head.*

7. Parental Lack of Agreement

Some families' control problems are compounded by a lack of agreement between the parents themselves about the need to control television.

A father of a five-year-old describes such a situation:

> *We had a lot of trouble saying no about TV because Peter would throw a real fit, an absolute tantrum, and that scared us, or at least me. I didn't really think television was so bad; I didn't think it was worth the struggle, since he wanted to watch so badly. But now the television stays off even if he throws a fit. An hour a day, that's the rule, and we stick to it. But it took us several years to establish it—[laughs] several years for my wife and me to agree enough to establish it. Once it was established, Peter caught on quickly. But when my wife and I were not completely in agreement about television, he saw right away that this was a great opportunity to bug us, to drive a wedge between us. He saw how easily he could get us going with the whole television thing.*

A mother notes:

I'm trying to kick the habit for my children but it's too hard. They want to see this and they want to see that and then there's all the specials they have to see because their friends are going to be watching. I try to be firm, but their father is not as disgusted with the whole children's television scene as I am, and so he tells them yes.

8. A Misguided Pursuit of Democracy

Some parents believe that it is somehow undemocratic to impose strict rules about television use. They fear that by laying down the law about television—or indeed, about anything else—they will cause their children to grow up overly rebellious or overly docile. As a result they find that their natural authority as parents and adults is undermined, and their ability to control television at home is weakened.

A mother admits:

I know it sounds weak, but I just hate to be the one to be constantly disappointing people, regulating them, stopping them from doing something they enjoy. I don't like to be the heavy in the family. I'd rather we were all on an equal footing. That's why I have so much trouble getting the kids to watch less television, even though I see it's not good for them to watch so much.

A British mother says:

The peculiar thing about American mothers is that they feel uncomfortable about many of the things their children do, but they won't do anything about it. They'll let them do anything. They're afraid of an authoritarian setup; that would be un-American. They don't like their children watching television

for so many hours, so they set up a family conference and discuss
setting up rules and so on. But the children end up watching
just as much television.

9. Devaluation of Parents' Rights

Related to parents' belief that democratic principles must prevail
in child-rearing, even with very young children, is a devaluation of
parents' rights that sometimes accompanies the acceptance of a
child-centered philosophy of raising children. A harried young
mother whose consideration of her children's wants and needs have
dimmed her awareness of her own rights reports:

> *When my kids are being awful and rude while I'm talking on*
> *the phone, instead of disciplining them there's a part of me that*
> *says, "Yes, I'm on the phone too long."*

She has lost her perspective and sees life exclusively from her
children's point of view. Such a mother will not turn off the television set when the child wishes to watch, even though she has a strong
feeling that too much watching may have detrimental effects, because the child's desires [to watch] take precedence over her own [to
turn off the set] in most daily confrontations.

A mother of two children aged eight and four reveals a similar
inability to assert her feelings and take action about television:

> *I wish I had the strength not to let my kids watch. I get home at*
> *five-thirty and make dinner—my husband comes home at six*
> *o'clock. So from five-thirty until seven or seven-thirty, the kids*
> *watch television. And there's the most horrible garbage on at*
> *those hours. Things I can't stand, like* The Flintstones.
>
> *"I just don't have the strength to make them turn it off.*
> *And these children have an almost unlimited supply of toys. But*
> *with the TV, they never touch a lot of them. Still, when I do*
> *turn the TV off, they go in and play with their toys.*

10. Sleep Deprivation

The last reason parents get hooked on using TV as a baby-sitter may be the most compelling, and the one hardest to argue against. For parents desperately in need of sleep, families with a new baby, for example, or parents who must work extra hours in the evening, it is irresistible not to accept the few extra hours of sleep television offers, especially on weekends.

A mother of three boys says:

> *I practically beg them to turn on the television set on Saturday mornings so they'll be quiet and I can sleep. When they play with each other they're just too noisy. They always play Emergency and imitate the siren noises*—Weeeeoweeeowee! *When they play with each other every toy is out, every hat is on, every truck is moving*—*I suppose that's fine, but I can't stand it! I need my sleep. The six-year-old is usually up at the crack of dawn, and if it weren't for TV, he'd be playing with all the toys, too. But now he turns on the set and watches quietly until nine, when we get up.*

Of course parents in the pre-television era had some tricks up their sleeve that bought them that extra sleep—setting out special snacks in the kitchen the night before, or books or games or toys, for example, to keep the kids amused on those Saturday mornings. Bribery sometimes works—if you kids let us sleep until nine, we'll go to the zoo in the afternoon. None of these strategies are completely admirable (or necessarily as effective as TV). Even so, for a family dominated by television, in the long run it may be worth losing a bit of sleep to gain control of that powerful medium.

Ubiquity

Television control is not merely a matter of keeping an eye on the television sets at home. Nowadays the ever-increasing proliferation of video screens in public areas creates problems for those families striving to diminish the presence of electronic images in their lives.

There are television monitors at every large airport. Though parents may choose to sit in a "quiet zone" away from the TV sound, the kids gravitate to the TV monitors like bees to nectar. If Mom and Dad thought this vacation was going to be a nice break from a television-dominated home life, they are off to a bad start.

On the plane there are movies, usually augmented by another hour or so of segments from TV sit-coms. Even if the parents choose not to purchase the earphones for the soundtrack, the kids' attention often wanders to the soundless screen. Parents who had carefully planned for the plane trip with games to play and books to read find the movie screen will be an ever-present distraction for much of the family's time aloft.

Long-distance buses show movies and TV, and local buses may soon follow suit. For example, in a pilot program in Orlando, Florida, large television screens inside municipal buses entertain riders with news stories, nature and lifestyle features, and—surprise—numerous advertisements. Not all passengers are delighted, needless to say. "It's bad enough that you have to be riding in a crowded bus in the first place, but this is adding insult to injury," an Orlando resident grumbled.

There are televisions in restaurants, even in restrooms. Many doctors' offices now have televisions in their waiting room, often tuned to special features sponsored by drug companies. And in spite of the American Academy of Pediatrics' strong advisory against any TV viewing at all for toddlers, many pediatricians have VCRs in their waiting rooms that play cartoons to their captive audience, many of them under three.

And what about those huge TV monitors that dominate the sight lines of fans who have chosen to go to an honest-to-goodness live baseball game? At least at home, a viewer can zap the commercials with a remote control. In most if not all stadiums, the gigantic electronic screens at the outfield wall detract attention from the little human figures in old-fashioned uniforms running around the field. Meanwhile, thanks to the wandering news cameras zooming in on some segment of the audience, you can wildly wave and grimace at your friends and family who are watching the game on their home TVs. The baseball game has become a sort of TV show and you can be one of its stars. For a child attending a game, this can become as important as the game itself.

There are televisions in restaurants like the Paradiso Italian Restaurant in Franconia, Virginia, recently mentioned with admiration by a parenting magazine. There kids can eat with their fingers and slurp their sodas as they watch a movie on a big-screen TV. Meanwhile, their parents enjoy a peaceful meal in an adjacent room. But who's going to teach the kids how to behave in a restaurant? The civilizing process has run into a roadblock.

There are television sets in auto repair shops to keep you occupied while you wait for an oil change. Did you bring a book with you? Try reading it with the TV blaring. Television sets blare in school buses. Does anybody sing songs on the way home? There are television sets in public lobbies, in shoe stores, in gyms and health clubs (at every Stairmaster), in supermarkets. Everywhere.

It's not as if the unwanted TV images in an airplane or doctor's office or baseball stadium are going to blight a child's life or destroy a family's chances for togetherness. It may seem overly earnest of parents to object strongly to this incursion into their autonomy. Yet in the end, the ubiquitous presence of TV in public places can make a family's chosen style of life just that much more difficult to adhere to.

A Chilling Episode: The "Tired-Child Syndrome"

The extraordinary power of the television medium and the extent of parents' dependence on it is exemplified by the episode of the

"Tired-Child Syndrome," as reported in *The New York Times* a number of years ago.

Pediatricians at two air force hospitals, puzzled by the incidence of a syndrome of anxiety symptoms—chronic fatigue, loss of appetite, headache, and vomiting—in a group of 30 children whose parents had brought them in for diagnosis, discovered that the children were spending three to six hours watching television daily, and six to ten hours on weekends. Suspecting that excessive television viewing might have something to do with the children's condition, the doctors instructed the parents to cut out TV entirely.

The effects were dramatic for the 12 children whose parents followed the instructions fully: the symptoms vanished within two to three weeks. The parents of the other 18 children, however, were unable to comply and allowed up to two hours of viewing a day. Even so, this represented a significant reduction in their daily viewing, and these children were free of symptoms in three to six weeks.

A later follow-up revealed a dismaying situation: of the twenty-six children whose cases were followed for several months, only nine remained free of symptoms. These nine were still restricted in their viewing. Of the rest, restrictions had been lifted entirely for thirteen children, eleven of whom were again suffering severe symptoms. Four others were allowed limited viewing and had limited disorders.

What this episode reveals about parents' difficulties with television control is telling: more than two-thirds of the parents of the children involved were unable to restrict their children's viewing successfully even though they had been ordered to do so by their pediatrician and even though their children's symptoms returned as soon as they relented.

A further indication of these parents' dependence on television is seen in a chilling fact: chlorpromazine, a strong sedative often used as an antipsychotic medication, had been prescribed for some of the children to aid them during the early days of treatment. A number of the parents who had trouble restricting their children's television viewing asked for *further* sedation of their children, preferring that alternative to the difficulties of life without television.

A Longing for Passivity

Why is television so supremely important in children's lives? A part of the answer may lie in the fundamental human struggle between passivity and activity, a struggle that is particularly strong during early childhood when the human being makes the transition from psychological dependence and passivity to self-propelled activity and independence.

In their television experiences children return to that comfortable, atavistic passivity that was once their right and that they must renounce if they are to become functioning members of society. It is only while they watch television that they are freed of the risks of real life. Their progress in the direction of activity, of giving, of "doing," is impeded by their television involvement.

No wonder, then, that parents find it so hard to stick to their guns when they decide to limit their children's television viewing. In their children's wails and lamentations, in their pleas and entreaties, in the endless bargains they try to strike ("Just let me watch this extra program today and then I won't watch *any* TV tomorrow"), parents hear the true note of desperation. Without an unwavering conviction that the particular pleasures provided by the television are not in the same life-enhancing category as the basic gratifications of life, that television viewing does not foster growth but by displacing more valuable activities tends to inhibit it, parents quite simply do not have the heart to turn the television set off.

A mother who decided to eliminate television entirely two years ago thinks back to her former struggles with television control:

I guess like most mothers I just hated to spoil their pleasure, even though I felt they were getting pleasure out of something that was not strictly worthwhile. It just seemed hard and mean to deprive them of their programs when they wanted to watch so much. Now that we don't have a set, it seems different. Somehow I don't feel that they're being deprived. On the contrary, I get a feeling that the TV was actually depriving them of doing a lot of good things they do now. . . .

17

Gaining Control

Real Conviction

A mother of a five- and a six-year-old gives evidence that _real conviction_ is a basic requirement for successful television control:

> One day I got fed up with the children watching TV in the morning before school. Our morning scene was pathetic. The kids would be fixed in front of the television set and want to eat their breakfast there, hardly able to move their arms or legs to get their clothes on. They looked like little mummies.
>
> Well, I'd been complaining about morning television for a long time, turning it off sporadically, yelling at them to get dressed, fussing about it—but not very consistently. Nothing really worked. I just thought it was hopeless to control their television watching at all, especially since I do use the set in the evenings to give me a rest from them. Doesn't everyone, though?
>
> Well, this time I absolutely decided we couldn't live like this and morning television watching had to stop. And as usual when I deliver an ultimatum with real conviction, it worked! That's the most exciting thing I've learned as a mother. If I say, "I really think you'd better not," then it never works. Or if I haven't made up my mind that this is absolutely the only way to

*deal with something, then it's reflected in the static I get back
from the kids.*

   *But it only took a couple of days and the morning TV
problem was eliminated. Just gone. The kids knew I meant it.
And I guess I knew I meant it, too. Maybe that was even more
important.*

Firm Rules

There's evidence that families with rules about TV viewing are
better off than families without rules. In a recent study of children's
media use, the researchers assessed the personal contentedness and
social adjustment of a large group of children, then related the results
to their media use. It turned out that children from families with
rules about TV viewing scored higher (that is, were happier and better adjusted) than children in families without rules. Needless to say,
having rules meant there was less TV consumption, so one can also
say that watching less TV leads to higher scores on the "Contentedness
Index."

   Though the study only demonstrated a correlation between social adjustment and family rules, not a causal relationship, nevertheless the results support the idea that rules about TV are important.
The same study also noted that children in families with rules were
more likely to spend more time reading.

   Though setting up and then maintaining new family rules about
television is more easily said than done, there is one circumstance
that increases a family's chances for success: rules are easier to establish after a period of time spent without TV, either after a vacation or
trip, or after a deliberate TV Turnoff week (see chapter 18). Regular
viewing patterns are shaken up somewhat by a hiatus from television,
and children are almost certainly less resistant to change at such a
moment. If the time without television, however brief, has introduced
new family activities or pleasures, it will help to justify the new rules

to children who might not understand why this amusing pastime needs to be curtailed.

But what rules to set? Here are five possibilities, to adopt singly or in various combinations:

1. No TV on School Days

That's it. No counting hours, no checking listings for one or two permissible programs. No bargaining and haggling: "If I watch two hours today I won't watch anything tomorrow," and so on. Eliminating television on school days effectively eliminates television as a competitor for other, more fulfilling activities (lively family meals, conversations, games, reading aloud and, of course, studying and doing homework) during a good chunk of the week. Then on weekends there is no restriction on TV viewing. It's the easiest of all the rules to live with.

But won't the kids simply spend their entire weekend glued to the tube? Somehow it doesn't seem to work that way. Most parents who have set up such a rule observe that after five days without television, the kids seem to forget about viewing for much of the weekend as well. Since so much of television viewing is done by habit, a pattern is set during the no-TV period that often (although not always) lasts into the TV-permitted period.

There are no statistics available to show how many families cut off television on school days, but it is interesting to note that a former vice president in charge of children's programming at CBS told an interviewer that as his own children were growing up he did not permit them to view programs during the week . . . they were compelled to do something more intellectually alive.

2. No TV at dinnertime or bedtime

This is the rule that virtually every expert agrees about. Whatever rules a family decides to establish, this one should be included. With the exception of a brief, annual vacation, dinnertime is often the only regular time a family can spend together. Whatever cohesiveness and family spirit is to exist, the evening meal is where it is consolidated.

As for bedtime, there is nothing that can replace the bedtime story as a uniquely valuable experience in every child's life. Yet in great numbers of American homes it is eclipsed by television or a bedtime video. Letting a child choose between a story or video at bedtime never works: the deck is stacked—television's pull is too strong. This does not mean that it's preferable to a story, as most parents instinctively understand. As Jim Trelease states in his valuable guide, *The Read-Aloud Handbook:*

> Don't try to compete with television. If you say "Which do
> you want, a story or TV?" they will usually choose the latter.
> That is like saying to a nine-year-old "Which do you want,
> vegetables or a donut?" Since *you* are the adult, *you* choose.
> "The television goes off at eight-thirty in this house. If you
> want a story before bed, that's fine. If not, that's fine too. But
> no television after eight-thirty." But don't let books appear
> to be responsible for depriving children of viewing time.

3. A One-Hour-a-day Time Limit

Some families set a strict daily time limit of no more than one hour of viewing a day. This may work to "detelevisionize" family life considerably, although not as effectively as a real hiatus from television. The competition factor television poses to other activities continues to operate, for children can spend two or more hours simply marking time until their permitted program comes on the air.

Parents sometimes are persuaded by their children to set a time limit of *more* than an hour a day. Indeed, some families feel that they have asserted the proper parental firmness in restricting their children to as many as three hours a day. Perhaps compared to seven hours of television viewing daily, a diet of three hours is an improvement for a child; nevertheless such a liberal limit does not make enough of a difference in a family's lifestyle—television, television talk, television plans continue to dominate. A mother who has limited her children's daily viewing to two hours describes her continuing dissatisfaction with television's effects on her family life:

> *What concerns me so much is not how to control television, because we've set up some rules and the kids have to observe them. But what I can't stop them from doing is talking about television. I wish I could play you back an average conversation that goes on at our dinner table. The kids talk about nothing but what went on in this program and that program. Who did what to whom, who said what, and then what happened. Sometimes my husband and I will tell them to stop, that we don't want to hear any more about television programs. "What happened in school today?" we'll ask. So there's a brief interlude and they'll quickly tell us something about school and then right back to the TV, which actor played what part, and on and on and on.*

4. No Solitary TV watching

Make TV viewing a special event the whole family does together. No one may watch TV by himself or herself. This is a great rule if it doesn't lead to constant contention about who gets to pick what everyone will watch.

5. Fewer or No "Regular" Programs

A rule limiting or eliminating the watching of regular weekly series programs will usually reduce the quantity of TV watching considerably. (Many kids have numerous series programs they watch regularly.) It also helps discourage families from planning their lives around the TV schedule.

Control Devices and the V-Chip

Starting in the 1980s enterprising manufacturers, recognizing a potential market, came up with a variety of gadgets to limit kids' access to television. Sometimes called lock-boxes, these could be programmed to shut a TV down after playing a limited number of programs. They could also be programmed to block out certain channels selectively (such as cable channels that air explicit sexual material), and even prevent kids from using the set to play video games.

There may be something about the lock-box that is inimical to the American democratic spirit. Some parents feel that by using control devices, they are establishing an atmosphere of mistrust with their children, showing them, all too clearly, that they don't believe anyone will follow family rules about television unless the set is locked up. Thus a mother explains that while they've had a lock-box for almost a year, they are now planning to return it. "I don't worry about their judgment," she says of her children. "The lock-box is there but we don't even use it. The key just sits in the set."

The lock-box may simply be too obvious a sign of weakness for most parents to resort to it. As a television manufacturer once declared: "It's rather a sad commentary on our society if parents have to rely on electronic devices to control network programming." Perhaps for these reasons during the eighties and nineties few parents chose the lock-box as an easy method of TV control.

In the mid-1990s the V-Chip—V for Violence—was introduced. A small electronic device, the V-Chip can be coordinated with an electronically coded rating system (not unlike the rating system used for movies) to filter programs deemed unsuitable for children. If a program contains violent or sexually explicit material or bad language, parents can program their V-Chip to block that program from their TV set. The 1996 Telecommunications Act required that by the year 2000, all new television sets with screens over 13 inches must include a V-Chip, and it mandated that television networks devise an appropriate rating system for parents to use with their V-Chip.

Civil libertarians objected, saying the V-Chip law violates the first Amendment and leads to censorship, at least indirectly. The television industry, not surprisingly, also opposed the V-Chip, fearing it would affect their freedom to create programs. As the producer of the popular program *Friends* explained, advertisers would be less likely to support her program, or other strong programs like *Law & Order*, out of fear that too many consumers might block the program.

She may have worried prematurely. Perhaps for the same reasons that parents didn't go for lock-boxes, or because of the specific complexities of the V-Chip and the rating system associated with it, it never really seemed to catch on. Five years after the law was passed mandating a V-Chip in every new TV set, a survey of a nationally representative sample of parents by the Henry J. Kaiser Family Foundation revealed that 50 percent of families with the mandatory antiviolence chip installed in their sets didn't even know they had it. Of those who did, only one-third said they ever used it. All in all, the survey reported, while parents indicated that they were highly concerned about sex and violence on television, only seven percent of all families around the nation were using the V-Chip.

Nevertheless the V-Chip often seems a better alternative than no control whatsoever. Most family-centered organizations, including the American Academy of Pediatrics, recommend its use to parents. In view of the fact that television is out of control in the great majority of American homes, that the amount of time children spend before a screen—be it TV, video, video game or computer—is increasing every year, that almost half of all American families have no rules at all about children's television viewing, that kids under seven watch TV without adult supervision 81 percent of the time, even though the V-Chip may encourage parents to continue focusing on content alone, who can blame anyone for grasping at straws . . . or chips?

Natural Control

For parents who lack the reserves of strength necessary to set rules and stick to them in spite of wheedling, whining, pleading, or angry cries of "I hate you!" there are certain "natural" methods of television control that do not require discipline or any extensive change in child-rearing style. These have to do with physical factors concerning the sound and placement of the set, and the natural social setup of daily family life. Such factors often allow parents who cannot say "no" in an old-fashioned and seemingly undemocratic way to live in relative peace with their television sets.

The Set Itself

The set itself, its condition and location in the house, often serves as a natural limit to a family's television viewing.

An eight-year-old boy who watches little television says:

I don't like watching television much, because we have a terrible television set. It keeps messing up and either the sound is bad or the picture or both. Worst of all we sometimes get a double picture. Grandma's set is also pretty bad.

In some families the decision to live with a poor television set is made quite deliberately.

An English teacher and father of two young children reports:

We inherited an old set. The reception was terrible. My wife thought that perhaps we ought to have it fixed, or buy a better set, but I persuaded her to continue with the old set. We could still see a program if we wanted to, but it wasn't easily accessible. Most of all it made the whole experience less enticing

for us, and we needed that. We all tended to do a lot of
watching when we had a good set.

Location of Set

In deciding *where* to locate the television set, many families consider the problem of control and the effects of television on family unity:

Our set is in the living room because we feel it's less likely to
separate the family there. It also helps cut down on the kids'
viewing because when we have company the kids can't watch.
That's all there is to it, and they accept that better than if we
tried to make rules about when they can watch and when
they can't.

Some families go even further in their efforts to find a way to limit their children's television viewing:

We used to have our television upstairs in the living room, but
it was just too accessible and tempting there. We were having
all sorts of problems with it and felt that the kids—all of us,
really—were just watching too much. We didn't want to get
rid of the set altogether, so we put it down in the basement.
It's pretty dilapidated and unpleasant down there, not the
sort of place you want to lie around all evening watching
television.

Another family made a similar decision:

We keep our set in the basement to have it out of the way. It's
there because we don't like to talk over the TV, as happens at
our friends' houses, or to have other people distracted by it and
lose the thread of the conversation. Also, in the basement there's
less of a temptation to just flick it on when you enter the house.
You have to make a special trip down there to watch something.

Operating on the "out of sight, out of mind" principle, some families go so far as to put their television in a closet after each use. The effort required each time the family wants to watch ensures a certain amount of selectivity. It also effectively prevents the children from overindulging in television when the parents are out, even though baby-sitters sometimes go to the trouble of bringing the set out of the closet in order to watch their own programs.

A slightly less radical but nevertheless effective method is used by this New York family:

> *One of the things that helps us not watch so much television is that we have a small black-and-white set and it's not stationary. It stands in a corner and it has to be especially put out on a table in order to watch. That makes watching a little inconvenient. The set's not right there, ready and waiting. In some homes I've noticed that the television set is so central that you can practically not do anything else but watch when it's on. But since ours is so small and you have to go to all the trouble of setting it up, we tend to use it only for special occasions.*

How Many Sets?

The number of sets a family possesses makes a considerable difference in how well parents can control their children's viewing. In a study of the factors affecting parental television control, researchers observed that the number of television sets in a home was "the crucial family variable" predicting whether parents were successful in controlling television. The more sets, the less control parents achieved, the researchers discovered.

The number of sets proved a more important indicator of a family control problem than the parents' educational level, income, or their own television habits, it turned out. The authors of the study conclude: "For parents who wish to exhibit more control over the

TV habits of their offspring, the easiest method would appear to be neglecting to fix the TV set the next time one breaks down."

A recent study of children's media use provides clear evidence that American parents have not taken this advice. Of the 99 percent of American families who had television at home in 1999, 88 percent of them owned two sets and 60 percent had three or more. Add to that the ever-increasing number who also own a VCR, a video game player and a computer, and the difficulties of controlling all those screens becomes all too obvious.

• Less Choice

Canceling the family's subscription to cable is an effective form of natural control. In most communities, eliminating the cable stations leaves only three or four channels of available television—in some large cities, thanks to the interference of high buildings, only one channel with clear reception might remain. A family in Tallahassee, Florida, found they were down to the three network channels and PBS when they dropped their cable hook-up. "We still have a VCR and the kids get to watch their programs on PBS, so we don't starve," said the Florida father. "But we're not glued to it the way we used to be."

Not in the Children's Room

A reverse example of natural control is the natural *decontrol* that occurs when a television set is located in a child's own room. The principal of an elementary school states:

> Sometimes parents mention in the course of a conference that
> the kids have a set in their own room. I'll say, "For heaven's
> sake, why do you have to give your child his own television set?
> That decontrols the situation completely." And their answer
> always is "Well, we don't want to have to hear their programs in

the living room." But when they don't hear the programs, they completely stop trying to cut down on television.

Keeping the television out of kids' bedrooms is an eminently sensible form of natural control. A 1999 Policy Statement by the American Academy of Pediatrics, directed to an audience of pediatricians, recommended that they encourage the creation of an "electronic media-free" environment in children's rooms. In February 2001, the Academy's new Policy Statement rephrased "media-free environment" to make sure its meaning was crystal clear. Pediatricians were told to tell parents: "Remove television sets from children's bedrooms."

According to a major survey of children's media use in America, children with their own TVs watch more television than those who share a family set. Since almost half of all children's reading takes place in their bedrooms, a TV there will inevitably cut down on reading. No TV in children's rooms, educators agree, is the single, most important rule parents should establish in order to encourage academic success.

Yet this basic rule is widely observed in the breech. The same survey of media use shows that 53 percent of all children aged two to eighteen have a television set in their rooms. Though older children are more likely to have their own TV sets than younger ones, nevertheless, a substantial percentage of the youngest viewers—at least one-quarter of all children between the ages of two and four and one-third of the two- to seven-year-old population—have a set in their bedrooms.

A Rich Social Life

A rich social life may also serve as a natural limit to children's television viewing. A family with two children eight and ten years of age, who live in an ample apartment in New York, find that the television set is infrequently used in spite of a permissive attitude toward it. The parents feel this is because there are always a number of extra children in the house, temporarily or semipermanently. The mother of that family reports:

> *I'm terrible about organizing the children's social lives, but there's always an enormous amount of activity going on. We usually have one or two older kids living with us, daughters of friends who live out of town. Also we live on the way to Lucy's school and she almost always brings girls home with her, sometimes ten at a time! Jeremy usually brings home a couple of kids since his school is nearby, too. But he has a friend who lives upstairs, an only child, and that child watches television a great deal. Maybe there's a connection.*

A psychiatrist agrees that the television problem depends on a family's social circumstances:

> *The television problem is related to small families. Amusing small kids would be perfectly easy if you had four or five kids of various ages around at all times to amuse each other. The whole idea of a mother entertaining a small child is kind of crazy, anyway. It never happened prior to 1900.*

A child therapist discusses her own need for an extended family and relates such a need to the television problem:

> *When you have children, then that small nuclear family life ought to come to an end. It's painful to end it. It's hard to have much less privacy. But I don't feel I can give my child all the attention that he deserves to have, that's good for him to have, that he needs if he is to flourish. I need my husband's interest and activity, and I also need my sisters and my mother and so on. It provides relief for me, a change of scene, it eliminates that stuck feeling, it's great for the baby. Maybe this is the great underlying reason for television's powerful hold on parents—it's sitting in for the extended family. There aren't enough resources within a single family to give your children. Television fills a vacuum.*

In the past, the economic functioning of the home necessitated an organization in which a number of people were available to share in child care. In today's small family, the lonely, isolated parent turns to the television set for the sort of service once provided by ever-present family members, neighbors, and friends.

Decontrol as a Means of Control

A word is needed about a prevalent myth: if children were allowed to watch unlimited amounts of television, encouraged, even, to "pig out" on the tube, they would lose interest in the medium and become self-regulating. Everybody seems to have a neighbor or friend whose children have "gone off television" after a period of "overdose," as the phraseology of the myth often puts it, suggestive of the intuitive connection people make between television and drugs. Undoubtedly this method of control seems attractive to parents engaged in a daily struggle with their children over television viewing, a struggle, moreover, that is often quite alien to their generally easygoing child-rearing philosophy.

There is some truth behind the myth. Undoubtedly a natural falling-off of interest in television does occur after a period of unlimited viewing. It's also true that a heightened interest in television may occur as a result of stringent family regulation. The problem with decontrol as a means of achieving ultimate control, however, is one of time.

If it were a matter of days or weeks or even months of unlimited watching that would bring about a loss of interest and a more balanced life, then a family might well consider adopting such a course. The reality, however, is more likely to involve years of constant viewing, not days or months. Somehow it seems too heavy a price to pay.

Sad evidence of the consequences of a parental laissez-faire policy toward television is found in the rueful testimony of so many children who were allowed to spend their childhood years "glued to the tube," without any parental restrictions. Such children may indeed be fed up with television viewing as they approach adulthood, but great numbers of them feel a sense of loss. They express regret about a childhood that was curiously monochromatic, though their television sets may have produced the most glorious living color. Yet this may be a hopeful sign for the future. Many of these former TV addicts now say they want to do things differently with their own children. Some of them give up television altogether.

Help from the Outside

Parents respond with gratitude and relief when help is offered by powerful outside institutions. When the American Academy of Pediatrics stated point blank that children under two should not watch television at all, suggesting that the experience might affect their brain development, many parents, especially those at the onset of their child-rearing journey, began to think about television in a new way. The deeply ingrained belief that some programs are educational, actually *good* for children, became harder to sustain. Consequently it became easier to resist the temptation of turning on *Teletubbies*.

When a well-known nursery school in New York City sent a letter to its entire parent body advising them to limit their children's viewing time to a maximum of one hour a day, the step was greeted with unusual enthusiasm. An article in the *The New York Times* quoted one mother:

> *That letter gave me the final push into curtailing television.*

Another mother described her three-year-old son's campaign to watch *Planet of the Apes* and other popular cartoons instead of his daily diet of *Mister Rogers*:

> *I was under heavy pressure, so when the letter arrived I was relieved to tell him the school didn't want him to watch.*

According to the head of the school, some parents used the actual letter itself to stop their children from watching, saying, "See, here is a letter from the school saying too much TV is bad," even though the children were too young to actually read it.

She observed:

> Parents feel guilty about their use of television. They feel that somehow they oughtn't to be doing this. We hope that by taking a position on this issue the school will give parents that extra little push. We hope they will finally decide to do something about it.

A teacher at the school who was a member of the committee that drafted the anti-television letter does not condemn those parents who needed a letter from school to find the courage to control television. She explains:

> I'm sympathetic to the parents' plight and I've softened incredibly since I've had children of my own. I feel that parents are often doing the best they can but they don't quite know what to do. They're bullied by their kids, afraid to stand up to them, and then they get into patterns that are hard to break. If those parents have the help of someone with authority so they can say, "Look, the school tells you to turn off the television set," that's great. It might be better if they could trust their own instincts and use their own authority. But if the same end is served this way, I can't help but feel that the means are worthwhile.

Videoholics Anonymous

Just as the first step in dealing with alcoholism is to make the addict face the existence of a drinking problem, so the first step in dealing with an inability to control television must be the widespread recognition that such a problem is real and has serious consequences. I once proposed that a new organization on the order of Alcoholics Anonymous was needed to alert the general public to the existence and nature of television addiction and to help families in their struggles to control the medium.

Such an organization, I imagined, would focus on problems of television dependence among adults as well as young viewers. While encouraging parents to deal with television problems, their children's as well as their own, it would serve to encourage the revival of family activities designed to fill the vacuum temporarily created by the absence of television, such long lost pastimes as reading aloud, storytelling, family singing. It would help parents find ways to make the family dinner hour a more enjoyable event, and help them relearn the lost art of conversation. It would encourage all people-centered rather than machine-centered activities.

Its most valuable role, I dreamed, would be to help parents of young children understand the nature of the television experience and the possible adverse effects of too much television viewing on their children's development: on their evolving verbal and social skills, for instance, their creativity, their resourcefulness, their sensitivity, their love of reading, and, ultimately, on their outcome as productive adult members of society.

Although a Videoholics Anonymous has yet to be organized, one national organization active today has achieved most of the same goals: TV-Turnoff Network. Since its creation in 1994 it has become a unique advocate for television control, always from a non-content point of view.

The TV-Turnoff Network held its first national TV Turnoff during the last week of April, 1995, and has continued to organize a similar event every year since. So far, more than 24 million people have participated, at least partially, in the national Turnoff, with 6 million signing on in 2000 alone.

Today TV-Turnoff Network leads an alliance that counts among its supporters medical organizations like the American Academy of Pediatricians, diverse groups like the Girl Scouts of America and the American Hiking Society, educator groups like the National Education Association, parent groups, environmentalists, health professionals (including the Surgeon General of the United States), and others concerned with television's impact on American life. In the year 2000 over seventy groups supported the annual TV-Turnoff week.

PART VII

No Television

"You know, when you come to think of it, all they really lack is a television set."

18

TV Turnoffs

One way to study television's effects on family life would be to compare families who watch TV regularly with similar families who don't watch at all. Since the overwhelming majority of American families fall into the category of television owners, however, there simply aren't enough no-television families for a well-matched comparison.

A simpler and yet scientifically valid experiment involves the before-and-after approach. Take a television-viewing family and eliminate television entirely for a period of time, keeping careful track of the changes in daily life experience without the medium. Such experiments are commonly called TV Turnoffs. Since each family is compared only with itself, the results are far more likely to reveal television's effects than those of a study comparing different families.

In the past, many individual families found themselves involuntarily involved in such before-and-after experiments, either when their one and only TV set broke, or when they moved into areas without TV reception. Today the great majority of families have more than one set, and the geographic pockets without TV reception have been completely eliminated

Many families organize brief TV Turnoffs deliberately, in hope of gaining understanding about television's role in their lives, or of gaining more control over the medium. The next section describes three such before-and-after experiments, the first involuntary, the other two deliberately set up.

Three Family Before-and-After Experiments

1. The Cable Vision Truck Never Came

Having read about my interest in families that gave up television, a mother in Glenwood Springs, Colorado, sent me the following report:

We are a family of five who lived for two and a half years without television. I am twenty-eight and a registered nurse and my husband is thirty-one and in the insurance business. Our daughter is now eight, and our sons are five and six.

Before we moved to Vail because of my husband's work, we lived in Colorado Springs. The children were TV addicts even though I consciously tried to monitor what they watched and limit them somewhat. I was very concerned about their TV watching. I'd watch my daughter go into a trancelike state whenever the TV was turned on—it made no difference what she was viewing. The boys were generally much more active than their sister and at first seemed less keen on television. However, as time went on, they, too, seemed to become totally passive in front of the television set.

In November we moved to Vail—actually five miles east of Vail. Soon we learned that our house was beyond the reach of Cable Vision, and without the cable there was no reception at all. The mountains simply blocked all signals.

At first we thought it was a temporary state of affairs and tried to fill our free time as best we could, always with the idea that television would be restored any day. We played our record collection until I was sick of every record. We talked about television a lot.

Before long we began to realize that we'd probably never see that Cable Vision truck pull in to hook up our set. We became resigned to our fate. Then life began to settle down into a more normal pattern. We began to read books, not just magazine stories. We'd play with the children for over an hour at a time sometimes, and they'd play by themselves for increasing periods of time, too. We entertained other couples much more than we used to. I started some serious sewing and experimented with new recipes. There just seemed to be much more time in a day.

Our daughter became quite good at entertaining herself by trying to read. She painted, drew pictures, modeled clay, wrote "letters" to all the family and her playmates. Several times a week she helped me bake cookies and cupcakes. Daddy taught her to play a serious game of checkers before she was six. I read at least one story a day to her and to the boys. We had a book on children's crafts and hobbies and several times a week we'd set aside an afternoon to make or play something new. Also I kept a large box of Halloween costumes and old dresses that my daughter and her friends and even the little boys loved to play with and never seemed to tire of. They loved best playing store and school and hospital. Many, many broken legs, heads, and arms did I bandage with cloth from the special costume box! Of course there was outside play, but on many winter days we couldn't go out for more than a few minutes, and all the swings and playground equipment were buried under snow for several months.

We did get to see some television during our Vail stay, however. Three or four times a year we'd go to visit Grandma, and we'd get to watch television. It was a real treat for all of us, just like going to the movies used to be before I ever saw television.

Then after two and a half years without TV in Vail, we moved again, because of my husband's work. We swore we'd never get addicted again. But even though we may not watch TV to the extent of many families I know, still I'm afraid we're caught again. I use the TV as a baby-sitter maybe two hours every day. We're in an apartment complex with no play facilities and having the television is just too tempting sometimes.

I try not to watch too much myself, but if I'm too tired to do anything else, I'll watch. Our daughter is addicted to the seven A.M. *Lassie* reruns and *The Lone Ranger*. If she starts watching an evening show, she has to watch it through to the end, even if she doesn't understand the story.

My husband isn't home much because of his new business, but if he sits down in the living room at all, the TV has to be on. He hasn't played with the children at home since we've moved here. We have gone out as a family on picnics, jeep trips, and fishing, but at home there is no more family roughhousing, piggyback rides, et cetera. No more checkers, either.

2. All the Good Things Disappeared

Some years ago (in the mid 1970s) Don Brawley, a young policeman on the New York City force, began work in a special program for police officers at Brooklyn College. One of his courses that year was sociology, for which he was required to devise a simple research experiment. He decided to disconnect his television set for two weeks and observe the effects on his own family life.

Brawley got an A for his illuminating, and ultimately heartbreaking paper, parts of which are included below:

First, a few things should be known about my household. The annual income is $20,000 a year, the education level of the adults is one year of college. We live in a suburban area about 35 miles from the city limit. My family consists of myself, my wife, and two sons, aged five and six years old. My two sons, who share the same bedroom, have their television located there. My wife and myself have a television located in our bedroom.

As a prerequisite for this experiment, I charted the time in which each television was in use for the period of one week. The children's television was used for a total of 41 hours, which is approximately 6 hours each day, and my wife's television was used for a total of 18 hours. However, some consideration could be given to the time of year in which this experiment took place; it was in the month of April. I was on vacation for three weeks.

At the start of the actual experiment, I had to devise a way to put both televisions out of service. The first was the portable television, which belongs to the children. I removed the fuse from the rear. The second was a large color console, in which I found a main control for the horizontal hold in the rear of the set. By turning the button, I rendered the television useless.

The first day of the experiment showed no real effects of the loss of television from the household. My wife went about her daily routine and the children spent much of the day playing in the backyard. It was that night when I noticed the first effects of not having a television set working. It was now too dark to send the children out to play and my wife found it quite impossible to do her evening work with the children in her way. This resulted in the children retiring early. This was a solution to the first problem but caused a greater one.

The very next day the children woke up at 6:30 in the morning. When the television is working, the children turn it on about 7 A.M. Each day the television would perform the duties of a baby-sitter from the time the children woke up until the time my wife got up from bed. The children constantly annoyed my wife until she got up and made breakfast. My oldest son was off from school because of the Easter holiday. What caused the major problem that day was the rain. By twelve o'clock my wife left the house to visit a neighbor and watch the stories that come on television each afternoon. As the day progressed, each member of the family became more and more annoyed over small things. Each day thereafter became more and more routine.

The children spent a great deal of time doing creative things that their mother planned for them each day, learning to write their alphabet, cutting out the letters and drawing on their blackboard. The puzzles came from out of the closet, and soon other toys that the children never had the particular interest to play with before took up much of their day. I could begin to see where the children spent more time doing things which would be of importance to them in their school work in the future.

The amount of time that my wife now spent actively with the children increased considerably. Also she now did a lot more tasks around the home. The closets that stored old clothes and other useless things were cleaned out. The guest room that had not been used for over three months got a thorough cleaning. She used to make her own clothes and sewed very well. With nothing to do in the evening, she started to sew again. By the middle of the second week of the experiment, she had completed a dress and started another one.

As a participant observer in the experiment, I found myself becoming completely bored at times. And like the rest of the family, I made certain changes in my daily activities. I also started to do those chores that somehow always got put aside until the next week. For the first time since I had been in school, I was completely caught up with all the reading for my courses.

After the long winter of not seeing most of the neighbors we began to visit different families who, during the winter months, we lost contact with.

During the experiment I noted a positive effect on our sex life. I attribute it to the early hours that we kept and the amount of rest we received each day. In the past we went to bed after the eleven o'clock news or one of us would watch the late show or some other show that would keep us apart.

The children seemed to fight among themselves more often. However, there is the possibility that it was noticed and paid more attention to because my wife and I were bothered by small things. At the same time the children became closer to us as we participated in doing things together. An average weekend at my house would consist of Saturday morning doing all the work around the house that was necessary and Saturday night taking the wife out. Sunday morning was Sunday School for the boys and church for the wife. In the afternoon, I would have some kind of activity with the boys. During the second week of the experiment, we went out three times in one week. As a family, we worked together on the lawn and preparing the garden for the summer; doing things the family had not done before as a unit.

At the end of the second week both televisions were operating. I wanted to once again compare the differences of having a television and not having one. All of the good things that had flourished because of the absence of a television set now disappeared. Everything reverted back to its old routine.

3. How *Not* to Do a TV Turnoff

A number of years ago Tom Valeo, a reporter on the *Daily Herald* of Arlington, Virginia, wrote an amusing, painfully honest account of his family's two-week TV Turnoff. It was published in the Sunday section. Though the Turnoff was not a happy experience (to put it mildly), Valeo's narrative demonstrates that a successful before-and-after experiment of this sort involves more than simply unplugging the television set. In many ways the Valeo story serves as a cautionary tale of how *not* to do a family TV Turnoff.

Valeo begins his story:

> It started, as it does with so many small children, with *Sesame Street*. Soon my daughter was watching *Mr. Rogers* and introducing her younger sister to the habit. Under the influence of the older kids in the neighborhood, they developed a taste for *The Flintstones, Popeye,* and Saturday morning cartoons. *Sesame Street* was too tame for them; they needed stronger stuff. Then they discovered reruns of *Three's Company* . . . When they moved on to *Taxi, Happy Days,* and *Diff'rent Strokes,* I knew things were out of hand. On top of that, they had a little brother toddling around, and he was getting hooked too. Drastic measures were needed. . . .

Valeo reveals the source of his anxiety about TV: a haunting suspicion that excessive television viewing during his childhood had "damaged [his] mind," an odd conclusion considering the high level of prose writing shown in his article. He explains further:

> I read a lot but I wouldn't say I like to read. I like to find out about things, so I read, but the act of reading is a lot of work for me. My wife, however, can spend hours lost in a good novel . . . for her, reading is easy, rewarding and fun. . . .
>
> I never knew a time without TV. I learned to read well, but reading was never as easy or exciting as watching those flickering images on the TV screen. My wife, on the other hand, watched little TV as a child. Her parents had a TV but they didn't let their children watch it much.

Consequently, my wife spent hours as a child curled up in a chair with a book, and she learned how to read for pleasure, a skill that still eludes me.

With these and other anxieties about television's effects in mind, Valeo proposed the experiment to his wife: "two weeks without TV just to see what happens." He elaborated on his fantasy of family life without television: "our children playing together, drawing, using their toys and blossoming under the extra attention they'd get from us." He felt confident that his book-loving wife would welcome the idea. "We knew we were using TV as a baby-sitter and we both felt guilty about it," he says.

His wife was unexpectedly cool to the proposal. "I'm the one who's going to bear the brunt of this," she observed. "Let's see you try to make dinner without the TV on."

Valeo prevailed. "Pulling the plug seemed the only right thing to do," he explains. And pull the plug they did, with no particular plan or preparations. Valeo describes the first days:

> The first thing I noticed was that all three kids were eating breakfast with me. "That's wonderful," I thought until I realized it meant the end of my morning meditation with the newspaper. My wife also found herself doing more things with the children, although there were moments when she was tempted to turn on the TV just to keep them occupied while she unpacked the groceries or carried laundry downstairs, but she resisted.
>
> The first weekend was brutal. In the absence of television, it is very difficult to keep three children occupied from sunup to sundown. We were desperate for relief. A note I made on the first Saturday captures the ambiance of the household: "I'm so exhausted I could vomit . . . Toys are being scattered faster than I can pick them up."

Without the TV my wife and I became butlers responsible for fetching, playing, and answering questions all day. Instead of watching TV, the six-year-old was drawing, the three-year-old was painting her nails, and the toddler was climbing the furniture all the time. The teasing and arguing among them was almost incessant, and the competition for our attention was becoming ferocious. . . . Dinners were particularly hectic because the kids would hang around after they finished and talk instead of dashing off to watch TV.

So it went for nearly two weeks, until we left for vacation. When we returned, we were tired from the hectic trip and desperate for a little peace. We stumbled through the door, hoping to rest for a few minutes, but the toddler was raring to go. We took the easy way out—"Let's see if *Sesame Street* is on." It was, and the TV was back.

I'm ashamed to admit it but the TV is on in our house as much as before. What's worse, we have a VCR too. . . .

What went wrong with the Valeo experiment?

The Valeos had been using television as a survival strategy from the time their children were babies. Now they were dependent on TV to keep the kids in hand.

Well, so what? Why shouldn't parents avail themselves of any help they can get during the trying years of parenthood. The answer is a hard one to face for parents who rely on television for child care. Using TV as a baby-sitter cuts down on kids' socialization. They become harder to handle without TV. By giving over some of their authority to the mechanical substitute, parents may have more serious trouble handling the kids when they get older, stronger-willed, and even more in need of firm guidance.

In his article Tom Valeo reflects a bit ruefully on the decision to go back to a television-dependent life:

In the diary I kept during the experiment is a line that
startles me with its conviction: "I'm clearly interacting more
with the kids. I'm convinced that television is one of the
most divisive influences on our family." I still believe that.
We were much better off without TV, but I also know that
we'll never be without it again. I still feel guilty when I see
the kids watching the same videotape again and again, but
it's just so much easier to let them watch. I know they'd be
better off without a TV in the house, but I don't think I
could handle all the togetherness.

Underlying that resigned conclusion is the assumption that
without TV, life would always be the same nightmarish, chaotic mess
the Valeos endured during their two-week Turnoff; the children
would be endlessly resentful and demanding, and the parents would
forever be forced to take the roles of butlers, maids, and entertainers.

But Valeo's wife had only to look back at her virtually TV-free
childhood to see that parents *can* survive perfectly well without using
television for relief. They might have looked back just a little further
at generations before 1950 who managed to cook dinner, unload
their groceries and live a normal life without being driven crazy by
demanding children.

It's not hard to see why the Valeos went back to television so
swiftly: their experience had been a terrible ordeal. All Tom Valeo's
idealistic notions about the children's blossoming in TV's absence
went down the drain in the awful reality of those two weeks.

Could the Valeos have managed their Turnoff differently? What
did they do wrong, and what might they have done instead to make
their experiment successful?

• *They didn't plan in advance.*

If the Valeos had understood that they needed support and help
in making a transition from heavy dependence on TV to "cold

turkey," they might have made some plans for their two weeks without television. These might have included social activities, inviting another family over for some meals, planning a child-friendly day trip, and, certainly, borrowing a great supply of books from the library, including one containing new family games or pastimes to fill time in the absence of TV.

• They didn't "sell" the Turnoff to the kids.

The six-year-old was naturally resentful at having the Turnoff foisted on her and inevitably passed this resentment along to her younger siblings. Surely some of their trying behavior during the Turnoff was based on their desire to sabotage this hateful project. If it had been presented as a scientific experiment, if there had been a few amusing rituals connected with it, if there had been a reward waiting for everyone at the end—the kids might have behaved differently during the no-TV period.

• They expected miracles.

It takes time to establish those play patterns that allow children to play on their own successfully, time to establish those parent-child relationships that allow a family to get along peacefully and harmoniously. The Valeos expected miracles to happen instead of setting things up in advance to make their transition easier.

• They were ambivalent.

Tom Valeo longed for a better family life and dreamed of having more resourceful children. And yet he included in his catalog of grievances that the six-year-old was drawing, the three-year-old was painting her nails and the toddler was climbing the furniture. After dinner, he complained, "the kids would hang around and talk."

Well, maybe nail-polishing is not the perfect activity for a three-year-old, but climbing furniture is certainly an honorable toddler pastime, and drawing is a most desirable occupation for a six-year-old. Having the kids hang around after dinner wanting to talk to their parents is a dream of fine family life. Without recognizing that being a good parent calls for the development of some new abilities, among them being able to find more pleasure in talking to a noisy bunch of kids than reading a paper in peace and quiet, Tom Valeo cannot in fairness accuse television of being a "divisive influence." His own divided feelings about being a parent and having a family need resolution before he can deal with the problem of television.

Postscript

I included the cautionary story of the Valeo's no-TV experiment in a book published in 1987. Shortly thereafter, Tom Valeo wrote another newspaper article about his family's television adventures. This time, however, a happier picture emerged. Referring to the miserable turnoff the family had endured two years earlier he wrote, "Yes, we lost that battle, but we ultimately won the war through a campaign of passive resistance that seems to have broken television's hold on our family."

How did the Valeos manage to free themselves from "the tyranny of the tube," as the reporter put it, after having been so solidly hooked?

The seemingly disastrous TV Turnoff proved to have been far more useful than the beleaguered parents had realized while in its throes. As Mr. Valeo explained, it provided the illumination they needed about their dependency on television as a child-rearing device, and led them to make some changes in their family routines to help control television.

For example, when the Valeo family moved to a new house not long after their TV Turnoff, instead of installing the television set in their living room once again, they picked a new location: a back room upstairs, outside the normal flow of traffic. As Mr. Valeo explained in his follow-up article.

So the TV is out of sight—it's also out of mind. If our children want to watch TV they have to climb the stairs and go to this distant room, which they don't like to do.

Moving the TV to a less-than-central location is an effective strategy for deemphasizing TV (see Natural Control, page 231). But would that really do the trick to transform a family once dominated by television into a virtually TV-free family? The follow-up article revealed another great change that had occurred as a result of the Valeo's TV Turnoff.

Oh, there's another element to our passive resistance to TV, and this is probably even more important. If you want this to work, you'll have to curb your viewing habits. My wife and I don't watch television, so our children never see us watching it. It's not part of our lives—we never initiate TV-watching, and we rarely suggest a program the children might like to see. Television has gradually evaporated from our routine, and no one seems to miss it.

Organized TV Turnoffs

An organized TV Turnoff is a simple experiment in which a group—a class, a school, a community, or a nation-wide conglomeration like the one put together by the TV-Turnoff Network (See Videoholics Anonymous, page 239), agrees to go "cold turkey" from television for a limited period of time. Its purpose is not to attack television or to create guilt about watching it. Rather, it is meant to help parents, teachers, and children better understand the role television plays in their lives so they can learn to control it more effectively.

The organized TV Turnoff has become fairly common, with hundreds of schools and communities around the nation setting up such events regularly. Besides gaining insight into their use or abuse of TV, the participants usually reap some publicity, have unexpected amounts of fun, and experience a feeling of adventure akin to camping in the wilderness.

The following comments and observations are taken from parents' and children's diaries kept during a number of organized TV Turnoffs I have been involved with personally. The earliest one, in 1974, took place in Denver, Colorado, for a period of a month. The others, taking place over the next two decades, were all one week in duration:

Why people choose to participate:

My own TV watching has become too much. I use it as a substitute for everything.

We rarely do things we mean to do—television is just too much of a habit.

I'd like the children to be aware of how much TV they watch and how many more exciting things there are to do.

I'd like to eliminate some of the hassle connected with television in our family.

My nine-year-old watches about four or five hours a day and it really worries me.

Why some do NOT participate in a Turnoff:

I'm afraid that if I gave up television the kids would take up a whole bunch more of my time—and I don't have time to spare.

My husband doesn't share my opinion of television viewing. When he's home, he watches almost continually.

If it weren't for Mister Rogers *and* The Electric Company, *I'd never get dinner ready or the entrance steps vacuumed.*

My child has a broken leg and needs to watch television. Maybe I'll try it next *summer.*

The "withdrawal" period:

The first week was hard for all of us. The kids sort of hung around and didn't know what to do with themselves. I suggested reading, which we did a lot of, but still time was long sometimes. After the first week it began getting easier and easier for all of us. By the end of the month we really didn't miss TV at all.

At the beginning the children kept asking to watch TV. They really seemed to miss it and we began to wonder whether the whole thing wasn't too hard on them. But gradually they found other things to do that we thought were a lot better than watching television.

Sometimes, the first few days after Dad unplugged the set I'd just go and look at it, even though it was off. I really missed watching. Then as the summer went on, I stopped thinking about TV so much.

I'd keep going to somebody's house and I wanted to know what day of the week it was. I always know what day it is from what programs are on.

Changes in family life noted by parents during the Turnoff:

• A greater feeling of closeness as a family
The children and I became closer because we did more things together. We discovered many things about each other during the experiment, hidden talents and interests.

• A more peaceful atmosphere in the home
I've enjoyed the quietness of life without TV. Maybe after the experiment we ought to find another place for the set besides the family room.

*There seems to be so much more time. Perhaps part of it is that
there isn't that frantic, hurrying sound of the TV always in the
background.*

*I would say that not having to adjust between watching TV
and playing made for a more restful atmosphere in the home.
I'd noticed that the "coming out" of the television spell and
adjusting to a play situation was often a lengthy process, full of
antagonism between children.*

• More help by children in the household

*I used to let the kids watch TV after dinner because their fa-
vorite programs were on then and it seemed too mean to deprive
them. Then I had to do the dishes alone. Now they have time to
help. We do a lot of talking while doing dishes. It's a very
comfortable sort of time when it's easy to talk—maybe the soapy
water makes us all relax.*

*Betty helped Dad with yard work and then helped him wash
the truck.*

*Both children cleaned their rooms more thoroughly than usual,
and spent a lot of time alphabetizing the books in their
bookcase and arranging the things on their desks.*

• Better sibling relations

*The children seem to deal with each other more without the TV.
When there's nothing to do, they're likely to play with each other,
really do things together.*

*When the kids had nothing to do, they went out and made a
secret hideout—played there for many days.*

*The girls are apt to play regular, organized games now that the
TV is out. And the older one is more willing to play with the*

younger, whereas before it was easier to just watch TV and not take the extra trouble of explaining the rules of a game to a younger sister.

Our children are playing together, real old-fashioned playing. The two middle children made up an entire musical today entitled Dolphins in the Desert.

• More interaction with adults by children
Cathy had a girl friend over and they sat around with the adults in the evening, listening and joining in the conversation. We enjoyed that and realized that in the past the kids always watched TV when we had company.

• More reading
Although the children have always enjoyed reading, we noticed a definite increase in the number of books read during the no-television period.

Joey will start reading in the middle of the afternoon and read through the time to go to bed. He wouldn't have done that with the TV available.

• More outdoor play
In the past we couldn't get the kids outside if my husband held open the door and I booted them out. Now they're going out in all sorts of weather with no television to keep them inside.

We noticed there's a lot more outdoor play, even when the weather isn't great.

• Changes in bedtime and meals
We found we were all going to bed much earlier.

Dinners are longer now since the children don't leave to watch their programs.

Mealtimes are given to general conversation, instead of arguments about how soon they could get up and watch TV.

• Better relations between parents
My husband misses the sports events, but I enjoy talking to him.

Personally I find I can tolerate Saturday housework as a working mother a lot better when I don't see my husband loafing near the TV.

• More crafts and hobbies
We have more time for games, crafts, model building, and reading.

We did several alternate activities: planted a large vegetable garden, various arts and crafts.

I did more sewing during the no-TV period than I've done in years.

Problems related to a Turnoff, mentioned by parents and children.

• Missed programs
I've missed not watching Masterpiece Theatre. *We had a ritual of watching it on Sundays.*

I really miss Wild Wild West.

• Social Pressure
I asked my friend Clark to come and sleep over and he said, "What are we going to do at your *house, sit around and listen to the radio?"*

I'm ashamed to ask anybody over. It just feels weird because all the other kids have TV.

• Loss of Effective Punishment

No TV was always our most effective threat. Of course we couldn't use it during the experiment.

After the Turnoff

Parents' reports:

All four kids were fighting over what to watch. My husband and I looked at each other and realized how nice the summer had been without TV—we had forgotten about all those fights that centered around the television set.

Turning off the TV for the summer was relatively simple. The kids just accepted the fact, with the few exceptions noted in the diary. Our problems began when we turned it back on. Our eight-year-old (the family addict) went back to sneaking programs at times he wasn't supposed to watch. The kids went back to watching cartoons before school, and that took care of those nice family breakfasts we had all enjoyed.

When we resumed watching, the kids didn't seem nearly as interested in TV—but they're getting into the old pattern as time goes on. And I know I am! That's why I think it's a good idea to do this once in a while.

When the TV blackout was over, I tried limiting the kids' viewing to two hours a day, but as time goes on, I find them turning on the TV when they get up and only turning it off at bedtime. It's not that they're particularly interested in TV, but they're bored with the season and biding time until school opens again.

Children's reports:

It's really harder to do other things when the TV is around. I just want to watch it.

During the experiment I got my mind off TV so I didn't keep
thinking about it. Then I had more fun. I had to kick the
habit.

Why Did They Go Back?

In light of the reported improvements in family life during various TV Turnoffs, why did virtually all the families resume their old patterns of television viewing when the Turnoff was over? Why didn't they try to perpetuate the improvements by getting rid of television permanently?

"Did you ever consider living without television for good?" Don Brawley, the New York policeman, was asked. He answered after a few moments of thought:

> No, I really never even considered that. You'd wonder why, wouldn't you? It reminds me of the time I was sick, a while back, and had to give up smoking. I said, "Oh, I feel so much better because I'm not smoking. I've got my wind back and I feel great!" But as soon as the doctor said I was all right again, I went right back to cigarettes. Well, I suppose TV's a habit, too. You enjoy it, but when you think about it, television doesn't offer much that you couldn't replace by yourself, or do a lot better. But still, once you've got the habit, it's hard to do without it. Like cigarettes.

Clearly a family trying to change a habit as addictive and passively gratifying as television-viewing needs more than a successful TV Turnoff to bring about a permanent change. A break from television may provide the initial push, but new and more favorable patterns must then be established if a family is not to settle back into the same old comfortable grooves.

When asked to give an opinion as to why various successful TV Turnoffs did not lead families to give up television, a psychologist suggested that the parents were in fact kidding themselves, that while they thought they *ought* to engage in the activities they took up during the no-television period—reading, playing games, conversing—these didn't fulfill the needs that television viewing did. That, he suggests, is why they went back to television.

But what *are* the needs that television fulfills? The need for passivity, for regressing to a state of dependence . . . surely habitual television viewing serves few needs more auspicious than these. Perhaps a life of activity, of self-searching and growth, seems too difficult to attempt in our fragmented modern society. And yet the tone of regret with which parents described their return to a television-dominated family life suggests one of the oldest conflicts of human nature. In the Bible Paul puts it in these words: "For what I would, that do I not; but what I hate, that do I."

19

No-TV Families

Most people believe that television wouldn't be a problem if only parents were firmer and took the trouble to monitor the programs their kids watch. But television control is devilishly difficult to achieve and blaming parents is not entirely fair.

Parents who use television to buy free time from child care are giving in to a temptation that is nearly irresistible. It's not unlike the problems people have trying not to eat some delicious but fattening morsel sitting in their refrigerator. They resist and resist, and then succumb. And then they feel terrible, as if they were weak-willed and self-destructive. Yet most people give in to such temptation. To be sure, if the fattening morsel weren't there, they wouldn't find it hard at all not to eat unhealthy food. The problem arises *when it's there*.

Social analyst Joshua Meyrowitz is one of the few experts who pins the rap on the medium more than on a lapse in parental authority and responsibility. Citing the many difficulties of television control, he concludes, "With television . . . the important decision is whether to have a television or not have one, whether to expose children to almost *all* of television's offerings or *none* of them." A look at statistics of television households in America makes it obvious that a vast majority—99 percent of the population—make that important decision in the direction of having television.

Yet some families *do* choose to live without television. Of these, some begin family life without a television set and bring up their children without ever having one in the home. Others (a casual survey indicates that their number is far greater) get rid of their sets after a period of ownership, though not necessarily forever.

Getting Rid of Television: Four Families That Did It

Often the decision to get rid of the set for good is precipitated by an involuntary period of no television—the set breaks, the roof aerial blows down during a storm. Sometimes the decision follows a long trip during which television was unavailable. It is during such television-free periods that parents seem to gain perspective on their television problem and come to the realization that something can be done about it. A Denver father describes such a moment:

> The set was controlling our lives. We argued with the kids about what they should watch. The kids argued with each other about what to watch. The kids didn't want to come to dinner because they were watching something. The biggest arguments we had in the family were over the damn TV set. When it broke down one day, we came to our senses. Let's see what happens, we said, and we never had another set after that.

Like the TV Turnoff families, those who have given up television for good are valuable sources of information about the changes that occur when television is eliminated. But while the Turnoff families soon returned to the "before" condition in the before-after conjunction, most of those who decide to get rid of their sets for good have the strength, for as yet undetermined reasons, to hang on to the "after" for longer periods of time. The following brief histories describe four families who decided to live indefinitely without television.

Too Hard to Control

The Gerbers were a family who found television too hard to control and decided to do without it. At the time of my interview, Jim Gerber, a writer, and Barbara Gerber, then a graduate student in sociology, lived in a large apartment in New York City with their children, Ned and Annie, aged fifteen and thirteen. Barbara described their family struggles with the television problem and their solution: no television at all. At the time of the interview (without Jim Gerber, who was out of town), the Gerbers had been without television for almost a year.

> When we had the television it was always the source of complaints and terrible fights. We kept trying out new systems to deal with it. Each system would break down and then we'd fight about the system itself. The whole thing was terrible. The government, the regulation, of television was consuming an enormous amount of time and energy.
>
> At first we had no rules. But it turned out that Ned would watch all day if he could. And then the kids would argue about what programs to watch, who would have first choice. But besides the squabbling, television caused other problems. For one thing, family dinner used to be arranged around television programs. Either somebody said, "I can't eat until eight o'clock because I'm watching Mission Impossible," or "I've got five minutes to eat dinner because Mission Impossible is coming on." So dinner always turned out to be something sandwiched in between two programs.
>
> And when the kids had friends come over, they were very likely to watch television together instead of playing. I'd come in and find them all in the zombie position, huddled around the television set. That would bother me and I'd turn it off and tell them to play. But do you know something extraordinary? Sometimes they'd sit there and stare at the set for minutes after I'd turned it off! It just amazes me to think that we could have lived in this horrible style for so many years.

How did this highly educated family get into so sorry a situation? I asked Barbara Gerber how the family's television problem developed. Her answer was revealing:

I sometimes wonder why we didn't get rid of the television set long ago. But actually I know the answer to that question. I really and truly needed television when the kids were little. I was stuck with two small kids, a year and a half apart, in a New York apartment, with no help of any kind. There was no backyard. There was no kind of activity around except what I could dream up for them to do around the house. And so I used the television set a lot. I don't think I would have survived without it.

In those days I let the kids watch as much television as they wanted, mostly because I wanted them to watch just as much as they did. But it turned out that Ned watched a lot more than Annie. He'd sit for hours in front of the set, sucking his thumb. He'd go into a real trance when he watched TV. Sometimes he'd watch for six, seven hours. He never got tired of watching television. Of course, I felt terribly guilty about it. I didn't think all that TV was good. But I rationalized. I was exhausted. I needed it. My husband was working day and night making ends meet in those days, so he couldn't help me.

A year ago we came back from a summer out in the West, two months completely away from television. And we just decided we'd had it. We unplugged the set and put it away in a closet. And it's been there ever since, except for the World Series and special things like that, when we go to all the trouble of bringing it out again.

I asked each of the Gerbers how they felt about life without a television set in their house.

The mother's answer:

I love not having television, even though I used to enjoy watching quite a bit. I feel as if I've been handed a gift of a few extra hours every day. Not just the time I myself spent watching, but all the time I spent adjudicating fights about it and dealing with it. I love not having to feel resentful that I have something to do instead of being able to watch some program I wanted to see. I love not having to read TV Guide, *not having to* look *for* TV Guide. *I love not being mad that I missed a program I could have watched last night. I don't feel sorry about not having TV, not one little bit.*

What about Ned, the most avid watcher in the family? His mother reported being surprised that Ned had not complained about the decision to eliminate television. Ned described his feelings about it:

I think it's a lot better now. See, what Annie does is she'll do her homework right away when she gets home from school and get it all over with. Not me. I'd always wait until the last minute. It was always such a temptation when the TV was around—I'd just keep putting off my work. I always felt guilty. I knew I should be doing my work. But I'd watch TV anyhow.

Now I usually end up reading one of my books for school, especially science, which I really like. Before, when we had TV I'd never read a book. Never. If I had reading to do for a course, I'd put it off and figure I'd just listen to the discussion in class and take it from there. But now with no TV, I'm sort of forced to read. There's nothing else to do.

Annie was not as emphatic, but did not disagree:

Yes, I guess we're better off without television. We talk more at dinner. Everybody tells what they did all day, and all that. But I never watched as much TV as Ned, so it doesn't make so much difference to me whether we have it or not. And I do miss some programs. And also it's hard sometimes because teachers sometimes assign things to watch on TV. But I'm pretty satisfied with our life without television.

The Gerbers presented a fine picture of family harmony and contentment. Did all those years of television viewing have no damaging effects? For if they did not, why not use television without limit when children are young and troublesome, as Barbara Gerber did, and then get rid of it when the going is easier? A final comment by Ned left the question in the air.

> *The way it used to be I didn't care what program I watched as long as I was watching* something. *It could have been* Popeye *or* Sesame Street *or the United Nations, anything. But now I spend more time out of the house. I* do *read more when I'm home, but mostly I try to stay out of the house as long as possible. Because I have a feeling that I have nothing to do at home now. I'm just not used to figuring out things to do. See, when we had the TV, I didn't notice I was doing nothing when I watched all those hours. But now I notice.*

It Takes Time to Get Television Out of Your System

The four Davis kids live with their parents in a large farmhouse surrounded by woods and fields in northern New York State. They are aged four, seven, ten, and thirteen years. On a warm spring day two years ago, instead of romping outdoors climbing the fruit trees nearby or peering into the woodchuck hole or watching the fish swim in the clear stream behind their house, the four children sat in a row on the long sofa in the living room and stared at a small table where a short time ago the television set had stood. It was gone.

Mrs. Davis described the scene to an interviewer:

> *The kids really sat there for quite a while, just as if they were watching. It was pathetic. But it made us absolutely certain that we'd done the right thing by chucking the set out.*

How had they reached the decision? Mrs. Davis told how it began and described the family's transition from a heavy-using TV family to a no-TV family.

The aerial on the roof blew down and broke in a storm, and without it there was no television reception. It would have cost an arm and a leg to buy a new one and get it installed. Besides, we were fed up with all the television watching we were doing—the kids and us, too. We were pretty addicted. The set was on most of the time. So we decided to get rid of the set and see what happened.

The first few weeks without the set were hard. The kids wandered around like lost souls. They stayed indoors a lot and got in my hair. I'd send them out and they didn't know what to do with themselves.

Saturday mornings was when I missed the set the most. That was when we used to stay in bed a nice long time while the kids sat in the living room, glued to the set, quiet, not moving hardly. Now they were after us for this and that, or they'd be fighting or getting into some kind of trouble.

But gradually things got better. They began playing games with each other, something they'd never gone in for much, even though we had all the games—Chinese checkers, Monopoly, Parcheesi.

They sort of had to learn to play with each other, and after a while they began to fight a lot less.

Then they began to spend more and more time outdoors. This happened gradually. The oldest boy began fishing a lot. And he and his younger brother got interested in the woodchuck and spent lots of time waiting for him to come out of his hole. They'd never been interested in anything like that before. They asked for one of those traps that catches live animals and got one for Christmas. And after that they hardly set foot in the house before dark.

This happened two years ago, and really, I think they're different kids now. They even think so themselves. And they know our getting rid of the television has something to do with it. Nowadays, when they come back from a visit at a friend's house they feel critical. They'll talk about how much TV their friends watch, and how they don't do many interesting things.

The funniest thing of all is that here we are all living in the country, and the kids are just beginning to be country kids. They talk about their friends as "indoor kids," can you imagine? But it took time. You can't just turn off your set for a few days and expect anything to change much. It takes time to get television out of your system.

"Like Old-Fashioned Living"

One July some years ago, Paul and Bea Warner and their boys closed up their house on the outskirts of Pittsburgh, left their dogs at a neighbor's, and went to Africa for six months. Adam was eleven, Peter nine. It was Paul's sabbatical from his university's music department, and with the help of a small grant, he intended to spend the time away from his teaching duties writing music. He needed a change of scene, he felt; his best works had been written far from home.

Bea described their television situation:

Before we left for Africa, the boys were really addicted to television. The *Three Stooges* after school, endless cartoons. I'd be in the kitchen cooking and I could hear the dialogue from the set. Without ever seeing the show, I could tell it was the fifteenth time they'd watched the same damn program. It made me furious. I'd yell at them to go outside and I don't think they ever heard me—they'd be in a stupor.

We tried to get them not to watch so much. We were always laying down all sorts of rules and regulations: You can't watch until you finished practicing or until your homework is done or whatever. It was a real struggle. The way they'd practice when they were rushing to see some program was probably worse than not practicing at all. It really upset us, especially Paul. Because both kids really wanted to play an instrument. It wasn't as if we were pushing them. But you've got to practice if you want to learn an instrument and practicing is hard. If there's something easier to do, like watch TV, what kid is going to want to practice?

When the Warners arrived in Africa, they stayed, as prearranged, in the comfortable house of another academic American family who had returned to the States for a year. The house was filled with books and games. But there was no television set. Television had simply not come to that area.

Of course, we were in a foreign country, a pretty exotic one at that, and there was a lot for the boys to see and take in. It wasn't as if we had gone cold turkey from television back home. But still, six months is a long time and we were all thrown on our own resources quite a lot. The first thing we noticed was that the kids began to do a lot more reading than they had ever done at home. I guess it was out of sheer boredom. Peter had always been a good reader, but Adam had never liked to read much. Now he started reading like a house on fire. He read all the nature books around and got really interested in the wild life around us. There was a junior encyclopedia in the house, and they started with "A" and began to plough through it! It was really amazing. Paul and I couldn't believe it.

But the biggest difference was that we began to do a lot of talking together. It was like old-fashioned living, somehow. The four of us sat around and just talked about everything. We talked and talked. We talked about socialism because we were in a socialist country. We talked about racial problems. We talked about music, about books.

Actually, the timing was perfect. The kids were old enough to talk to, but still young enough to be dependent on us. And so they had to adhere to our routine, in a way. And they couldn't just go off somewhere and do their own thing, like watch television, because they had no special thing of their own there. We had to find common *things, if you see what I mean. I'll never forget those months.*

When we came home we decided that there was no reason why we shouldn't keep on talking together, why the boys shouldn't keep on reading a lot of books. We made up our minds to get rid of our set. It's not the same as in Africa, of course. The kids across the street have television, and so on. But things are better. The kids still read more. They seem to have a lot more time on their hands. They do hang around the house a lot, it seems, and sometimes they drive me crazy. But sometimes, just out of nowhere, they'll start to do something interesting, like make up a crossword puzzle, or start a collection. And they do a lot more practicing nowadays, pretty much voluntarily.

Ousting the Stranger from the House

Colman McCarthy, a *Newsweek* columnist, described the results of eliminating television in an often reprinted article. The drug metaphor he uses to describe his relationship with television, though lighthearted, lends a particular power to this piece:

When I turned off the television for the last time about a year ago and dumped the set for good, some friends, relatives and unasked advisers on the block predicted I would not last long without it. Few disputed the common gripe that TV is a wasteland, with irrigation offered only by the rare trickle of a quality program. Instead, they doubted that the addiction of some twenty years before the tube could be stilled by this sudden break with the past. It is true that an addiction had me, my veins eased only by a fix of 30 to 35 hours a week; my wife's dosage was similar, and our children—three boys under seven—already listened more to the television than to us.

Now, a year later—a family living as cultural cave men, says an anthropologist friend—the decision we made was one of the wisest of our married life. The ratings—our private Nielsens—during this year of selflessness have been high, suggesting that such common acts as talking with one's children, sharing ideas with one's wife, walking to the neighborhood library on a Saturday morning, quiet evenings of reading books and magazines aloud to each other, or eating supper as a family offer more intellectual stimulation than anything on television.

The severity of an addiction to TV is not that it reduces the victim to passivity while watching it but that it demands he be a compulsive activist to get in front of it. If I arrived home at 6, for example, and dinner was ready at 6:25—my wife's afternoon movie had run late—I would shove down the food in five minutes. The deadline, falling like a guillotine, was at 6:30. Chancellor came on then, Cronkite at 7; if CBS was dull, Smith and Reasoner were on ABC. If I hadn't finished dinner, I would sprint back to the table during the commercials for short-order gulps, then back to cool John, Uncle Walter or wry Harry. My wife, desperate Mav, was left at the table to control the bedlam of the kids, caused by my in-and-out sprints. The chaos I heard coming from the dining room was fitting: it was matched by the chaos in the world reported on the evening news, except the latter, in the vague "out there," was easier to handle.

With the set gone, these compulsions and in-turnings have gone too. We eat dinner in leisure and peace now. We stay at the playground until the children have had enough fun, not when I need to rush home to watch the 4 P.M. golf. Occasionally, my wife and I have the exotic experience of spending an evening in relaxed conversation, not the little half-steps of talk we once made in a forced march to Marital Communications. In those days, we would turn off the set in midevening and be immediately oppressed by the silence.

What had been happening all those years of watching television, I see now, was not only an addiction but also, on a deeper level, an adjustment. All of us had become adjusted to living with a stranger in the house. Is there any more basic definition of a television set than that?

No Television Ever

The number of families in America who choose to live without television is small indeed. An even smaller number of these no-television families have never owned a set.

Among them are those who have decided to live without television because they simply don't like it. "We didn't want TV because we felt we had no time for it," and "As newlyweds we saw no real need for a TV, and after periodic reconsiderations we still feel the same—TV just isn't important to us" are among the reasons given for the decision to eschew television completely. Some avoid acquiring a television out of fear that they will not be able to control it. "I was worried that I might watch too much. That's what used to happen when I lived at home. I'd sit in front of that thing all day," explains a Denver father.

Yet whatever the motivation for their televisionless state, the no-television-ever families interviewed for this book present a solid front: not a single parent or child among them expressed the desire to acquire a television set.

No-television-ever parents are often asked if they find the job of bringing up children much harder in the absence of a television set.

But these parents believe their life is easier, partly because their children are more resourceful, and partly because an area of conflict has been eliminated.

A Denver mother says:

> *I object to people who think that I must have a lot of patience to manage my kids without TV. I don't have a lot of patience at all. But the kids have plenty of things that keep them occupied. I never hear them say, "What shall I do now?"*

A New York mother of three children notes:

> *There is that hour or so when you're trying to prepare dinner when it might be nice to send the kids off to watch TV. That's the time of day they're most obnoxious. They're hungry and tired, and I'm hungry and tired, too. But a little bit of healthy mayhem and yelling and screaming at each other works up our appetite, I guess. By dinnertime everything is all right. It's a small price to pay for all the advantages of life without television.*

One disadvantage no-television-ever families often mention is the difficulty of attracting baby-sitters to a televisionless home:

> *My biggest problem is baby-sitters. If you don't have a television, they come with great reluctance. I try to lure them by telling them about the stereo and allowing them to make all the phone calls they want, but it's a big problem. If anything would cause us to get a set, it would be to make it easier to get baby-sitters.*

Do these families spend a lot more time with their children than other families? Not necessarily. Unlike the families that get rid of their sets, who often try to replace viewing time with games and family activities, no-television-ever families give little evidence of playing more with their children than other parents. "We don't really play games at all, as a family," says a mother of two school-age children. "To tell the truth, I don't like to play games."

How then *do* these families spend their free time, especially those hours that other families spend watching television? Besides reading (the major leisure-time activity replacing viewing), practicing a musical instrument takes up children's time in many of these households. Pianos were played in four out of the ten households surveyed by *The New York Times* in an article about no-television families.

Some no- television-ever families spend considerable time listening to the radio and to stories and books on tape. Though these may seem similar activities to watching dramas on television, these parents consider them different, and preferable. One mother noted:

> *You use your imagination in listening to records or stories on the radio.*

Another parent observed:

> *Sometimes my five-year-old is tired and uses a record to relax, but she often falls asleep before the record is over. I don't think kids who zonk out with television actually fall asleep while watching. They just sit there in a daze.*

These televisionless families seem to spend considerably more time eating together than other families and their meals are characterized by more family conversation. As one mother relates:

> *We have house guests who are always surprised when they come down to breakfast and find us all there talking together. Sometimes we sit at the breakfast table for an hour and a half. But we all go to bed terribly early, shockingly early, and get up early as well.*

Other no-television-ever families report a similar tendency to linger at mealtimes, more frequently dinner than breakfast. That this is related to their lack of television is suggested by the reports of former television-owning families, who frequently mention longer and more chatty meals after television has been eliminated. Early bedtimes are also commonly mentioned by no-television-ever families, as well as by those who have given up television.

Unlike families who give up television after years of viewing and often feel evangelistic about their new way of life, no-television-ever families tend to be reticent about their televisionless status. As one father says:

> We seldom mention it to people, although neighbors discover our TV-less home from their children.

A mother says:

> We just don't talk about TV with our friends. Most people don't even know we don't have a set, except for our closer friends. They'll ask if we saw such-and-such program and we'll say no, we missed it, without going into our not having a TV.

Perhaps the reserve of no-television-ever families is an acquired defense against the prickly reactions of many parents when confronted with an anti-television argument, especially when voiced in the somewhat self-righteous tone that characterizes converts to a cause.

Yet reticence does not completely eliminate self-satisfaction. One mother does not hesitate to air her low opinion of television and her delight in her family life:

> We have been accused many times of culturally depriving our children by not having a TV. You'd be amazed at how emotional and angry people can become when you express the idea that you don't approve of television. It's worse than attacking motherhood or apple pie. We take our four children to concerts and museums and don't feel they're deprived of culture. On the contrary, I'm well pleased with their physical, mental, and emotional development—they're active, eager, curious,

independent doers. *They love to read, do well in school, and have good imaginations. They never run out of things to do.*

Though occasionally guilty of smugness, no-television-ever families may well have something to be smug about. As one such parent reports:

People always ask me accusingly, "Don't you want your children to watch Sesame Street*?" But we're a very close family and we don't want any built-in separaters cutting us off from each other. We read a lot, talk a lot, listen to music. Once in a while we'll rent a set for a special occasion like a big sports event. But for us television is like junk food—a once-in-a-while thing.*

Coda

The Television Generation

Who Is the Television Generation?

One aspect of television distinguishes it from all other past technologies that have affected society. No other advance had ever affected the lives of children under the age of six—the most impressionable segment of the population—as swiftly, pervasively, and directly as the coming of television to the American home.

The invention of the electric light, the automobile, or the telephone changed most adults' lives significantly, but not the lives of the youngest children. They continued to spend their days in pretty much the same way small children have spent their days throughout history. They slept, they ate, and the rest of their time they engaged in the enormously varied complex of activities that falls into the category of *play*.

At some point during the late fifties and early sixties small children began to spend a significant chunk of their day engaged in an activity that was neither sleep nor play but fell somewhere in between, an activity characterized by a novel intake of visual and auditory materials accompanied by behaviors quite uncommon among young children—silence, inactivity, mental passivity.

The amazing swiftness with which television was adopted makes the time television began to have its impact easy to pinpoint. Within a narrow period of four years, between 1948 and 1952, television ownership in America rose from a few thousand to fifteen million. Thus one might expect to see within a narrow period of time signs of television's effects upon the first generation of children to grow up with it as a formative influence.

A logical proposition follows: that children who have watched television for a quarter of their waking hours during the critical years between two and six, who will have spent a total of at least five thousand hours (and perhaps double that much) watching images on a screen by the time they start first grade, will be different, in discernible ways, from those who have not watched television. If this proposition is accepted, it inevitably follows that an entity called *the television generation* exists, and that it differs from previous generations in ways related to its early television-watching experiences.

As the first children who grew up watching considerable amounts of television—that so-called television generation—came of age in the late sixties and early seventies, certain across-the-board changes began appearing throughout America. Notable among them was a decline in young people's verbal skills, both reading and writing, and a widespread decline in community involvement throughout society. Many have connected these changes to the arrival of television as a mass medium.

To this day these declines have not been reversed. But of course the television generation never really ended. It is still with us today. Year after year, decade after decade, children who grow up watching extensive amounts of television throughout their childhood— that is to say just about all children—belong to the television generation. If indeed television has been instrumental in bringing about these inauspicious societal changes, then we must resign ourselves to their permanence. They will be with us until viewing patterns change.

Mystery of the Declining SATs

There is an old, unsolved mystery regarding scores on the SATs, those tests of verbal and mathematical abilities that high school students must take to be accepted into most colleges. In the mid-1960s the average scores on the verbal part of the SATs began an almost twenty year decline. In a range from 200 to 800 points, the average scores went from 478 in 1964 to 424 in 1980—a drop of 54 points. At the beginning of the 1980s the scores began to level off, and have stayed within five points of 424 to this day.

What brought about this troubling decline? Why did it begin just when it did? People have been trying to find the answer to these questions for years. Yet no one seems to have pursued a related question that may offer a clue to the mystery: What caused the decline to end around 1980, with no significant decreases or increases after that? Juxtaposing the SAT scores of high school students during the last forty or so years with some statistics about TV ownership and viewing times during those years, may help to answer all three of these questions.

In 1977, when the scores had almost reached their lowest point, a panel commissioned by the College Board concluded that a major factor for the lower scores was the greater diversity of students taking the test—more minority students, some of them not native speakers of English, were now striving to get into college. Yet the great increase in minority test-takers cannot be the explanation: the verbal scores of white, middle-class, native-speaking students had declined along with everyone else's scores.

Various other explanations have been offered for the decline. A Cornell sociologist blamed it on the dumbing down of text books. He showed that latter-day sixth-grade texts are on the same level of difficulty as fourth-grade McGuffey readers were in 1896 and pointed out that the decline began when the first wave of Baby Boomers, who had used those simplified text books, sat down at the SAT test tables.

But he didn't explain why the decline suddenly ended around 1980, though the same texts remained in the classrooms.

Others have suggested less effective teaching in the schools. Yet that wouldn't explain why the decline has been greater in verbal skills than in math skills. And even if it turned out that only reading and language arts teaching had fallen off, while good teaching, for some reason, had managed to prevail for math, it still would not explain why the decline leveled off after a number of years.

How about television's arrival in American homes as a primary cause? The timing is right. The first generation of children who had watched television during a significant part of their childhood sat down to take its first college boards during the mid-1960s, just as the decline began.

The fact that the verbal scores went down far more than the math scores lends support to the theory that television was a causal factor. As chapter 7 argues, extensive television viewing affects young children's verbal development more than the development of their visual or spatial abilities. And as we have seen, numerous studies have shown a strong negative association between television viewing and school performance. Reading achievement seems especially vulnerable to the effects of excessive television viewing. Meanwhile reading, it is universally acknowledged, is the key to academic success.

If indeed television viewing, whether directly or through the experiences it displaces, adversely affects children's verbal abilities, then the steady decline of verbal SAT scores starting in the mid-1960s may be explained by the steady increase in television ownership year after year from 1950 on. In 1950 fewer than 8 percent of American families owned TV sets. By 1954 more than half had televisions. By 1957, 78 percent of families were set owners, and by 1964, almost everyone—92 percent of families—had become TV viewers. The saturation point had just about been reached, though set ownership would inch up another 4 percent over the next twenty years.

The decline in scores began in the mid-1960s. That's exactly when the first children who had spent their formative years watching TV—those who were about three in 1950 turned sixteen or seventeen and took the test. Every year through the sixties and seventies, thanks to the increase in set ownership, a larger cohort of TV watchers took their SATs, and every year, the scores went down, down, down: from 478 in 1964 to 471 in 1966 to 460 in 1970 to 445 in 1973 to 434 in 1975 to 429 in 1978 and finally to 424 in 1980. That's the year when the scores stopped going down. Why? At least partly because the saturation point had been reached around 1964. So sixteen years later the scores bottomed out. They have stayed at about the same level ever since.

Another explanation for the steady, two-decade-long decline lies in the steady increase in children's viewing time from 1950 through the 1970s. The students who scored 478 in 1964 had watched virtually no television during their formative years, having been born before TV became a mass medium. They probably didn't acquire a time-consuming TV habit until they were in high school, with a lot of reading and other verbal experience under their belts by the time they took their SATs.

After 1950 children's average weekly television-viewing time began to rise, year after year. One study indicates that first- and sixth-graders (the two groups chosen for that particular study) were watching about an hour more television daily in 1970 than in 1959, and that Sunday viewing had increased by more than two and a half hours for the sixth-graders. The rise in viewing time eventually leveled off—after all, there wasn't that much more time left in the day, after schoolwork, chores, sports, and a few other activities that continued to compete with television for children's time. At that point the decline leveled off as well.

Another suggestive pattern emerges when noting that the decrease is characterized by changes in the two extremes—fewer high scores and more low scores—rather than an across-the-board slippage.

Why the decrease in high scores? In 1959 the brightest sixth-graders were found to be among the heaviest users of television while the brightest high school students were found to be lighter viewers (and heavier readers) than their less gifted classmates. Anxious parents were reassured, figuring that television would have little effect on their children's destinies since by tenth grade the bright students turned to books just as they had always done.

But by 1970 this comforting trend had been reversed. The Surgeon General's report showed that now *more* of the brighter students in tenth grade were heavy users of television than heavy users of books. Television now reigned supreme in the lives of the group that had once contained the most avid readers—the most gifted students.

As these brightest students watched more TV, their college board scores began to decline. Year after year the number of students scoring in the 600 to 800 range on the Verbal SATs dropped steadily, going from 112,000 in 1972, to fewer than 72,000 in 1990, a decrease of more than a third.

Why had the scores of those best and brightest test-takers taken a dive? It seems likely that before they succumbed to television, their verbal and analytic abilities had been sharpened and deepened by extensive reading. As more of these students replaced books with TV viewing, their scores decreased dramatically.

Making Inferences

Since the early 1970s the federal government's National Assessment of Educational Progress (NAEP) has been administering tests in various subjects to representative groups of schoolchildren throughout the nation. Its purpose: to monitor changes in school achievement patterns over a period of time. The picture emerging from the NAEP surveys has not been an encouraging one—a steady decline in academic skills at all grade levels during the 1970s and 1980s and a leveling out since then.

One particular skill measured by the NAEP that showed a significant decline—an advanced reading skill called "inferential reasoning"—has caused particular concern among parents and educators. Inferential reasoning is the ability, beyond the mere mechanics of reading, to draw conclusions, form judgments, and create new ideas out of what one reads. The ability to make inferences is essential to meaningful reading in literature, history, science, and other subjects. Without this complex ability, reading becomes a superficial exercise.

Is there reason to connect the decline in inferential reasoning with children's time-consuming television experiences? As it happens, an ingenious project carried out by a Harvard University research organization named Project Zero helps us make this very connection.

The experiment was designed to investigate the effects of different media on children's comprehension of story material. As it happens, it cast particular light on the vital ability under discussion here—to make inferences.

For the study, the experimenters prepared two versions of a children's story, *The Three Robbers,* by Tomi Ungerer. The "book version" was simply the illustrated storybook, which was to be read to one group of children by an experimenter. The "TV version," to be shown on a video screen to a second group of children, used the book illustrations for its visual material, animation being provided only by a camera moving over the pictures in the book. The narration for the TV version, moreover, was spoken by the same experimenter who read the story in real life to the "book-version" children. Thus the two versions were virtually identical in all aspects save the medium of transmission. In this way the researchers hoped to ferret out any differences in children's response to material transmitted by different media.

The results were startling. Compared to the children who saw the presentation on TV, the "book-version" children remembered more of the story when tested at the end of their session and were able to recall more details when asked to do so on their own. In addition, the "book-version" children were far more likely to repeat the exact words or phrases that had appeared in the book, while the video children were prone to paraphrase.

But according to Howard Gardner, then the director of Project Zero, "the most intriguing media differences concern the ability to make inferences." As he described it, although the TV-version children and the book-version children tended to reach the same conclusions about the story in the course of their subsequent testing, the lines of reasoning each group used to reach that conclusion were significantly different. The television children, Gardner reported, seemed to rely overwhelmingly on the visual aspects of the story as seen on the screen. Rarely did they go beyond that specific reality to interpret the story's meaning. In contrast, "book children are far more likely to draw on their own personal experience or apply their own real-world knowledge," explained Gardner.

"In all," Gardner concluded, "television emerges as a much more self-contained experience for children, and within its boundaries, the visual component emerges as paramount. The book experience, on the other hand, allows for greater access to the story's language and suggests greater expanses of time and space. Books may encourage readers to make connections with other realms of life."

Of course there is no scientific proof to show that the thousands of hours American children spend watching television have caused a deterioration in their complex thinking skills. But again, common sense alone makes the strongest case—that if the ability to interpret verbal material in a meaningful way is not developed during the course of television viewing, then a population of children habituated to a different way of processing material will be deficient in that particular skill when it comes to taking in material via another medium—that is, via reading. That decline will be measurable on standardized exams.

Writing Is Book Talk

A corollary of the decline in reading skills since the mid-1960s is a similar, if not more pronounced, deterioration in *writing* skills of American students: "Plagued by increasing numbers of students who are unable to write coherent sentences . . . more and more colleges and universities are finding they have to offer remedial work in such basic skills," began a 1976 article, one of the first to comment on this decline.

According to past surveys by the National Assessment of Educational Progress, the writing performance of American students has been steadily deteriorating. The majority of students tend to use only the simplest sentence structure and the most elementary vocabulary when they write. The essays of thirteen- to seventeen-year-olds are far more awkward, incoherent, and disorganized today than the writings of their counterparts of previous decades.

Especially telling among the findings of the NAEP are those concerning advanced writing skills. Among the high-school students who have acquired the basic mechanics of grammar, spelling, and syntax, who can produce at least "marginally acceptable narratives," the percentage able to handle the more difficult task of organizing an argument and writing persuasively dropped dramatically between 1969 and 1979, from 21 to 15 percent.

For example, a test requiring students to write an "open-ended" analysis of two poems, found that 51.2 percent of seventeen-year-olds wrote adequate analyses in 1971, while by 1980 only 41.2 percent were able to do so. As education critic Diane Ravitch noted after examining the writings of one group tested by the NAEP: "The students wrote as if they were writing commercials. There was no continuity from sentence to sentence, no sense of what makes a paragraph; no sense of an underlying connection from one paragraph to the next."

Students' writing skills have not improved since the 1980s. The latest writing assessment by the NAEP, conducted in 1996, found scores for fourth- and eighth-graders relatively unchanged during the last two decades, while eleventh-graders' scores were lower in 1996 than they were in 1984.

The connection between the decline in children's reading abilities and the decline in their writing skills is not hard to make: educators understand well that a student who cannot read with true comprehension will never learn to write well. "Writing, after all, is book talk," said a teacher of language education, "and you only learn book talk by reading."

A high-school English teacher observes:

> *There is no question that your success as a student depends enormously on your vocabulary, both in what you can understand as you read and in how you reason as you write, and there is no way to build up a good vocabulary except by reading—there just is none.*

"Learning to write," wrote Carlos Baker, author and educator, "is the hardest, most important thing any child does. Learning to write is learning to think."

Professor Baker was undoubtedly referring to the logical, verbal kind of thinking that is required for intellectual efforts. For such work the skills involved in learning to write effectively are surely necessary. But a child can learn other ways of thinking, those characterized by rapid scanning and visual receptivity. Learning to write well will neither encourage this nonverbal form of thinking, nor, conversely, will nonverbal thinking be helpful in acquiring writing skills. Quite the contrary, the two work at cross-purposes. It is, however, nonverbal thinking that is nurtured by television watching.

A professor of English at a Midwestern university observed:

> *So many of my students can't seem to hear when a sentence should end or where a semicolon should go as against where a*

comma should go. It's not a physical loss. Their ears hear words. But the mechanism that recognizes a complete thought and distinguishes it from an incomplete thought seems to be missing. Their thinking doesn't seem to have a subject-verb structure built into it, and they are not able to measure incoming sentences against that subject-verb structure and either declare that they need a period at the end or that they mustn't have a period at the end. And mind you, these are bright students. There's nothing wrong with their thinking. It's just different in certain ways.

The role television has played in the national decline of reading and writing skills has not been precisely assessed—perhaps it never can be. But the nonverbal nature of the television experience, and the great involvement of children with television from their earliest years to the end of their school careers, makes a connection between television watching and inadequate writing skills seem inevitable. In this regard, one of America's most beloved writers, E. B. White, once said, "Short of throwing away all the television sets, I really don't know what we can do about writing."

Television and the Social Chill

Starting in the late 1960s or early 1970s, Americans seemed to grow considerably less community-minded than they had been in years past. Club membership and church attendance went down. Political participation decreased sharply. Time spent in informal socializing went down. The trend was not a temporary blip accompanying the social upheavals of that era; it only accelerated during the next two decades.

In a meticulously documented book, *Bowling Alone: The Collapse and Revival of American Community,* Harvard social historian Robert Putnam points out that the first television generation was precisely the one that marked the beginning of the decline.

It seems mysterious at first. As the highly civic-minded population that grew up around the time of World War II began to face retirement, you'd expect the Baby Boomers following in their footsteps to become even more involved in community activities and to grow even richer in that form of wealth Putnam calls "social capital." After all, education had always been considered the best predictor of civic engagement, and the Boomers, as a group, were the best educated generation in America's history.

But it did not happen that way. The generation that came to maturity in the late 1960s proved to be more individualistic, more inner-directed, more likely to emphasize the personal and private over the public and collective. The Boomers did not join organizations or churches or clubs as much as their mothers and fathers had, nor did they get involved in community affairs at anywhere near the level of the preceding generation. The generation that followed them, the Gen X-ers, as they have been dubbed, were even less community minded. More interested in accumulating individual wealth, more focused on self-improvement than on the improvement of their local schools or government, they were even less likely to join civic organizations or volunteer in their neighborhoods.

What caused the great difference? According to Putnam's careful investigations, television emerges as the major instrument of change.

Why should the entry of television into American life bring about a reduction in civic engagement? In a certain sense it's a simple matter of time: time spent watching television is time not spent at social activities outside the home. Putnam sums it up: "More television watching means less of virtually every form of civic participation and social involvement."

But the answer may be more than a simple time equation. Though social scientists may never discover exactly how the experience of watching television works to alter old patterns of social involvement, it is hard to deny that a major social change has occurred, and that television is part of its etiology. As Putnam points out: "Men and women raised in the sixties, seventies and eighties not only watch television *more* than those born in the thirties, forties and fifties; they even watch television differently—more habitually, even mindlessly—and those different ways in which television is used are linked in turn to different degrees of civic engagement."

Putnam uses data from demographic comparisons of heavy and light viewers to bring television's role in civic participation into sharp focus. Surveys reveal that light viewers are far more active in their communities than heavy viewers, across all socioeconomic boundaries. They attend more public meetings, they play leadership roles in local organizations more frequently. The heavy viewers, on the other hand, are less involved in every social aspect. They spend less time visiting friends, less time writing letters, less time volunteering, less time joining clubs: the catalog of diminished activities is long. The most important statistic of all is this: in the general population there are many, many more heavy viewers than light viewers. Putnam concludes unequivocally: "A major commitment to television viewing—such as most of us have come to have—is incompatible with a major commitment to community life."

Concrete evidence that television plays a major role in reducing community involvement was amply provided by the Canadian "natural experiment" described earlier. The researchers studying the effects of television's introduction into a town that had never had TV (Notel), found that before TV's introduction Notel inhabitants were much more active in community activities than their counterparts in towns having only one or many TV channels available. Once TV was introduced into Notel, participation in community activities diminished significantly, not only among those who were peripheral members of groups or organizations, but among those who had been centrally involved as well. With television's entry into Notel's homes, children played fewer outdoor sports. Attendance at dances, parties, and suppers decreased.

What Is to be Done?

Well, so what if people are less socially involved? Society may be different but is it necessarily worse? In *Bowling Alone* Robert Putnam proceeds to document a fascinating link between a community's level of civic involvement and the outcome of its citizens, especially its children: the greater the community involvement, the better the outcome.

There's much evidence to show that a community rich in social capital provides benefits far beyond the satisfactions that social activities generally offer. To give one of many examples, statistics show that when parents are actively involved in their children's schools, the kids do better—at every grade level, and in every socioeconomic category. "At Harvard as well as in Harlem, social connectedness boosts educational attainment," Putnam writes.

In addition, social cohesion leads to safer neighborhoods, to greater economic prosperity, improved physical and mental health, a greater sense of fulfillment. Altogether, there's a strong case to be made for the important benefits conferred by community involvement.

The last part of *Bowling Alone* tackles the inevitable. "What is to be done?" Putnam remains hopeful that social connectedness can be restored to American society and proposes that the television industry itself might spearhead a movement toward greater social involvement. "No sector of American society will have more influence on the future state of our social capital than the electronic mass media. . . . If we are to reverse the adverse trends of the last three decades, the electronic entertainment and telecommunications industry must become a big part of the solution instead of a big part of the problem."

Continuing in that direction, Putnam issues a challenge to that industry: "Let us find ways to ensure that by 2010 Americans will spend less leisure time sitting passively alone in front of glowing screens and more time in active connection with our fellow citizens. Let us foster new forms of electronic entertainment and communication that reinforce community engagement rather than forestalling it." Similarly, Putnam calls on software designers and communications technologists to make the Internet a force for rebuilding community in America.

Putnam's hope that the industry will provide an answer to the problems it has created seems over-optimistic, to say the least. As Brandon Centerwall, a physician, once observed, "if someone were to call on the tobacco industry to cut back production as a matter of social conscience and out of concern for public health, we would regard that person as being simple-minded, if not frankly deranged." Why, he asked, do people persistently assume that the television industry operates according to a higher standard?

The solution cannot be sought from the telecommunications industry. For if indeed those who grow up watching great amounts of television prove to be less civic-minded when they come of age, there is nothing the industry can do about it. Even if they were to try to "reinforce community engagement rather than forestalling it," it would be too late. For as Putnam has noted earlier in his book, "The more fully that any given generation is exposed to television in its formative years, the lower its civic engagement during adulthood."

If a new generation is to come along that will once again be rich in social capital, then the challenge must be made to parents, not to TV moguls or electronic techies. Only parents can find ways to ensure that during the most vulnerable stages of development, children spend less time staring at the flickering screen. Only if great numbers of parents heed the challenge by limiting their children's viewing time, encouraging them to play with other kids, to read, to daydream, to practice musical instruments, to become involved with hobbies that might lead to lifelong interests—only then might a different, more public-spirited generation emerge. Perhaps this is another form of unrealistic idealism—but at least this one has a modest chance of working.

The Passive Pull

Controlling television or even eliminating it entirely will not automatically lead to family happiness. While television's presence often puts serious obstacles in the way of a fulfilling family life, its mere absence does not guarantee that parents and children will suddenly coalesce into a real family. There's always the passive pull to contend with, that deep-rooted inner force that too often makes it so hard to pull oneself together and *do* something—to read, to write a letter, to go to a meeting, to play with one's children—anything.

Television's attraction is so powerful precisely because it gratifies the passive side of human nature that everyone is endowed with in differing degrees. Thus an important step toward a more satisfying family life is to become aware of this passive pull, to assess its power, and to consciously struggle against it. For most parents this requires a true dedication to the family over all personal pursuits, and a firm resolve to make their children's childhood a rich and distinctive experience, one that will serve as a resource for the rest of their lives. With television under control, this can become an achievable goal.

Yet a feeling of helplessness often surrounds the issue of television control. It seems a formidable undertaking, far easier said than done.

If parents would recognize the ultimate toll a time-consuming investment in television takes on young children's ways of thinking and behaving, they might change their focus from *what* their children are watching to why and how much time they are spending at this single activity and especially to what they are missing as a result.

If parents would understand that they are likely to end up with less manageable kids when they replace direct, confident child-rearing strategies with the electronic baby-sitter, they might resist the powerful temptation to use the plug-in drug as a respite from child care.

If parents would open their eyes to television's undermining effects on family meals, conversations, games and rituals, they might finally decide that the price of accepting TV as a dominant force in the family is too high to pay.

In the complex age of technology, we may feel powerless in the face of the uncontrollable machine that modern society seems to have become. But we can still assert our wills in the face of that real and tangible machine in our homes, the television set. We can learn to control it so that it does not control us.

Helpful Organizations

TV-Turnoff Network
1611 Connecticut Ave NW, #3A
Washington, D.C. 20009
www.tvturnoff.org

Founded in 1994, this ground-breaking group was the first to organize a National TV-Turnoff Week, now a highly successful annual event. Also offering a pro-literacy grammar school program, "More Reading, Less TV," the organization's stated goal is "To encourage children and adults to watch much less television in order to promote healthier lives and communities."

Center for Commercial-Free Public Education
1714 Franklin St, Suite 100-306
Oakland, CA 94612
www.mediaandthefamily.org

This watchdog organization addresses issues of commercialism in public schools. Founded in 1993 in reaction to the introduction of Channel One into schools around the country, it still focuses much of its attention to this program, providing information about it, and offering ideas to schools and communities for challenging it.

The Television Project
2311 Kimball Place
Silver Spring, MD 20910
www.tvp.org

A support organization for families, it offers workshops and opportunities for families struggling with television control.

Learning in the Real World
725 Main Street, Suite 232
Woodland, California 95695
www.realworld.org

A California-based organization, Learning in the Real World questions the assumption that computers play a valuable role in early childhood education, and advocates reality-based experiences in place of the virtual kind. Its Web site includes links to other organizations questioning the rush to computerize the classroom.

Alliance for Childhood
P.O Box 444
College Park, MD 20741
www.allianceforchildhood.net

A consortium of educators, physicians and others concerned about the negative effects of computers on young children, Alliance for Childhood addresses the fact that our emphasis on technology is diverting us from promoting children's urgent social and educational needs. These include: the need for more personal attention from caring adults, for a closer relationship to nature, for access to creative play, and for involvement with the arts.

National Parent Information Network
http://ericps.ed.uiuc.edu/npin

This Web site offers access to material from ERIC, the federally funded Educational Resource Information Center. In addition to providing full texts of recent studies about children's TV, computer, and video game usage, NPIN also offers general information about child development and parenting.

Read Across America
www.nea.org/readacross

An annual pro-literacy initiative of the National Education Association, Read Across America calls for every child in America to celebrate reading on March 2, Dr. Seuss's birthday. In 2001, thirty-five million children and adults participated, spurred on by a roster of celebrities that included first lady Laura Bush, actor Morgan Freeman and pitcher Pedro Martinez. The NEA website offers ideas and information for schools, communities, and parents wishing to plan and organize a reading event on Dr. Seuss's next birthday.

Brief Bibliography

Alison Armstrong and Charles Casement. *The Child and the Machine: How Computers Put Our Children's Education at Risk.* Beltsville, MD: Robins Lane Press, 2000.

Jane M. Healy. *The Endangered Mind.* New York: Touchstone Books, 1999.

———. *Failure to Connect: How Computers affect Our Children's Minds— And What We Can Do About It.* New York: Touchstone Books, 1999.

Robert Kubey and Mihaly Csikszentmihalyi. *Television and The Quality of Life: How Viewing Shapes Everyday Experience,* Hillsdale. NJ: Lawrence Erlbaum Assoc., 1990.

Joel Meyrowitz. *No Sense of Place: The Impact of Electronic Media on Social Behavior.* New York: Oxford University Press, 1985.

Robert D. Putnam. *Bowling Alone: The Collapse and Revival of American Community.* New York: Simon & Schuster, 2000.

Jeffrey Scheuer. *The Sound Bite Society: Television and the American Mind.* New York: Routledge, 2001.

Jim Trelease. *The Read-Aloud Handbook, 4th Edition.* New York: Penguin Books, 1995.

Tannis MacBeth Williams, editor. *The Impact of Television: A Natural Experiment in Three Communities.* Orlando, FL: Academic Press, Inc., 1986.

Endnotes

Preface

ix   D.W. Winnicott, *Mother and Child*, New York: Basic Books, 1957.

Chapter 1. It's Not What You Watch

Page

4   ***Nielsen statistics:*** Nielsen Media Research, 2000, Report on Television.

4   ***School-aged children's viewing statistics:*** National Center for Education Statistics, NAEP, 1999 Long Term Trend Assessment, Washington, D.C., 2000.

8   Urie Bronfenbrenner, "Who Cares for America's Children?" address presented at the Conference of the National Association for the Education of Young Children, 1970.

8   Tannis MacBeth Williams, editor, *The Impact of Television: A Natural Experiment in Three Communities*. Florida: Academic Press, Inc., 1986.

10   ***"According to a recent comprehensive survey":*** Jeffrey Stanger and Natalia Gridina, "Media in the Home 1999: The Fourth Annual Survey of Parents and Children." The Annenberg Public Policy Center, Washington, D.C., 2000.

10   ***Quote about ACT goals:*** Evelyn Kaye Sarson, "How TV Threatens Your Child," *Parents' Magazine*, August 1972.

12   ***"A network executive once stated":*** Norman Morris, *Television's Child*. Boston: Little, Brown, 1971.

13   ***Quote by 20-year-old:*** Joyce Maynard, "Growing Up with TV," *TV Guide*, July 5, 1975.

14   Jack Gould, "Family Life 1948 AT (After Television)," *The New York Times,* August 1, 1948.

Chapter 2. A Changed State of Consciousness

page

16   ***Dr. Edward Palmer quote:*** personal interview, May 7, 1975.

18   T. Berry Brazelton, "How to Tame the TV Monster," *Redbook,* April, 1972.

19   Letter from Matthew Dumont, M.D., *American Journal of Psychiatry,* Vol. 133, April, 1976.

19   ***Quote from "another psychiatrist":*** Dr. Werner I. Halpern, quoted in Philip Jones, "The Educational TV in Your School May Be Anything But Educational," *The American School Board Journal,* March 1974.

19   Gerald Lesser, *Children and Television.* New York: Random House, 1974.

Chapter 3. The Power of the Medium

page

26   Much of the material in the section "Why Is It So Hard To Stop Watching?" is based on a reading of Julian Hochberg and Virginia Brooks's "The Perception of Television Displays," a prepublication draft of a survey and analysis of the basic perceptual determinants that may affect viewers' responses to the television experience. It was commissioned by the Television Laboratory at WNET/13 during the mid 1970s. Twenty-five years later a diligent search did not discover any published version of the final book.

28   ***Quote about "early experiences with electronic displays":*** Hochberg & Brooks.

28   ***Quote from "an early commentator" about HDTV:*** Raymond Sokolov, "The Best TV Picture You've Never Seen," *The Wall Street Journal,* March 20, 1997.

29   ***Quote by a BBC executive:*** Martin Mayer, *About Television.* New York: Harper and Row, 1972.

29   ***Experiments demonstrating the importance of outside stimuli:*** J. Gewirtz, "A Factor Analysis of Some Attention-Seeking Behaviors of Young Children," *Child Development,* Vol. 27, 1956.

31   ***Survey reporting on use of TV deprivation as punishment:*** Stanger and
      Gridina, op. cit.

33   Lawrence Kubie, *Neurotic Distortion and the Creative Process.* Lawrence:
      University of Kansas Press, 1958.

36   ***"Media Burn":*** Cyclops, "The West Coast—Is It Live or on Tape?" *The
      New York Times,* July 20, 1975.

37   Robin Smith, "Television Addiction," in Jennings Bryant and Dolf Zill-
      mann's *Perspectives on Media Effects.* Hillsdale, NJ: Lawrence Erlbaum As-
      sociates, 1986.

38   ***Source of Smith's definition of addiction:*** Solomon R.L and Corbit
      J. D., "An opponent-process theory of motivation: I. Temporal dynamics
      of affect." *Psychological Review,* 81, 1974.

38   Robert Kubey & Mihaly Csikszentmihalyi, *Television and the Quality of
      Life: How Viewing Shapes Everyday Experiences.* Hillsdale, NJ: Lawrence
      Erlbaum, 1990.

38   ***Kubey explains further:*** Robert Kubey, "A Body at Rest Tends to Remain
      Glued to the Tube," *The New York Times,* August 5, 1990.

Chapter 4. The Experts

page

39   ***Quote beginning "In general":*** Benjamin Spock, *Baby and Child Care.*
      New York: Pocket Books, 1963.

40   ***Quote beginning "come to a reasonable but definite"*** Ibid., 1976 edi-
      tion.

40   ***Quote beginning "Of all the media"*** Ibid., 1998 edition.

41   ***In 1984:*** American Academy of Pediatrics, Task Force on Children and
      Television, "Children, Adolescents and Television," *News and Comment,*
      1984.

41   ***In 1995: "Children, Adolescents and Television,"*** Policy Statement, *Pe-
      diatrics* Vol. 96, no. 4, October 1995.

41–42 ***New policy statement by AAP:*** Media Education, Policy Statement, *Pe-
      diatrics,* Vol. 104, no. 2, August 1999.

42–43 ***Study monitoring metabolic rates:*** Tufts University Diet and Nutrition
      Letter, June 1992.

43   ***Diabetes report:*** Denise Grady, "Diabetes Rises; Doctors Foresee a Harsh Impact," *The New York Times,* August 24, 2000.

43   ***Decline in fitness attributed to excessive TV watching:*** Jane Brody, "Fitness Gap is America's Recipe for Fat Youth," *The New York Times,* September 19, 2000.

43   J. Owens, R. Maxim et al., "Television-viewing Habits and Sleep Disturbance in School Children," *Pediatrics* Vol. 104 No. 3, September 1999, p. e27.

44   F. Balague, M. Nordin et al., "Non-specific low-back pain among schoolchildren," *J. Spinal Disorders,* October 1994.

5. Television and Violence: A different approach

page

47   ***Review of research undertaken by American Psychological Society:*** *Big World, Small Screen* Lincoln: U. of Nebraska Press, 1992, citing research studies : Freedman, J.L., "Effect of television violence on aggressiveness," *Psychological Bulletin* 96[2] 1984, and Liebert, R.M. & Sprafkin, J. *The Early Window: Effects of Television on Children and Youth.* New York: Pergamon, 1988.

48   ***Selma Fraiberg quote:*** from an address to Child Study Association of America, 1961.

48–49   ***Television critic's quote:*** Edith Efron, "Does Television Violence Really Affect TV Viewers?" *TV Guide,* June 14, 1975.

49   Victor Cline, *The Desensitization of Children to Television Violence.* Bethesda, MD: National Institute of Health, 1972.

50   ***New Study on TV and Agression:*** T. N. Robinson et al., "Effects of Reducing Children's Television and Video Game Use on Aggressive Behavior," *Archives of Pediatrics and Adolescent Medicine,* January 2001.

50   ***Program that found imaginative ways to motivate children to cut down TV:*** Although I didn't know it until doing research for this edition, the researchers used my book *Unplugging the Plug-In Drug* [Viking/Penguin, 1987] as a model for their Turnoff period. For the months after the turnoff, parents were provided with a commercial device called "TV Allowance" to limit TV and video game use.

6. Television for Tots

page

56   ***1986 Japanese survey:*** S. I. Kodaira, "Television's Role in Early Child-
            hood Education in Japan." Tokyo: NHK Broadcasting Culture Research
            Institute, 1987.

56   ***Survey about "With Mother" viewing:*** S.I. Kodaira and T. Akiyama,
            "'With Mother' and its Viewers: Behavior Monitoring of two- and three-
            year-olds," NHK Broadcasting Culture Research Institute, 1987.

56   ***Survey about TV sets in baby's room:*** N. Kobayashi, "Infants in the Age
            of Television—Effects of Audio and Visual Broadcasting on Pre-birth Ba-
            bies to Early Childhood." Newsletter of the Hoso-Bunka Foundation,
            No. 29, December 1989, cited in "Television and Children: Towards the
            Millenium," by W. Cordellan, *Communications Research Trends*, Vol. 10,
            no. 3, 1990.

56–57   Nicole Wise, "A Video Made Just for the Diaper Set." *The New York
            Times,* May 17, 1990.

57–58   Susan E. Linn and Alvin F. Poussaint, "The Trouble with Teletubbies,"
            The American Prospect, May–June 1999.

59   S. Ball and G. Bogatz, *The First Year of Sesame Street: An Evaluation,* and
            The Second Year of Sesame Street: A Continuing Evaluation. New Jersey:
            Educational Testing Service, 1970, 1971.

59   Thomas D. Cook, Hilary Appleton, Ross F. Conner, Ann Shaffer, Gary
            Tamkin, and Stephen J. Weber, *Sesame Street Revisited.* New York: Russell
            Sage Foundation, 1975.

61   ***1995 study:*** John C. Wright and Aletha C. Huston, "Effects of educa-
            tional TV viewing of lower income preschoolers on academic skills, school
            readiness and school adjustment one to three years later," Center for
            Research on the Influences of Television on Children, Dept. of Human
            Development, U. of Kansas, 1995.

61–62   ***Dorothy Cohen quote:*** Edith Spiegel, "Yes, Sesame Street Has Its De-
            tractors," *The New York Times,* August 5, 1979.

62   ***Jerome Singer update***: personal communication, January 19, 2000.

62   Jane M. Healy, *Endangered Minds: Why Children Don't Think—and What
            We Can Do About It.* New York: Touchstone Books, 1999.

63   Tannis MacBeth Williams, The Impact Of Television, op. cit.

64   ***Study of preschooler's comprehension:*** Bernard Z. Friedlander, Harriet S. Wetstone, Christopher S. Scott, "Suburban Preschool Children's Comprehension of an Age-Appropriate Informational Television Program," *Child Development,* Vol. 45, 1974.

64   ***"In another study:"*** Leifer, Collins, Gross, Taylor, Andrews, and Blackmer, "Developmental Aspects of Variables Relevant to Observational Learning," *Child Development,* 1970.

64   ***"In a third study":*** Coates and Hartup, "Age and Verbalization in Observational Learning," *Development Psychology,* Vol. 1, 1969.

64   ***"More recently researchers . . .":*** Couch Potato Chronicles, volume 2, no. 4, Television Viewing Lab, a service of WGBH Research, Boston, MA—617-492-2777

65   ***"Even children as old as eight":*** S. L. Calvert and B. A. Watkins, "Recall of Television Content as a Function of Content Type and Level of Production Feature Use," paper presented at the meeting of the Society for Research in Child Development, San Francisco, 1979.

7. Television and the Brain

Page

68   ***An experiment published in 1972:*** Mark R. Rosenzweig, Edward L. Bennet, and Marian Cleeves Diamond, "Brain Changes in Response to Environment," *Scientific American,* February 1972.

69   ***Marian Cleeves Diamond's quote:*** Television and the Preparation of the Mind for Learning, Conference Proceedings, Dept of Health and Human Services, 1992.

69   Harry I. Chugani, M. E. Phelps and J. C. Mazziotta, "Positron Emission Tomography Study of Human Brain Function Development," *Annals of Neurology,* vol. 22, 1987, p. 487–497.

69   ***"According to other neuroscientists":*** Sandra Blakeslee, "Studies Show Talking with Infants Shapes Basis of Ability to Think," *The New York Times,* April 17, 1997.

70   ***"One of many such experiments":*** Wiesel and Hubel, "Effects of Visual Deprivation on Morphology and Physiology of Cells in Cats' Lateral Geniculate Body," *Journal of Neurophysiology,* Vol. 26, 1963.

70   ***"Other experiments with chimpanzees":*** A. Riesen, "Arrested Vision," *The Nature and Nurture of Behavior,* ed. Greenough. San Francisco: W. H. Freeman Co., 1973.

70   ***Among the studies of the effects of institutionalization are:*** H. Skeels, "Adult Status of Children with Contrasting Early Life Experiences," *Monographs on Social Research in Child Development,* vol. 31, 1966; Coleman and Provence, "Environmental Retardation in Infants Living in Families," *Pediatrics,* vol. 19, 1957; R. Spitz, "Hospitalism," *Psychoanalytic Study of the Child,* vol. 1, 1945; W. Goldfarb, "Effects of Psychological Deprivation in Infancy and Subsequent Stimulation," *American Journal of Psychiatry,* vol. 102, 1945.

70   ***Head Start's effectiveness:*** Maya Pines, "Head Head Start," *The New York Times Magazine,* October 26, 1975, and Urie Bronfenbrenner, "Is Early Intervention Effective?" report for Department of Health, Education, and Welfare (Washington, D.C., 1974).

71   John T. Bruer, *The Myth of The First Three Years: A New Understanding of Early Brain Development and Lifelong Learning.* New York: The Free Press, 1999.

72   ***"Researchers have demonstrated":*** Jerome Kagan, *Change and Continuity in Infancy.* New York: John Wiley & Sons Inc., 1971.

74–75   ***"Many of the evident dualities in human nature":*** See Eric H. Lenneberg, "On Explaining Language," *Science,* May 9, 1969, for a discussion of brain lateralization.

75   See Howard Gardner's, *Frames of Mind.* New York: Basic Books, 1993, for discussion of multiple intelligences.

75   The idea of two disparate forms of mental organization was suggested by Arthur J. Deikman's "Bimodal Consciousness," *Archives of General Psychiatry,* December, 1971.

76   ***Quote from director of a Harlem Center:*** Ned O'Gorman, "The Children," *The New York Times Magazine,* June 1, 1975.

77   ***Study of relationship between TV viewing and preschooler's spoken language:*** Selnow and Bettinghaus, "Television Exposure and Language Level," *Journal of Broadcasting,* 26:2, spring, 1982.

8. Television and Play

page

78   *1972 survey:* Lyle and Hoffman, "Explorations in Patterns of Television Viewing by Preschool-age Children," *Television and Social Behavior,* Vol. IV. National Institute of Mental Health, Rockville, MD, 1982.)

82   Edward Norbeck, "Man at Play," *Natural History,* December 1971.

86   "The Child and Television Drama: The Psychological Impact of Cumulative Viewing," formulated by the Committee on Social Issues, Group for the Advancement of Psychiatry, Mental Health Materials Center, New York, 1982.

86–87   Stephen J. Suomi and Harry F. Harlow, "Monkeys at Play," *Natural History,* December, 1971.

9. Television and Reading

page

92   A discussion of the "acoustic" image of words is found in H. J. Chaytor, *From Script to Print.* London: W. Heffer and Sons, 1950.

93   Bruno Bettelheim, "Parents vs. Television," *Redbook,* November 1963.

94   *The phenomenon of "aliteracy":* Beers, Kylene G., "No Time, No Interest, No Way! The Three Voices of Aliteracy," *School Library Journal,* March 1996.

96–97   *Preschooler's comprehension of the nature of TV images:* Lyle and Hoffman, "Explorations in Patterns of Television Viewing by Preschool-age Children," *Television and Social Behavior,* Vol. IV, op. cit.

97   *Survey of more than 500 fourth and fifth graders:* J. Feeley, "Interest and Media Preference of Middle Grade Children," *Reading World,* 1974.

97   *Poll of sixth graders:* California State Department of Education, "Student Achievement in California Schools, 1979–80 Annual Report," Sacramento, California, 1980.

97–98   *1992 Government report:* "Bush Says Schoolchildren Watch Too Much TV" *The New York Times,* May 5, 1992.

99   *Evidence from TV-Turnoffs:* "It's Cold Turkey for the Families on 89th Street," *New York Post,* April 22, 1977; "Kicking the TV Habit," *The New*

York Times, March 16, 1982; "Is There Life Without TV?," *The Wall Street Journal,* February 8, 1984.

99 **Study of the role of home environment on reading achievement:** Christine M. Bachen et al., "Television Viewing Behavior and the Development of Reading Skills: Survey Evidence," paper presented at the Annual Meeting of the American Educational Research Association, New York, March 1982.

100 George Steiner, "After the Book?" *Visual Language,* Vol. 6, 1972.

100–101 **Donald Barr quoted in:** Norman Morris, *Television's Child.* Boston: Little, Brown, 1971.

104 Rudolph Arnheim, *Visual Thinking.* University of California Press, 1972.

104 **Study at U. of California comparing radio and TV:** Greenfield P. et al "Is the medium the message?" *Journal of Applied Developmental Psychology* 7, 1986.

104 **Book review about Joe DiMaggio:** John Gregory Dunne, *The New Yorker Magazine,* October 30, 2000.

107 **Quote by an education writer:** Grace and Fred Hechinger, "Can TV Lead Children to Reading?" *The New York Times,* June 29, 1980.

107 **Jerzy Kosinski quote:** Horace Newcomb, *Television: The Critical View.* London: Oxford University Press, 1976.

10. Television and the School

page

108 **Summary of TV research:** *Television and Behavior: Ten Years of Scientific Progress and Implications for the '80s,* Vol. 1, Summary Report, National Institute of Mental Health, Rockville, Maryland, 1982.

108–109 **The Canadian study:** The Impact of Television: A Natural Experiment in Three Communities, op. cit.

109 **1997 study in Netherlands:** Cees. M. Koolstra et. al, "Television's Impact on children's reading comprehension and decoding," *Reading Research Quarterly,* Newark: April–June 1997.

109 **"Children who had been allowed to watch many hours":** G. Burton, J. M. Calonico, and D. R. McSeveny, "Effects of Preschool Watching on First-Grade Children," *Journal of Communication,* 29:3, 1979.

109   **High I.Q. students:** M. Morgan and L. Gross, "Television Viewing, I.Q.
           and Academic Achievement," *Journal of Broadcasting,* 24:2, Spring, 1980.

109–110   **Large scale California survey:** "Coast Survey of Students Links Rise in
           TV Use to Poorer Grades," *The New York Times,* November 9, 1980.

110   National Center for Educational Statistics, NAEP, 1999 Long Term As-
           sessment.

110   **1999 survey:** *Kids and Media @ the New Millenium.* Menlo Park, CA:
           The Henry J Kaiser Family Foundation, 1999.

111   "French Schoolchildren Found to Eat Little and Work Too Much," *The
           New York Times,* October 27, 1976.

111   **Quote by N.Y. administrator:** "Helping Kids with TV," *Daily News,*
           January 2, 1979.

111–112   Walter Goodman, "Literacy Does Not Mean Looking at the Pictures,"
           The New York Times, December 27, 1990.

113   **Teacher who assigned Lou Grant:** "The Decline in Homework,"
           Newsweek, January 8, 1979.

114   Joel Meyrowitz, *No Sense of Place: The Impact of Electronic Media on So-
           cial Behavior.* New York: Oxford University Press, 1985.

114–115   **Quote by high school journalism teacher:** *Television in School.* The
           Quarterly of the National Council for Families and Television, Spring
           1989.

116   **Quote from the American Academy of Pediatrics:** "Required TV pro-
           gram in schools encourages poor lifestyle choices," *AAP News* November
           2000.

116   **"As one parent complained to a reporter"** Constance L. Hays, "Chan-
           nel One's Mixed Grades in School," *The New York Times,* December 5,
           1999.

117   William Hoynes, *News for a Captive Audience: The Case of Channel One.*
           Poughkeepsie, NY: Vassar College, January, 1997.

117   Center for Commercial-Free Public Education, *www.commercialfree.org*

11. Before Television

page

121   Lloyd de Mause, "The Evolution of Childhood," in *History of Childhood.*
        New York: Psychohistory Press, 1974.

122   **Children literally frightened to death:** ibid.

12. Free Time and Resourcefulness

page

138   Russell Hoban, *Nothing to Do.* New York: Harper and Row, 1964.

143–144 **Research on the quality of attention:** J. Gewirtz, "A Factor Analysis of
        Some Attention-Seeking Behaviors of Young Children," *Child Develop-
        ment,* Vol. 27, 1956.

144   **"A later research study . . .":** R. R. Sears, L. Rau, and R. Alpert, *Identi-
        fication and Child Rearing.* Stanford: Stanford University Press, 1965.

13. Family Life

page

152   **Quote from writer in 1949:** Dorothy McFadden, "Television Comes to
        Our Children," *Parents' Magazine,* January 1949.

152   **Another commentator:** Henrietta Baffle, "TV and Your Child," *Parents'
        Magazine,* November 1949.

152   **Television critic:** Jack Gould, "What Is Television Doing to Us?" *The
        New York Times,* June 12, 1949.

153   **Set ownership in 2000:** Nielsen Media Research, 2000.

153   **Early study of TV's effects:** Himmelweit, Oppenheim, Vince, *Television
        and the Child.* London: Oxford University Press, 1958.

155   **Quote by writer and mother of two boys:** Eleanor Dienstag, "What Will
        the Kids Talk About? Proust?" *The New York Times,* December 24, 1972.

156   **Definition of ritual:** James H. Bossard and Eleanor S. Boll, *Ritual in
        Family Living.* Philadelphia: University of Pennsylvania Press, 1950.

156   **"Another text notes":** Bossard and Boll, *The Sociology of Child Develop-
        ment.* New York: Harper and Row, 1960.

158   **Studies of eye-to-eye contact:** Ralph V. Extine, "Visual Interaction: The Glances of Power and Preference," in *Nonverbal Communication—Reading with Commentaries,* ed. Shirley Weitz. New York: Oxford University Press, 1974.

158–159 Bruno Bettelheim, *The Informed Heart.* New York: The Free Press, 1960.

160   **"One survey showed that 78 percent":** E. Maccoby, "Television: Its Impact on School Children," *Public Opinion Quarterly,* vol. 15, 1951.

160   **"Thirty-six percent of the respondents . . .":** R. Hamilton and R. Lawless, "Television within the Social Matrix," *Public Opinion Quarterly,* vol. 20, 1956.

160   **Statistics:** *Kids and Media @ the New Millenium.* op. cit.

161   Urie Bronfenbrenner, "The Origins of Alienation," *Scientific American,* August 1974.

161   Robert Kubey and Mihaly Csikszentmihalyi, *Television and the Quality of Life.* Hillsdale, New Jersey: Lawrence Erlbaum Associates, 1990.

14. Computers in The Classroom

page

166   Stanley I. Greenspan, *The Growth of the Mind and the Endangered Origins of Intelligence.* New York: Perseus Books, 1998.

166   **Long term trends in reading performance:** National Center for Educational Statistics, NAEP 1999 Long-Term Trend Assessment.

166   **Survey of computer use in writing:** U.S. Department of Education, National Center for Education Statistics, *The NAEP 1998 Writing Report Card for the Nation and the States,* Washington, D.C., 1999.

166–167 **Latest NAEP math assessment:** US Department of Education, National Center for Education Statistics, *Pursuing Excellence: A Study of US Fourth Grade Mathematics and Science Achievement in International Context.* Washington, D.C., 1997.

167   **Heritage Foundation analysis:** Kirk A. Johnson, "Do Computers in the Classroom Boost Academic Achievement?: A Report of the Heritage Center For Data Analysis." The Heritage Foundation, Washington, D.C., 2000.

167   "A survey indicated that 90 percent of all parents": Samuel G. Sava, "Maybe Computers Aren't Schools' Salvation," op. ed. piece, The New York Times, September 6, 1997.

168   *"In 1999 schools spent an estimated $6.9 billion":* Glenn M. Kleiman "Myths and Realities about Technology in K–12 Schools" *Leadership and the New Technologies Perspectives,* April–June 2000.

168   Panel on Educational Technology, "Report to the President on the Use of Technology to Strengthen K–12 Education in the United States," Washington, D.C., 1997.

169   *Investment in technology compared to dot.com stocks:* Glenn M. Kleiman, op. cit.

169   *Technology director of the Bank Street School, quoted in:* Jane M Healy, *Failure to Connect: How Computers Affect Our Children's Minds— And What We Can Do About It.* New York: Touchstone Books, 1999.

170   *Suburban school board president's quote:* Katy Moeller, "No Magic Wands" *The Sunday Gazette,* Schenectady, NY, April 1, 2001.

170–171 *Computer programmer's letter:* Dave Davis, Letter to the Editor, *The New York Times,* March 8, 1992.

171   *International test of science and math:* "Worldwide Survey Finds US Students Are Not Keeping Up," *The New York Times,* December 6, 2000.

171   *Addendum:* Just as this book was going to press, the results of a later international exam were published, this one measuring knowledge in math, science and reading of a quarter-million high school students in 32 industrialized nations. Once again American students did not excel, scoring lower than all but four of the participating countries. (Source: Diana Jean Schemo, "U.S. Students Are Middling on Test in 32 Nations," *The New York Times,* December 5, 2001.

172   *Schools eliminate various programs for technology:* Samuel G. Sava, op. cit.

172–173 Clifford Stoll, "Give them Clay," *grok,* October 2000.

173   *Diane Ravich quote:* Bob Davis, "Internet in Schools: A National Crusade Backed by Scant Data," *The Wall Street Journal,* June 19, 2000.

175   *Quote from the head of a Palo Alto organization:* Sandy Banks and Lucille Renwick, "Technology Is Still a Promise, Not a Panacea," *Los Angeles Times,* June 8, 1997.

178   ***William L. Rukeyser quote:*** Banks and Renwick, ibid.

179   ***Andy Carvin quote:*** Lisa Guernsey, "O.K., Schools are Wired. Now
          What?" *Education Life, The New York Times,* January 9, 2000.

179   Michael Wolff, "Honey I Wired the Kids," *New York,* June 12, 2000.

180   ***"If your child is captivated by certain writers":*** Adam Bryant, "Book-
          worms Click Here," *Newsweek e-Life,* winter, 2001.

181   ***Sylvan Learning Centers:*** Adam Bryant, ibid.

182–183   ***The case of Trinity High:*** Jacques Steinberg, "As Teacher in the Class-
          room, Internet Needs Fine-Tuning," *The New York Times,* July 7, 2000.

183–184   ***Swarthmore sophmore's op-ed piece:*** Nate Stulman, "The Great Cam-
          pus Goof-Off Machine," Op-ed, *The New York Times,* March 15, 1999.

184   ***Yale law professor's report:*** Ian Ayres, "Lectures vs. Laptops," *The New
          York Times,* March 20, 2001.

15. Home Electronics

page

186   ***Viewing statistics:*** *Kids and Media @ the New Millenium.* op. cit.

190   ***"The kids can't wait to hit the road":*** Julie Halpert, "Hey Ma, Pass the
          Popcorn,"*Newsweek e-Life,* winter, 2001.

191   ***"Baby Wow":*** Deborah Branscum, "Click Baby Click," *Newsweek e-Life,*
          Winter, 2001.

191–192   ***David Elkind and Jane Healy quotes:*** ibid.

193–194   ***Quotes by Diane Levin and Mary Pipher:*** "Robotic Baby Dolls Named
          Worst Toy Idea of the Year," Alliance for Childhood press release, College
          Park, MD, 2000.

194   Jerome Singer and Dorothy Singer, *Make Believe: Games and Activities to
          Foster Imaginative Play in Young Children.* Washington, D.C.: Magination
          Press, 2000.

194   ***Quote by Joan Almon:*** "Computers and Children: 'Smart' Toys, Dumb
          Idea," Alliance for Childhood, College Park, MD, 2000.

195   Eugene F. Provenzo Jr., *Video Kids: Making Sense of Nintendo,* Cambridge,
          Massachussetts: Harvard U. Press, 1991.

195   **Hammersmith Hospital study:** "Nintendo Neurology," *Scientific American,* Science and the Citizen, August 1998.

196   Robert Johnson, "Arcade Fans Discover New Use for Skee-Ball: Fighting Video Fatigue," *The Wall Street Journal,* February 22, 2001.

196   **"One survey found":** J.B. Funk, "Reevaluating the Impact of Video Games," *Clinical Pediatrics,* February 1993.

197   **"As one parent wrote in a magazine article":** Ralph Gardner, Jr. "Is AOL Worse Than TV?" *New York,* June 12, 2000.

16. Out of Control

page

207   **Largest long-term study of child-care:** Sheryl Gay Stolberg, "Researchers Find Link Between Behavioral Problems and Time in Child Care," *The New York Times,* April 19, 2001.

218   **Orlando pilot program:** "Ad-Packed TV's May Soon be Boarding City Buses," *The Wall Street Journal,* February 21, 2001.

219   **Paradiso Italian Restaurant:** "Bright Idea," *Parenting* June/July 2000.

219–220   "Doctors Find TV Makes Child Ill," *The New York Times,* October 27, 1964.

17. Gaining Control

page

224   **Recent study of children's media use:** *Kids & Media @ the New Millenium,* op. cit.

225   **Quote from former vice president of CBS:** Norman Morris, *Television's Child.* Boston: Little, Brown, 1971.

226   Jim Trelease, *The Read-Aloud Handbook, 4th Edition.* New York: Penguin Books, 1995.

228   **Quote from television manufacturer:** Lesly Berger, "TV Devices Limit Children's Viewings," *The New York Times,* May 27, 1982.

228–229   **1996 Telecommunications Act:** Federal Communications Commission V-Chip Homepage: *www.fcc.gov/vchip*

229   ***"As the producer of Friends explained":*** Chris Roth, "Dossier on V-Chip Mess," 12/29/96, *www.cep.org/roth.html.*

229   ***V-Chip survey:*** "Parents and the V-Chip 2000," The Henry J. Kaiser Family Foundation, Menlo Park, CA, 2001.

229   ***Statistics about family TV use:*** *Kids & Media @ the New Millenium,* op. cit.

232   **Study about number of household sets:** Lynne Schaffer Gross and R. Patricia Walsh, "Factors Affecting Parental Control Over Children's Television Viewing: A Pilot Study," *Journal of Broadcasting,* Summer, 1980.

232–233   ***Recent study of children's media use:*** Stanger & Gridina, op. cit.

233   ***"A family in Tallahassee":*** Sharon Rauch, "TV Time Out" *Tallahassee Democrat,* December 31, 1996.

233–234   "Policy Statement—Media Education," *Pediatrics,* August 1999 and "Policy Statement—Children, Adolescents and Television," *Pediatrics,* February 2001.

234   ***Survey of media use:*** Stanger & Gridina, op.cit

238   ***"When a well-known nursery school in New York City":*** Nadine Brozan, "Film and TV Violence: A Nursery School Takes a Stand," *The New York Times,* June 1, 1975.

18. TV Turnoffs

page

246–249   Quotes from Don Brawley's report used by his permission.

249–250   ***Tom Valeo's TV Turnoff article:*** "Television and Kids: Breaking the Habit." *Daily Herald,* Arlington, IL, July 18, 1985.

255   Marie Winn, *Unplugging the Plug-In Drug.* New York: Viking Penguin, 1987.

255   ***Tom Valeo's follow-up article:*** "Curbing a Bad Habit," *Daily Herald,* Arlington, IL, December 23, 1987.

264   ***Quote from the Bible:*** King James version, Romans 7:15

19. No-TV Families

page

265   Joshua Meyrowitz: _No Sense of Place: The Impact of Electronic Media on Social Behavior._ op. cit.

266   Author's note: In a follow-up call on April 15, 2001, I learned that the Gerbers had not remained a No-TV family. After the passage of more than two decades, however, no one in the family could remember exactly when they had resumed watching. It may have been less than a year after the interview.

274   Colman McCarthy, "Ousting the Stranger from the House," _Newsweek,_ March 25, 1974.

278   New York Times **_article about families without TV:_** Nadine Brozan, "No TV in the House and They Want It That Way," _The New York Times,_ December 20, 1974.

CODA: The Television Generation

page

283   Any discussion of the SAT score decline must begin by clearing up some confusion about the scores as they are published today. In 1994 the College Board, the organization that administers the tests, decided for various reasons that the average American student was not the same as the student of the 1940s, when the standard was set. So the Board "recentered" the SATs by taking the scores of the year 1990, finding what score was the average of all the kids tested that year, and making that figure the new average, rather than the higher figure previously used. Since the average of a range from 200 to 800 is 500, that automatically became the score for 1990, and all scores thereafter were refigured from that point. The actual 1990 verbal average, based on the old scale, happened to be 424. So 424 suddenly became a nice fat 500 on the new "recentered scale." Every year thereafter the scores were raised in the same way. The test had not changed—the scores were simply made higher. In consequence, anyone comparing today's SAT scores with past decades might gain an impression that American kids' verbal scores are higher today than they were in the 1950s and '60s, and might assume that we have solved the problems of poor academic achievement. This, of course, is not so. That student in 1990 who scored 500 was still scoring 54 points lower on the exam than the student who had scored 478 in 1964. I have re-converted all scores

back to the old form here in order to make comparisons between pre-television and post-television test takers and to try to assess if, indeed, the presence of television should be considered a factor in the decline.

283   **SAT statistics before 1965:** P. Whitty, "Studies of the Mass Media, 1949–1965," *Science Education,* 1966.

283   The source of all statistics about SAT scores after 1965 is: US Department of Education, National Center for Educational Statistics, Washington, D.C.

283–284 *"A Cornell sociologist":* Jerry E. Bishop, "Lab Notes," *The Wall Street Journal,* November 29, 1993.

284   **Statistics about set ownership over the years:** "Number of TV Homes by Season," Nielsen Media Research 2000.

285   **Study of viewing time of first- and sixth-graders between 1950 and 1970:** Lyle and Hoffman, "Explorations in Patterns of Television Viewing by Preschool-age Children," *Television and Social Behavior,* Vol. IV, op. cit.

286   **1959 statistics:** Schramm, Lyle, Parker, op. cit.

286   **1970 statistics:** Lyle and Hoffman, op. cit.

286   **Decline in high scoring students:** U.S. Dept. of Education, op. cit.

287–288 **Harvard study of effects of different media:** C. A. Char and L. Meringoff, "The Role of Story Illustrations—Children's Story Comprehension in Three Different Media," Technical Report 22, Harvard Project Zero, January 1981.

288   **Quotes by Howard Gardner:** "Reprogramming the Media Researchers," *Psychology Today,* January 1980.

288   Update: Twenty years after the study was performed, Howard Gardner responded to a query asking whether the study had stood the test of time: "I think it still holds up . . . If no one has complained to you, that's probably a good sign!"

289   **1976 Article about decline in writing skills**: Gene Maeroff, "Rise in Remedial Work Taxing Colleges," *The New York Times,* March 7, 1976.

289   **Drop in skills between 1969 and 1979:** *Writing Achievement, 1969–1979: Results from the Third National Writing Assessment.* The National Assessment of Educational Progress, Princeton, N.J., 1980.

289   ***"A test requiring students to write an 'open-ended' analysis":*** Edward B. Fiske, "Reading Analysis Is Called Lacking," *The New York Times*, November 21, 1981.

289   ***Diane Ravich quote:*** "Teachers Say They Expect Less from Homework and Get It," *The New York Times*, May 4, 1978.

290   ***Latest writing assessment by NAEP:*** The National Center for Education Statistics, *Long-term Trends in Student Writing Performance*, 1996.

290   ***Carlos Baker quote:*** "Why Johnny Can't Write," *Newsweek*, December 8, 1975.

291   ***E. B. White quote:*** ibid.

291–292   Robert D. Putnam, *Bowling Alone: The Collapse and Revival of American Community*. New York: Simon & Schuster, 2000.

293–294   Tannis MacBeth Williams, editor, *The Impact of Television: A Natural Experiment in Three Communities*, op. cit.

295   Brandon Centerwall, "Television and Violence," *Journal of the American Medical Association [JAMA]*, June 10, 1992.

Acknowledgments

For the 2002 edition:

For their time, interest, and brilliant comments I owe a debt of gratitude to my three advance readers—Anne Malcolm, Steve Miller, and Sarah Paul. As representatives of a new generation of young parents, their role in updating and improving this anniversary edition of *The Plug-In Drug* was enormous.

Many thanks to Sheila Baird for providing an inspiring workspace—a room with a view and without a telephone

And to Helen Steiner for using her network as a veteran third-grade teacher to arrange interviews for this edition in Scotia, New York.

Acknowledgement is also due to:
Arthur Bienenstock; Jack and Dani Carr; Jennifer Durand; James Garbarino; Howard Gardner; Janet Malcolm and Rose Botsford; Mike Miller; David Olds; Jerome Singer.

Anita Andersen; Brian Aylward; Gayle Blumenberg; Mary Cloutier; Cathie Currin; Cheryl Gottwald; Vera Weiss.

Sherry Atwell; Kathleen Beeman; Mary Held; Karen Hess; Hali Holmes; Karen House; Wendy Luft; Lynn Macan; Cindy Maiuccoro; Carolyn Manor; Caron McGraw-Peters; Gwen Mitsche; Joseph Perrella; Rodney Rosenberg.

And the kids: Justin Bariteau; Sean Black; Marina Boschi; Laura Burbank; Matthew Bynon; Sophia Cardinali; Dennis Caringi; Emilia Carosella; Aubree Cristello; Amy Douglas; Carson Drake; Todd Drake; Joseph Ferrari; Lori Fisher; William Gibbons; Leon Graves; Cat Hadcock; Nicole Himpele; Shane Janssen; Michael Kautz; Caitlin Mackey; Greg Manning; Matthew McKenna; Tyler Paluba; Katherine Robinson; A.J. Schnore; Lisa Silvestri; Victoria Sitterley; Elizabeth Stiffen; Andrew Suttliffe; Andrew Swab.

At Penguin Books, thanks to Caroline J. White, the editor of this new edition.

Above all thanks to Allan Miller, whose encouragement, enthusiasm and help at every stage of this book transformed the task into a true collaboration.

For the 1977 and 1985 editions:

Belated thanks to Dick Grossman, who first accepted this book for publication, and to Dan Okrent and Kathy Matthews at the Viking Press for their faith in its future.

Special thanks for help and encouragement to Dorothy Cohen, Nina Mack, Elspeth and Nick MacDonald, Janet Malcolm, Peggy McIntosh, Ellen Posner, Peggy Steinfels, Arthur and Mary Ellen Wang, Joan Winn.

Acknowledgment is due to: Irene Abosch; Karen Andres; Linda Asher; Chris and Margaret Beels; Candace Berger; Mrs. Charles Bohons; Marilynn Bonato; Mr. and Mrs. Jack Carey; Danielle and

Jack Carr; Ellie Caulkins; Carol Cohen; Elizabeth Rogers Cohen and Ezekiel; Reneta Cuff; Mr. and Mr. R. S. Culver and Joe, Bobby, Tommy, and Lisa; Naomi Danzig and Alexis and Adrian; Donnamae Davidson; Mrs. Margaret Davis; Ken and Barbara Eisold and Katherine and Elizabeth; Jill Frisch and Madeleine; Mrs. Perry Fersko; Carol Gelber and Jed and Amy; Linda Gottlieb and Andrew and Nicholas; Sally and Wayne Halloway; Earl and Pat Hauck; Mrs. Darrell Harrison; Sue Heath; Dinny Howard and Nugget and Maggie; Nina Knyphausen and Anton and Julie; Arthur and Leslie Kopit; Betty Kramer; Penny Littell and Fanny; Clara Longstreth; Marcia Lowe; Ethan and Zachary MacDonald; Ken and Peggy McIntosh; Ginny Miller and Ivan; Mary Alice Murphy; Mr. and Mrs. Ralph Pederson and Arne and Amy; Mr. and Mrs. Paul Peterson; Florence Phillips; George Port; Mr. and Mrs. D. K. Porter and Randy, Laurie, and Michael; Mrs. J. Radinsky; Barbara and Jack Radosevick; Mary Beth Reed and Tracy and Toy; Mrs. John Robertson; Barbara Rosen and Sarah; Louis Rosenberg; Peggy Rosenberry and Flip; Mrs. William G. Ross; Lowell and Margo Rubin; Barbara Haddad Ryan; Irene Sample and Kate and Edward; Brandy and Aaron Schure; Jaclyn Shapiro; Mrs. David Sidorsky and Robert, Gina, and Emily; Mrs. Richard Sigfoos; Mrs. G. R. Spendlove; Mr. and Mrs. Fred Tanquary; Joan Turner; Bea Wernick; Mrs. John V. Wright.

C. Christian Beels, M.D.; Stella Chess, M.D.; Peter Crown; Jim Day; Marshall Haith; Desmond Heath, M.D.; Julian Hochberg; Paul Kaufmann; Edward Palmer; Lowell Rubin, M.D.; David Rush, M.D.; Rebecca Shannock, Suzy Sholz, M.D.; Diana Siskind; Joel Solomon, M.D.; Eleanor Townsend, M.D.; Sidney Werkman, M.D.; Joseph Winn, M.D.

Eleanor Brussell; Jerry Cascio; Betty Lou English; Esty Foster; Helen G. Garrison; Evelyn Halpert; Nancy Hedland; Aloise Heubach; Margaret Katz, Margaret Lawrence; Virginia Paulsen; Sheila Rowe; Kay Saelens; John Seeger; Terry Spitalny.

Index

Note: To avoid repetition, topics or names included in this book's detailed Table of Contents [i.e. **Brain Changes,** or **Computer Games** or **Harry Potter**] are not included in the Index.

$\rho \, \frac{33}{40}$